# THE 5 KICK-ASS STRATEGIES

WITHDRAWN

## Every Business Needs

## TO **EXPLODE SALES,**

### STUN THE COMPETITION,

# WOW CUSTOMERS,

### AND ACHIEVE EXPONENTIAL GROWTH

# ROBERT GREDE

**SOURCEBOOKS, INC.**
NAPERVILLE, ILLINOIS

Published by Sourcebooks, Inc.
P.O. Box 4410, Naperville, Illinois 60567-4410
(630) 961-3900
FAX: (630) 961-2168
www.sourcebooks.com

Library of Congress Cataloging-in-Publication Data
Grede, Robert.
  The 5 kick-ass strategies every business needs: to explode sales, stun the competition, wow the customers, and achieve exponential growth / Robert Grede.
    p. cm.
  Includes index.
  ISBN-13: 978-1-4022-0640-5
  ISBN-10: 1-4022-0640-2
  1. Management—Handbooks, manuals, etc. 2. Strategic planning—Handbooks, manuals, etc. I. Title: The five kick-ass strategies every business needs. II. Title.

HD38.15.G74 2006
658.4'012—dc22

                                              2006003650


Printed and bound in the United States of America.
VP 10 9 8 7 6 5 4 3 2 1

*For Cammy and The Nate, my reasons for being.*

# CONTENTS

This chapter introduces the concepts behind strategic planning,
the importance of defining your organization's strengths, and
how to translate those strengths into benefits for your customers
and prospects.

This chapter helps you understand fundamental marketing
principles used throughout this book, including product
differentiation and branding.

This chapter describes how a strategic marketing plan is written
and where to find the information necessary to develop reasonable
assumptions about your industry and its growth potential.

The fundamental principles behind the 5 Kick-Ass Strategies,
how they were developed, and why there are five and only five ways
to build your business. Each of the 5 Kick-Ass Strategies is then
explained in greater detail in the succeeding five chapters.

**CHAPTER TWELVE: Managing Your Human Assets** . . . . . . . . . . .275

Your people make or break your business. This chapter explores
human resource management, including hiring, termination,
leadership styles, motivation, corporate culture, and the benefits
of outsourcing your personnel needs.

**CHAPTER THIRTEEN: Social Profit** . . . . . . . . . . . . . . . . . . . . . .299

This chapter examines why ethical behavior is good business and
how to encourage ethical behavior at all levels of your organization.

# ACKNOWLEDGMENTS

As with any book, the written words often stem from ideas germinated in the minds of others.

My gratitude to Tim Blumentritt for his input on Succession Planning; to Phil McGoohan for his insight on Mergers and Acquisitions; to Bernard Hintzke for his explanation of Business Legal Entities; to Mark Ehrmann for his thoughts on approaching Merger and Acquisition candidates (and for his jump shot); to Tim Johnson for his Human Resources input; to Dick Grady for his creative contributions; to Marilyn Allen for her guidance and support; and to Dominique, Peter, and all the folks at Sourcebooks for their faith and patience.

A special thanks to Aye Jaye for sharing his Schmooz.

And, as always, I am grateful to Terry Firkins, who showed me how.

# INTRODUCTION

This is a book about strategy. More specifically, business strategy—how to grow your business exponentially.

Strategy is an important part of growing any organization. It is the careful method by which an organization goes from here to there. Strategies are the roads.

You run a successful business, and like scores of entrepreneurs before you, you want to see it grow and prosper—and ultimately achieve the level of success to which you aspire.

These aspirations can be measured in many different ways:
1. Wealth beyond all avarice.
2. An organization of which you can be proud.
3. An organization that will outlive you and continue to prosper for generations.
4. All of the above.

## WHY THIS BOOK WAS WRITTEN

More than how to increase sales, this book tells you how to develop the infrastructure that needs to be in place to accommodate growth.

The past two decades of my professional life have been devoted to fostering and nurturing the growth of small businesses. The Grede Company advises men and women at various stages of their organization's growth, from start-up to the next level.

I also teach at various university levels, from undergraduate to executive MBAs. It gives me access to textbooks, scholarly journals, and advance-degree theses from which I can extract the best and most applicable business theories and apply them in my practice (and in this book).

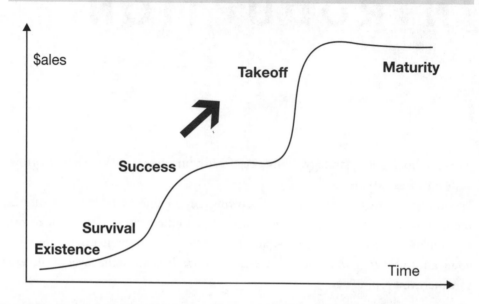

# ORGANIZATION LIFE CYCLE

> Like people, organizations go through stages.
>
> Takeoff refers to a period of rapid growth typically characterized by sales increasing in multiples.
>
> Surging customer demand must be balanced with the limitations of the manufacturing, financial, and human resources.
>
> Source: Churchill and Lewis, Harvard Business Review

Our clients' growth has come primarily through the development and implementation of carefully prepared strategic initiatives. Rigorous study of the industry and target markets, coupled with an aggressive management approach, has led to substantial growth in sales and profit. We wrote a plan, and we followed it.

For each and every client, that growth came from executing the 5 Kick-Ass Strategies outlined in this book.

*The 5 Kick-Ass Strategies Every Business Needs* translates leading academic and corporate theories into terms you and I can understand, theories that help you analyze your company's four interdependent business functions:

1. **Operations** (property, plant, and equipment)
2. **Finance** (cost controls, borrowing capacity)
3. **Human Resources** (competent middle management)
4. **Marketing** (planning, promotion, sales)

Apply these 5 Kick-Ass Strategies over the four business functions to grow exponentially. Simple.

# THE PURPOSE OF THIS BOOK

The real purpose of this book is to relieve stress. Your stress. And the stress your business faces as it grows.

Stress can lead to poor health, both yours and your company's.

Some entrepreneurs confuse stress with challenge, but these concepts are not the same. Challenge energizes us psychologically and physically. It motivates us to learn new skills and master our fate. When a challenge is met, we rejoice. Problem solved.

At work, challenge is an important ingredient for a healthy and prosperous organization. Once the challenge is bested, we can all relax. We have accomplished our goal and can now enjoy a sense of fulfillment. Challenge is a good thing.

Stress, on the other hand, is not so good. In the human organism, stress sets off an alarm in the brain. Your nervous system goes berserk, sending out hormones to sharpen your senses, quicken your pulse, deepen your respiration, and tense your muscles.

Stress can lead to chronic health problems—cardiovascular disease, musculoskeletal

> *The Grede Company, in just a few days, analyzed my business; cut through the marketing and advertising chaff recommended by every trade organization, media salesperson, and "marketing specialist" that descends relentlessly on a small business; and recommended concise organizational changes and a marketing plan that, in two years, increased our sales by 58 percent; elevating us to the eighty-first largest quick printer in the United States from a field of over 65,000 companies.*
>
> —Dale Wilson, President
> Wilson Printing
> www.wilprint.com

> **Stress** *(n.) physical or emotional state resulting from an unexpected change; harmful physical and emotional response that occurs when requirements do not match resources.*

disorders, and psychological disorders. You're a ticking time bomb and there's nothing you can do about it. Your response is preprogrammed biologically.

A company under stress can suffer as well. Low morale, infighting, polarization, and even malfeasance are all signs of tension within a company. Unexpected changes in the work environment can cause individual stress, but the resulting stress on the organization can be critical.

Short-lived or infrequent episodes of stress pose little risk. But as an entrepreneur, your body (and your organization) may be under constant pressure, causing stress that may go unresolved for long periods.

Many entrepreneurs have the mistaken notion that it's more efficient to do it all themselves. They are so busy working *in* their business, they fail to work *on* it. It's like trying to keep a dozen ping-pong balls underwater all at once. This book will show you how to relieve some of that stress.

## THERE ARE FIVE AND ONLY FIVE WAYS TO GROW YOUR BUSINESS

If you are a small business owner or operator and you want to increase your sales dramatically, you must execute the 5 Kick-Ass Strategies.

Chances are you are using some of them right now and you may not know it, operating as most entrepreneurs do "from the seat of your pants" (or skirt, as the case may be), building sales through deeper market penetration or by exploring new markets.

Your success has come without any prescribed plan. You may never have had any formal training in marketing, strategic planning, or business administration. Rather, you have a technical skill, a proficiency that has propelled your organization to the success it enjoys today: a better mousetrap, a useful service, the Big Idea.

> *First say to yourself what you would be, and then do what you have to do.*
>
> —Epictetus

And it has served you well. You make a good living, a decent living. But you want to do better. You want to kick ass. You want to reach the next level.

# EXPONENTIAL GROWTH

It's out there, that brass ring, seemingly just beyond your grasp. Opportunities abound. Could you sell different stuff to each of your current customers? Or sell the same stuff to new customers? Build that innovative new product you've been designing in your head for ages? Triple your sales over the next five years?

Yes, you can. Using these 5 Kick-Ass Strategies, you can grow your organization exponentially.

This book was written for those who are responsible for the growth and development of their organization. If you are in charge, if you are to be held accountable for profit and loss, this book is written for you. It will make it easier for you to identify opportunities, increase your sales, provide strategies that will effectively (and efficiently) achieve your company's objectives within a manageable budget, and help grow your business.

Whether yours is a manufacturing company, distributor, retailer, service company, or not-for-profit organization, *The 5 Kick-Ass Strategies Every Business Needs* provides the blueprint for building your business using simple strategies designed to enhance your position in the marketplace.

But it also provides insight into managing that growth. The blueprint is multidimensional, digging deeper than just *sales growth*. It tells you how to prepare for that growth and how to manage it as it develops, layer upon layer—operations, finance, and human resources—in addition to marketing.

# PROVEN WINNERS

If you have decided to grow exponentially, this book will lead you through the process. Follow these 5 Kick-Ass Strategies and you will be amazed how simple it is.

# CHAPTER 1

# Defining Your Business

Purpose: *The purpose of chapter 1 is to establish the basis from which your company can begin to grow exponentially by: 1. defining who you are, 2. writing a growth plan, and 3. managing your company's greatest asset: YOU.*

———◦———

**F**ace it. It's a dog-eat-dog world out there, and your company is raw meat. Wily competitors growl at your door and will gobble you up if given half a chance.

It wasn't supposed to be like this, was it? You went into business for yourself because you had dreams of working at something you love, reaping the rewards, and never going back to that nine-to-five job again. You thought it would be exciting, invigorating, and lead to wealth and respect within the community. How did it get to be like this?

## Case Study

# WILSON PRINTING

### THE PROBLEM

While Dale Wilson was still in college, he began working in his friend's tiny print shop in Santa Barbara with the funny name: Kinko's.

Wilson soon became manager of Paul Orfalea's first store and began learning the trade. After graduation, he decided to open his own print shop and called it The Alternative, as it was the only other quick-print shop in town.

The firm began to prosper, growing to forty employees in just five years. Wilson expanded, adding two-color instant printing to his list of capabilities, targeting advertising agencies and large companies up and down the South Coast.

Despite his growth, Wilson had a problem. The company offered both copying and two-color printing, but did neither better than his competitors. To complicate things further, walk-in traffic took up an inordinate amount of his employees' time for their onesy-twosy copy requirements.

Dale Wilson needed to redefine his business.

Face it. It's a dog-eat-dog world out there, and your company is raw meat. Wily competitors growl at your door and will gobble you up if given half a chance.

It wasn't supposed to be like this, was it? You went into business for yourself because you had dreams of working at something you love, reaping the rewards, and never going back to that nine-to-five job again. You thought it would be exciting, invigorating, and lead to wealth and respect within the community. How did it get to be like this?

*Note: All of the case studies used in this book are real cases.*

*Each company is or was a client of The Grede Company, marketing and strategic planning consultants.*

Instead, you find yourself beaten down by constant chaos, reams of paperwork, obdurate employees, inspectors, tax collectors, and bankers all saying, "Show me the money!" Your family and friends complain they never see you anymore, and when they do, you're usually crabby or cantankerous.

So how did you get to where you are right now?

The fact that you're still in business means you are a survivor. But before you can grow your business exponentially, you need to assess where you are right now, and how you got here.

There are only three ways to become the owner of a business:

1. Start it.
2. Buy it.
3. Inherit it.

(Some will claim that "marry it" is another way to become an owner, but I liken that to buying. You pay for it one way or the other.)

Like many, you had that dream of being an entrepreneur, running your own show, at one time in your life. Or perhaps you were downsized, right-sized, out-sized, or capsized and found yourself scrambling to make ends meet. Your only option was to operate on your own.

However you came to be an entrepreneur, you cannot grow exponentially without help. You can't do it alone. No one is an expert at everything. Sure, you're accustomed to doing it all, from selling your products to keeping the books to emptying the wastebaskets. Even if you are a sole proprietor, you still need outside assistance from time to time for help in those areas where you lack expertise.

> ## DEFINE YOUR BUSINESS
> ...................................
> *1. Identify your company's core competencies.*
>
> *2. Hone them to perfection.*
>
> *3. Abandon all the other peripheral products that drag down profitability.*

## CORE COMPETENCY

What is it you do best? Before you begin to examine methods for growing your business, it is important to maintain focus on those areas at which you will be most successful.

Growth does not always lead to profitability. Critical to the success of any business is to direct your efforts where you will generate the most profit. Typically, they are the unique products or characteristics that made your organization a success in the first place, those that set it apart from any others.

Academics and business gurus refer to these as your **core competencies.** To identify your organization's core competencies, it may be necessary to refocus your business.

Over time, even a small company can lose its focus. It begins to offer too many products or services to too many diverse markets at too many different price points. Management cannot pay attention to all its product offerings. Customers lose interest in others. Margins begin to shrink.

Profitability declines.

Is your company like that? Maybe it's time to refocus, to find your core competencies again. To specialize in the things you do best. While most corporate management is focusing on growth, business is really driven by specialization.

And not just business; civilization was founded on specialization. Early families did everything for themselves: grew their own food, made their own clothes, built their own shelters.

It wasn't until families began to specialize, concentrating on their **core competencies**, making clothing and trading it for food prepared by others, or shelters made by still others, that the standard of living for all began to rise.

## Case Study ) WILSON PRINTING

### THE SOLUTION

Dale Wilson redefined his business as a commercial printer.

He changed the configuration of his shop so that there was no longer a street entrance, sold the smaller copy machines that were used by walk-in business, and began focusing solely on commercial customers.

As technology changed, he upgraded his equipment, using digital copiers (Docutech, color copiers) and conventional sheet-fed printing presses (Komori Lethrone 628p).

To emphasize this change in focus, he changed the name of his company to Wilson Printing. The company has grown to become the eighty-first largest quick-print shop in the U.S. (according to *QP* Magazine).

www.wilprint.com

# SPECIALIZATION

Specialization is probably what made your company a success in the first place. You picked your niche and became the very best at it. As you succeeded, you branched out into other niches that you didn't know quite as much about, and while some may be successful, others may be costing you dearly.

How specialized should you be? Typically, the larger your geographic trading area, the more specialization can help your business grow.

For example, if you lived in a small, isolated town of five hundred people, you could probably find one or two general merchandise stores that sold everything: pots and pans, shoes, tires, and toiletries. (Wal-Mart has successfully pursued this strategy to become the largest retailer in the world.)

In a big city, you'll find highly specialized stores. Not just a shoe store, but also a women's shoe store, men's shoe store, children's shoe store, and an athletic shoe store. Maybe even a store that just sells orthopedic shoes.

The size of the trading area determines the level of specialization. As our economy becomes more global, specialization becomes more critical. The most successful companies will be those that find their core competencies and focus on those.

Retailers lead the way. No other market segment is more sensitive to trends than retailing. The best have learned the benefits of specialization.

Think back a few decades, when department stores were king. Gimbels, Abraham

## SPECIALIZATION

*In the 1970s, Charles Lazarus started a children's toy and furniture store called Children's Supermart. As the store grew, Lazarus was tempted to broaden his product line, to add children's clothing, diapers, baby food, and bicycles.*

*But that isn't what he did. Instead, Lazarus decided to specialize. He threw out the furniture line and concentrated on toys only. He changed the name of his store to Toys "R" Us and the rest, as they say, is history.*

*Or is it?*

*By the late 1990s, Toys "R" Us (www2.toysrus.com) faced declining sales and eroding profit margins. Why? Because while warehouse clubs like Costco and Sam's began selling similar products at even lower prices, Toys "R" Us was busy expanding in new areas.*

*Corporate growth came from building new stores rather than from individual store growth. And Toys "R" Us left its core competency and expanded in new areas: Kids "R" Us, Babies "R" Us,*

(continued next page)

## SPECIALIZATION
··································
(continued from previous)

*and Geoffrey's. By 1999, losses were over $132 million on $11 billion in sales.*

*Since then, the company has regrouped and begun concentrating on what they do best: toys. The company has returned to profitability and remains the market share leader, selling nearly one in every four toys in the U.S.*

& Strauss, Bonwit Teller, and Ohrbach's were leaders in retailing. Today, all are gone. Macy's and Bloomingdale's have flirted with bankruptcy. Many experts believe the golden age of retailing may have past.

But people haven't stopped buying.

Enter the **specialty store** (sometimes referred to derogatorily by rivals as "category killer"). Virtually every department in the traditional department store is now a specialty category. Shoppers go to the Gap for basic clothes for younger adults, Foot Locker for athletic shoes, Staples for office supplies, and Home Depot for home-repair supplies.

How can you create a dominant presence in your category like Toys "R" Us, Staples, or Home Depot?

Here are five principles for specializing:

**1. Narrow your focus.**

You can't be all things to all people. Eliminate all unnecessary product lines or services. The U.S. Postal Service delivers mail. But Federal Express took the most profitable segment of that market, overnight delivery, and made it their own.

**2. Stock in depth.**

If you are going to specialize in selling model trains and model trains only, make sure you sell every kind of model train there is, every add-on, every accessory. If someone wants something for his model train set, he knows he needn't look any further. You will have it.

**3. Buy cheap.**

By specializing, you can often make large quantity purchases at big discounts.

**4. Sell cheap.**

Pass the savings along to your customers. By narrowing your focus to just one category, you limit your sales potential if you can't sell for less than some retailer who offers everything.

**5. Dominate your category.**

Focus your specialty so narrow as to dominate your niche. Whether you sell 22 percent of all the toys in America (like Toys "R" Us), or the best deli sandwich within a five-block radius, focus on your core competency to dominate your market niche.

# A MARKET PERSPECTIVE

Over time, all categories undergo change, changes in customer needs and wants, changes in technology, changes in economic factors.

Every category was once a growth category. Railroads, grocery stores, fax machines, and sushi restaurants all enjoyed their day in the sun. The fax machine was replaced by email technology. Supermarkets replaced the corner grocery store as consumers changed their shopping habits.

Railroads did not stop growing because the need for passenger and freight transport declined. The need, in fact, has continued to grow dramatically. Railroads are in trouble

| THINK GLOBALLY |
|---|
| *The Internet has allowed virtually any business to sell globally. Communication and trade have become easier and faster.* |
| *Your competitors are no longer those in your immediate neighborhood. Your organization may be competing simultaneously with companies in Argentina, China, India, or Zambia.* |
| *All the more reason to specialize.* |

today because they perceived themselves as railroads, instead of transport companies. So, cars, trucks, and airplanes filled the need.

Railroad executives, with miles of track and hundreds of rolling freight cars, saw only railroad solutions for passenger and freight transport problems. They had a product orientation rather than a market orientation.

Too often, businessowners view marketing as simply the task of creating a product and selling it. Case in point: contrast Proctor & Gamble Company with Union Carbide Corporation.

Union Carbide makes chemicals. As an advertising executive, I worked with their Consumer Products Division's Glad Bags business. Top brass had an excess of polyethylene plastic and told us to "come up with a way to sell more Glad bags."

We all sat around and thought for a while and eventually decided to develop a new product, Handle-Tie bags. We got lucky and they sold well, but only because we found a consumer need (convenience) and filled it. Had we simply advertised our current line of bags, or worse, offered deep discounts (in a category

The carpenter with only a hammer in his toolbox sees every problem as a nail.

with razor-thin margins already), we would have suffered severe losses. (More on the development of Handle-Tie bags in chapter 7.)

Proctor & Gamble, on the other hand, listens to its field sales representatives, supermarket managers, and the customers themselves. They develop a new product based upon their knowledge of customers' wants and needs. They test it in small markets. Then they spend sinful sums on promotion to create awareness and communicate the benefit (the satisfaction of those needs and wants) to consumers.

Proctor & Gamble is enormously successful. Union Carbide no longer has a consumer products division.

The secret to continued growth then is a two-step process:

1 Focus on your core competencies.
- Find what you do best.
- Abandon all non-related businesses.
2. Take a market perspective.
- Focus on consumer needs, not product capabilities.
- Broaden your thinking to take advantage of new growth opportunities.

If you know your organization's core competencies, why not make them a part of the stated mission of your business?

# THE MISSION STATEMENT

If you don't know where you're going, any road will get you there. So once you have defined your core competencies, it's time to put pencil to paper and describe exactly where you want your organization to go, how it will operate, what it stands for.

Every organization exists to accomplish something: design buildings, bake bread, provide transport, and so on. This may seem obvious when your start your business. But over time, your business has evolved and changed as the market changed, or as competition warranted.

To define your mission, you must first determine your core competencies (see above). As these may change over time, likewise your mission may change.

Successful companies continuously address Peter Drucker's classic questions (*Management: Tasks, Responsibilities, and Practices,* NY: Harper & Row, 1973):

- What is our business?
- Who is the customer?
- What is of value to the customer?
- What will our business be in the future?

These simple-sounding questions are among the most important your firm will ever have to answer. The result should be written down. Some companies refer to this as their Statement of Objectives. Others call it a Corporate Credo. Still others, the **Mission Statement**.

Whatever name you choose to ascribe to it, this written document represents the guiding principles by which your organization operates. It defines who you are as a company, sets the mood, articulates the corporate culture, and helps perpetuate favorable work methods. In short, it serves as a guide on the long road to success.

> ## A CHANGE IN MISSION
> ...................................
> *As the marketplace changed, Amazon.com changed its mission from being the world's largest online bookstore to simply the world's largest online store.*

Externally, the mission statement provides management focus when faced with difficulties due to corporate expansion, competitive pressure, or changes in industry regulations. As these changes occur, management simply refers to the mission statement as a guide, how to deal with the change, and how to manage employees.

Internally, it demonstrates leadership and helps to inspire independent thinking. It empowers employees to make decisions in accord with top management, guides geographically dispersed employees to work independently yet collectively toward the same goals, and it saves time.

If your employees live by these guiding principles, they don't have to run to some rulebook every time they make a decision. They can simply look at the mission statement to remind them what their boss would have them do. (This can avoid a lot of annoying meetings.)

## YOUR MISSION STATEMENT
··················

*Once written, don't change it every few years just because the economy changes or you introduce a new product, or simply because the urge moves you.*

*Change your mission statement only when you must redefine your company, if you have undergone a fundamental change in the way you do business.*

*For example, on September 29, 1997, Sara Lee announced an abrupt shift in its business. Manufacturing would be outsourced and henceforward, the company would become solely a marketer of brands.*

*The company's mission changed, and so did their mission statement.*

At Leo Burnett Advertising Agency, we had to know both Leo's mission statement ("The best advertising, bar none.") and motto ("Reach for the stars. You may not always get one, but you won't come up with a handful of mud either.").

The U.S. Air Force uses a mission statement as simple and direct as a B-52: "To defend the United States through control and exploitation of air and space."

EBay's mission statement simply says: "We help people trade practically anything on earth."

Good mission statements most often:

1. Focus on a limited number of goals.
2. Stress the principles and values the company honors.
3. Define the limited areas within which the company will operate (the core competencies).

Essential to the success of your organization's mission is a **brand focus** rather than a product focus.

Kodak defines itself as a provider of images rather than a film company. IBM defines itself as a builder of networks rather than a hardware/software manufacturer. Standard Oil no longer "sells gasoline" but "supplies energy." In one of the most dramatic changes from a product focus to brand focus, Encyclopædia Britannica went from selling encyclopedias to information distribution.

Coca-Cola evolved from a seller of colas to a marketer of soft drinks to a provider of products to anyone needing to quench thirst. As people's tastes changed, Coca-Cola decided to sell other beverages whose growth potential appeared to be more promising.

What is your mission? For any organization to have a mission statement, it must have a mission, one that is probably buried in the back of your mind and one that employees may (or may not) share. Writing a formal statement doesn't just voice this unspoken mission; it endorses it as company policy. If a mission statement is to inspire, it must speak to employees in such a way to galvanize them. It must grab their attention, inspiring them to work harder, smarter, in words that ring true for today, and for tomorrow.

Once written, use your mission statement. Share it with employees. Post it around the office. Display it at meetings. Distribute it to customers and suppliers. Print it on your letterhead, purchase orders, and invoices.

Use it as a direct mailing to all your customers and potential customers. Enclose a cover letter explaining how it was written and how you intend to live up to it today and in the future.

> ## HOW TO WRITE YOUR COMPANY'S MISSION STATEMENT
> ............................................
> *Ask yourself:*
> - *Why are we in business?*
> - *Why are our products unique?*
> - *Who are our customers?*
> - *What do we do better than anyone else?*
>
> *Keep it simple and direct. Phrase it just as if you were talking to a friend.*

The mission statement is more widely used than any other management tool. Why? Because the cost is negligible, and it works. If the function of a leader is to advance a clear and shared vision of the organization, what better way than through the stated mission of your business?

# THE STRATEGIC BUSINESS PLAN

To grow exponentially, start with a plan. You've probably heard the old marketing maxim that says 50 percent of all advertising is wasted. Don't believe it. It's a lot more than just 50 percent.

Knowing how to avoid that wasted 50 percent takes forethought. And that means planning. To grow your business, you need to have a plan, one that encompasses all four parts of your business:

1. Operations
2. Finance
3. Human Resources
4. Marketing

> ## PLANNING
> ............................................
> *Planning is all about vision. It is the eyes of your company.*
>
> *Execution is the feet.*
>
> —John Pepper,
> former president of
> Procter & Gamble

## STRATEGIC BUSINESS PLAN VS. STRATEGIC MARKETING PLAN

*A strategic business plan* encompasses all aspects of your business: operations, finance, human resources, and marketing.

*A strategic marketing plan* focuses solely on sales and marketing goals, goals you set after a thorough analysis of your customers, your competition, and your industry. The five strategies are part of the strategic marketing plan.

This is known as a strategic business plan, and it is the cornerstone of your company's growth. It is the blueprint that will allow you to grow exponentially. Whether your company is large or small, a good strategic plan is essential.

It must be well written, one that advertises you and your company to the debt and equity marketplace. That's your audience: the debt and equity marketplace, bankers and financiers whom you need to convince that your dream is a wise investment.

Skills you have acquired through years of work experience do not often translate well into a business plan. No matter how creative your product may be, no matter how great the need for your services in the marketplace, you will have difficulty obtaining the necessary funding without a well-written plan.

My brother, Don, is a partner in The Aspen Alliance (www.theaspenalliance.com), a Colorado-based venture capital firm specializing in expansion strategies for the entrepreneur. The sole purpose of his business is to help entrepreneurs grow their business. He reviews, on average, about thirty business plans each week. Most get a cursory glance before they hit the round file. He claims the worst are written by lawyers, but accountants are a close second.

Skip the legalese—too hard to plow through. And while accountants are necessary to assure your pro forma statements are accurate, they typically lack luster in their prose.

*Someone is sitting in shade today because someone planted a tree a long time ago.*

—Warren Buffet
American Investor

A **business plan** is an advertisement for your idea. And while I acknowledge my bias, the best are written by advertising professionals, those who understand how to snag a reader with the primary benefit up front, the supporting data clearly labeled, and the call to action at the end.

The well-written plan will garner notice among heavy hitters (those debt and/or equity providers who aren't funding a friend or brother-in-law). It will demonstrate to any reader how serious you are about your company and your idea. It is well worth the investment if your plan gets you the funding you require.

This is not to say your plan will never be funded without professional help. But the odds are a lot longer, that's all.

**Planning** is the process of anticipating future events and conditions, and then determining the best way to achieve your objectives. Yet planning is often met with resistance within an organization. This opposition is based upon:

1. A reluctance to commit to long-term goals in a rapidly changing environment.

2. Your employees' perception that planning is simply busywork and not useful.

3. Your sense that there are "more important" things to do.

If you want to grow, you have to make the commitment to plan. Then it is up to you to emphasize the importance of planning to your key employees. If the boss isn't sold on planning, nobody else will be either.

If you truly want to grow your business, consider the benefits of having a strategic plan:

- Encourages thinking ahead in a systematic manner.
- Sharpens the company's focus.
- Prepares for unforeseen developments.
- Leads to better coordination of everyone's efforts.
- Helps develop performance standards.
- Inspires a sense of commitment to the growth process.
- Allows investors to understand your financial needs and helps assure them they will receive a return on their investment in your company.

# SAMPLE STRATEGIC BUSINESS PLAN

Begin with an outline. I have found that most fill-in-the-blank software is a waste of money, and while many books and websites have standard formats that you can use, most carry an accounting bias, emphasizing the numbers more than intangible factors.

> **NOTE**
> ...................................
> *Instructions for writing your strategic marketing plan can be found in chapter 3.*

Here is a basic outline. It is suitable for any business, whether new or expanding, a manufacturer, distributor, or consumer service.

1. **Executive Summary:** A one-page summary with a twenty-five-word (or less) explanation of your product and its primary benefit. Devote most of this page to the financing sought and its payback schedule.

2. **The Industry, the Company, the Products:** An analysis of your industry and how you fit in it.

3. **The Market:** An analysis of market potential and trends, your target customers, competition, and most important, realistic sales estimates. The bulk of this section comes from the situation analysis section of your strategic marketing plan (see chapter 2).

4. **The Marketing Strategy:** Your business begins with customers. How will you get them? How will you position your company in the marketplace, price it, distribute it, and promote it? The bulk of this section comes from the remainder of your strategic marketing plan (see chapter 2).

5. **The Operations:** A brief description of operations, facility requirements, management organization, and support services (your accounting and law firms, and any other advisory services). Included in this section is a lengthy description of the management team, their past experience and industry skills. Include résumés in an appendix.

6. **The Risks:** An analysis of customer risks, labor and raw materials availability, economic factors, changes in technology, and government regulations affecting your company. Often the most neglected section, this is extremely important to investors who want to know you have considered potential risks, and your management team's response to them.

7. **The Financial Statements:** Pro forma balance sheet, income statement, and cash-flow analysis. Be sure to include *all* assumptions.

8. **The Financing:** This is the call to action: the amount of debt and/or equity funding required, its use, and payback schedule.

The biggest mistakes in business plans stem from a lack of focus on management. Serious investors assume your idea is sound. They assume your numbers make sense. What they really want to know is this: Who is going to manage my money?

Many plans lack an end game. Where is management taking the company? Franchising? Multiple locations? IPO? How will investors get paid out? And when?

# FOUR PARTS OF ANY BUSINESS

Your company's strategic business plan becomes the blueprint for your exponential growth.

It begins with market research, a study of the people who will buy your products. Until you understand your market, you cannot begin to organize the other parts of your business for growth.

Every business has four fundamental parts:

1. **Operations**
2. **Finance**
3. **Human Resources**
4. **Marketing**

You've heard it said: "Build a better mousetrap and the world will beat a path to your door!" Ask most entrepreneurs and they'll tell you that **operations** is the most important part of any business. "Without a good product, nothing else matters." They have a point. No business will be successful unless it satisfies its customers' needs and wants.

Entrepreneurs begin with the product. They invent something, a product, process, or service. They nurture it, modify it, and sell it to customers along the way. And their business grows. Consequently, they have an innate prejudice in the value of the product over the other essential elements of business.

But talk to the **finance** folks, your accountant, banker, or your company bookkeeper, and they will tell you that money matters most. "It's the blood that feeds the organization. Cash flow is everything." They, too, have a point. Over time, without sufficient income to pay expenses, your company is bankrupt.

Some managers will tell you that people make a business successful. After all, it's your **human resources** who do the work. "A business is only as good as its people."

**Marketing** always seems to get shuffled into last place. And that's wrong. Marketing is the most important.

I admit I'm prejudiced. But hear me out.

> ## START WITH MARKETING
> ·····················
> *When developing a strategic plan, marketing is the first part that needs to be written.*

Without customers, you have no business. It doesn't matter how good your product is if no one knows about it or where to find it. It doesn't matter how well financed your firm is if you have no customers. It's the customers who create cash flow.

## THE ROLE OF MARKETING

*The marketing manager is the most significant contributor to the planning process, with leadership roles in defining the business mission; analysis of the environmental, competitive, and business situations; developing objectives and strategies; and defining product, market, distribution, and quality plans to implement the business's strategies.*

*This involvement extends to the development of programs and operating plans.*

—Jack Welch, former president and CEO of General Electric

## MARKETING IS THE VOICE OF THE CUSTOMER

Marketing matters—now more than ever. Given product parity due to near-instant information and the ability to deengineer almost anything, the quality of an organization's marketing strategy becomes paramount.

Only marketing can set your products apart from your competitor's. Marketing is the voice of the customer within your organization. It is the cry of the consumer, telling you what he or she wants. Ignore the cries at your peril.

The other business functions have rallied ambitiously around their initiatives. **Operations** people have Six Sigma and TQM. **Finance** people apply Total Cost of Ownership principles, and accounting's Balanced Scorecard. A variety of leadership and management theories motivate and direct **human resources**.

## THE ROLE OF MARKETING

**Marketing** has, in the past, only been responsible for attracting customers. Now it must also be given the authority to retain and grow profitable customers.

Marketing more than ever must be accorded greater say over decision making in key areas formerly delegated to other departments.

Procurement, pricing, product development, and logistics all play important roles in satisfying the customer. Key suppliers can be an integral part of the marketing team, contributing long-range planning suggestions and product development ideas as well as providing delivery schedules to meet customer demands. Marketing plays a critical role in the planning process. A firm's marketing decisions affect all other aspects of the company.

Working with the finance department, marketing managers must determine optimal pricing, promotion budgets, and customer credit and payment terms.

Working with the operations department, marketing managers must determine product quality, quantities, features, and delivery schedules.

Estimate sales based upon five factors:

1. Last year's sales,
2. An estimate of your promotion campaign's effectiveness,
3. New products you will be introducing,
4. An analysis of your competition, and
5. The operating environment.

Once established, begin developing the operations and financial plans based upon those assumptions.

Too often, companies calculate their manufacturing capacity and tell the sales department how much needs to be sold. This is particularly true in capital-intensive businesses where capacity utilization is critical (e.g., airlines, foundries, printers). This method often results in deep price discounts and thin (or even negative) profit margins when sales quotas are not met.

## The Business Model

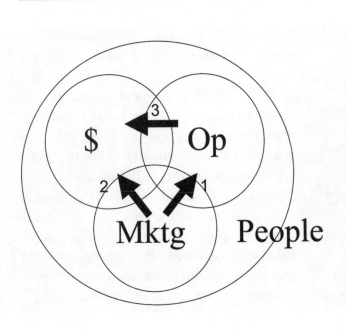

1. **Marketing** tells **Operations** how much raw material is needed, and how much labor to hire. Sales projections recommend how many wedgets to manufacture.

2. Those same sales projections (together with pricing projections) tell the **Finance** people how much revenue to expect.

3. Meanwhile, the **Operations** people, using sales projections received from the **Marketing** Department, tell **Finance** how much expense to expect from raw material and labor costs. **Finance** can then begin to plan capital structure, borrowing requirements, and payback schedules.

## A STRATEGIC MARKETING PLAN

*Serves three functions:*

1. *It defines the business strategy (primary and secondary target markets based upon analysis of market opportunities).*

2. *It specifies the marketing tactics (product features, promotion, pricing, distribution channels).*

3. *It provides feedback (measurement and analysis) that is then used to take corrective action, possibly leading to new strategies and tactics.*

## CONSISTENCY

*The message your employees convey must be consistent throughout the organization.*

*For instance, if you tout your outstanding customer service and inquiries to accounts payable are treated rudely, or your shop foreman is overheard using foul language during a plant tour, your reputation goes out the window.*

Had management begun by estimating their company's sales, they might have avoided those problems. Knowing in advance that sales may not utilize capacity can help companies plan cost-cutting methods in order to assure profitability.

Make it interactive. Planning should interact with both customer and employee. The plan is an opportunity to reflect customer input, your chance to tell your customers about your products and to listen and act upon their responses. Use the plan to build a relationship with your customers. It is your strategy for wooing them away from competitors. It is based upon listening and reacting to what they have to say.

As your customers' priorities change, your plan must change with them. Ten or twenty years ago, conventional wisdom suggested you write a five-year marketing plan and review it annually.

But change happens faster today than it did back then. Can you imagine companies like Cisco Systems, Intel, or Genentech using a five-year plan?

When I write a plan for my clients, we may look out three to five years, but I only recommend tactics for the first year. These we review quarterly (or even monthly) to identify problems and opportunities in the market.

Seek consensus in the planning process. Your employees are the ones who will implement your plan. While the planning process starts with marketing, your strategic business plan is a function of all the departments in your company, finance, operations, and marketing.

Requesting input from all departments helps develop a sense of ownership for all. If your bookkeeper sees ideas she suggested included in the final plan, she becomes invested, eager to implement the plan and help ensure its success.

# GETTING YOUR HOUSE IN ORDER

You are poised for success, on the brink of growing your business beyond its entrepreneurial state, and ready to reach for the stars.

But are you ready for exponential growth? There is reason for trepidation. The leap can challenge the most capable manager.

Start the process in the confines of your conscience. Make sure your house is in order. That means your operations are ready for the influx of new orders, your financial health is capable of supporting the additional working capital you will need, and your people are prepared for that increased workload. Each of these—operations, finance, and human resources—is covered in chapters 9, 10, and 11, respectively. But before tackling these weightier subjects, there is one tiny issue that needs to be addressed first before putting the rest of your house in order. That's *you*. Yours is the first ass that needs to be kicked.

Organize yourself first. Time management is one of the most talked-about, written-about subjects in business today. If I were to espouse all the theories and practices for better time management, you wouldn't have the time to read them.

---

### TYPICAL ENTREPRENEURIAL CHORES

Here is a checklist of duties you, as an entrepreneur, might perform in any given month. Just for kicks, put a circle by those you most enjoy, the reasons you had for getting into the business in the first place. And put an X by those you loathe, the ones you put off or simply hate to do.

| | | | |
|---|---|---|---|
| Correspondence | Ad production | Budgeting | Meet with staff |
| Inventory control | Website maintenance | Bill customers | Hire |
| Open mail | Customer contact | Pay bills | Terminate |
| Filing | Networking | Collection calls | Motivate staff |
| Answer phones | Press releases | Financial planning | Training (you) |
| Ship/receive | Promotion planning | Credit management | Training (staff) |
| Janitorial | | Pay taxes | Administration |
| Order input | | | |
| Quality control | | | |

You may see a pattern here. Those duties in the first column are typically Operations issues; those in the second column are Marketing; third column are Financial; and the last column are Human Resources.

With your business poised for growth, the areas that you have X'ed are the ones you should delegate first. That means either trusting someone within your organization to assume the burden of these tasks or hiring someone to assume them.

So let's boil them all down to two basic time management fundamentals:
1. Work more smart, less hard.
2. Delegate.

# WORK MORE SMART, LESS HARD

Time is a precious commodity. It can't be bought or sold. It can't be given or taken away. Once lost, it can never be retrieved. The secret then to more success and less stress is time management.

Experts agree that effective time management means allowing for a balanced lifestyle. Your overall health and that of your business require attention to five important life areas:
1. Physical (exercise, nutrition, sleep)
2. Intellectual (cultural, always learning)
3. Social (family and friends)
4. Professional (status and ego gratification)
5. Emotional (the higher quest for meaning)

A truly happy person will foster a balance in these five areas.

Start with exercise. Some people will plan a workout, but then something comes up and they don't get around to it. Do this often enough and the blood thickens, the gut broadens, and the heart stops pumping at the ripe old age of fifty-two.

Schedule exercise like any other meeting. You will find yourself more energized, sleeping better, and working more efficiently the remainder of your day. Physical exercise is a great stress reliever. Many executives claim they achieve their clearest thinking on the treadmill or while whacking a racquetball around the court.

Good entrepreneurs have a natural intellectual curiosity, and the mind needs exercise too. Attend the theatre or a concert now and then. Commit to an evening class in a field unrelated to your technical skill. You may meet some nice people (who could become part of your network), and you will refresh your intellect, gain new perspectives on life, experience some different kinds of pleasure, and perhaps focus more clearly on your job.

You may not need a specific set of activities in each of these life areas. But if you notice one area that you don't attend to at all, you may be ignoring an important part of yourself.

For example, here's a helpful little exercise: Take a big jar (with lid) and fill it with rocks. All the way to the top, until you can't fit in any more rocks. Screw on the lid and shake it until the rocks settle into the least amount of space. Unscrew the lid and put in a few more rocks. Can't fit any more? Good.

Now, add some gravel—little stones to fill up the spaces. Put the lid on and shake it again. Add some more gravel. Is it full? Okay, now add dirt. Keep pouring dirt in the jar until no more will fit. You think the jar is full yet? Nothing more will fit? Now add water.

We all have large priorities in life, like the larger rocks. We also have things that we enjoy doing, such as the gravel. Other things we have to do, like the dirt. And there are always those time-consumers that clutter our lives and drain our energies: the water.

This example is all about balance. Good time management means balance. You make time for everything, and everything simply fits where it is supposed to fit. The secret is to figure out what those big rocks are, and schedule time for them in your daily routine.

Email is not a rock. Seldom will an email be crucial in the grand scheme of things. Put it off till the end of the day or fit it in when you finish a "rock" earlier than expected.

Likewise, don't be afraid to put your phone on hold. If you think about it, rarely is there an instance when you absolutely need to answer your phone or email at that precise instant. On those rare occasions, make it a

## TIME MANAGEMENT

*If you find yourself solving problems and troubleshooting emergencies rather than planning and managing others, follow this handy guide for staying on task and managing your time better:*

- *Keep a list of your goals where you will see it easily.*

- *Review your long-term and short-term goals often.*

- *Eliminate tasks that are not related to your goals or to maintaining balance in your lifestyle.*

- *Don't be afraid to say no to people, including spouse, friends, children, and parents.*

- *Solicit cooperation from those around you. Let others know about your efforts to manage time.*

- *Do not set yourself up to fail. Set realistic goals.*

- *Make a daily "to do" list and stick to it.*

point to answer your phone and put it on hold for the rest of your day, rather than the other way around.

Grab your jar again and empty it. Fill it full of water. Now, try and add some rocks. You can't do it, can you? Not without spilling the water.

The point is this: You must first ensure that your large priorities (the rocks) are scheduled and completed before allowing smaller, less important things to occupy your time.

That doesn't mean you should not allow time for relaxing and having fun. Remember: Balance is key.

Set goals. The experts agree, the best way to keep on track is to establish goals and be mindful of them as you commit to various tasks throughout your day. Set both long-term goals and short-term goals.

As your day begins to clutter, continually ask yourself, "Does this contribute to my goals?" If not, put off the task or delegate it.

## DELEGATE

"If you want it done right, do it yourself." It's an often-heard axiom. Don't believe it. If it were true, no company would ever get larger than a one-person operation.

Delegation is simply allowing someone else the authority to act on your behalf. Simple enough.

But how do you ensure the person will perform the task in the manner you want it performed? The fact is, you can't. No one should be expected to perform

## JONCO INDUSTRIES

### THE PROBLEM

JONCO Industries, Inc. is a provider of customized packaging and product fulfillment in Milwaukee. After ten years in business, owner Tom Ryan embarked on a plan for rapid growth.

As JONCO began to expand, Ryan needed to delegate many of his duties. He could no longer afford the time to lead every sales effort, personally make every sample, develop costs, and write up estimates for prospective customers.

a task as you would perform it. But (and this is a big "but"), you can expect similar results. How?

Follow these simple rules:

1. **Describe the task** to be performed. Be as specific as possible.
2. **Outline the time frame** in which the task should be completed.
3. **Describe the level of authority** you are willing to grant.
4. **Establish checkpoints** for review along the way

### *1. Describe the Task*

Be as specific as possible. This does not mean you should dictate the methods used, though it may be helpful to offer suggestions. Rather, specify the end result you expect.

For example, this morning I asked my teenage daughter to "pick up her room." Big mistake. My vision of a clean room is far different from hers.

Later, as she was heading out the door for an evening with friends, we inspected her room. Clean laundry littered her unmade bed; dirty clothes could be found among them. Scraps of paper, jewelry, and miscellanea littered her desk and dresser in no particular order.

"But the room is picked up," she argued.

True, nothing remained on the floor except her shoes, thrown haphazardly beside her dresser. Nevertheless, I remained adamant she should finish putting away the laundry, make her bed, and organize her papers and bric-a-brac while her friends sat tapping their feet in the foyer. Meanwhile, I retired to my office to write about how to delegate. Talk about not practicing what you preach!

Had I clearly described the expected outcome, she would likely have had no problem accomplishing the goal, her friends would not have been left cooling their heels while she finished, and life in my household would have been far happier this day. My bad.

> ## ON DELEGATING
> 
> *"Has anybody given you the law of these offices? No? It is this: Nobody does anything if he can get somebody else to do it. As soon as you can, get someone whom you can rely on, train him in the work, sit down, cock up your heels, and think out some way for Standard Oil to make some money."*
> 
> —John D. Rockefeller, Sr., founder of Standard Oil

She deserves an apology. I should have asked her to repeat back to me what was expected to ensure we understood one another. I learned my lesson. Perhaps you will learn from my mistake.

## 2. Outline the Time Frame

Let your subordinate know how much time he has to perform the task. An hour, a week, a month?

If the project is time sensitive, be sure to say so. He may be fully capable of performing the task as you have described it and fully capable of delivering results you expect. But you may still be disappointed if he does not share your sense of urgency.

## 3. Describe the Level of Authority

Let's say you explained a project clearly, specified the time frame, listened while your subordinate repeated both back to you so that there is no misunderstanding, and still the project went awry. What happened?

You need to describe the level of her authority.

Once given the parameters of a project, your subordinate assumed she had been given the authority to carry out the task. She got other people involved you

## Case Study — JONCO INDUSTRIES

### THE SOLUTION

Ryan decided to delegate many of the sales responsibilities to Mike, his son.

At first, Mike was given responsibility for making samples. Later, he began developing costs for all new-customer pitches. As he proved himself, he was given more responsibility, including customer contact.

Not only did Mike prove capable, but many of the new customers looked to Mike as their primary contact. This freed up Tom for planning and administrative duties.

In addition, Mike is gaining valuable experience should he decide to take over the reins one day.

www.joncoind.com

would never have asked. She made decisions that were not hers to make. And ultimately she took action that may take more of your time to fix.

So you decide that from now on, you'll just do it yourself rather than delegate, and you're back to square one. But this wasn't her fault. It was yours. You did not define how much authority she had in making decisions.

Differing levels of authority extend from simple **investigation** to **recommendation** to **initiation** to **action**.

**Investigation** means simply having the subordinate gather information so that you can make an informed decision.

**Recommendation** is the same as investigation, with the addition of a recommendation by the subordinate for specific action.

**Initiation** allows the subordinate to make a decision and begin implementation, but only after informing you so that you might make suggestions or head off any problems.

**Action** gives complete responsibility for the implementation over to the subordinate.

Let's try an example: You've just hired an executive assistant. She is smart, personable, and anxious to demonstrate her competence. For the first several weeks, you ask her to gather information, prioritize it, and present it to you. You give clear directions and establish a time frame for gathering and presentation. You even ask her to repeat the instructions back to you so you're sure she understands them.

This works well for several months, so you ask her to begin making recommendations on much of the information she brings to you. You accept many of her recommendations without question; several of them you tweak a bit. You are pleased with her progress, and you tell her so. She beams.

After six months, she has learned how you would implement many of the more repetitive tasks, so she begins initiating action. She informs you of these activities so that you can troubleshoot any problems and keeps you abreast of their progress.

Within the year, she is making decisions on many of the routine tasks, and implementing them regularly. You take a month vacation to Bora Bora and enjoy the solitude. Upon your return to the office, you find you have barely been missed. You beam.

### 4. Establish Checkpoints

If the task is complex, it is a good idea to schedule meetings to monitor her progress. These checkpoints help you make sure things are headed in the right direction. The more complex the project, the more guidance may be necessary.

Schedule frequent meetings at first. Then, as she prove capable and shows you she is on the right track, the checkpoints can become less frequent.

In this way, you avoid a lot of time passing by while you are left in the dark. You review the project with her, make sure she's on the right track, and offer suggestions for any problems she may encounter.

Delegating means relying upon others to make decisions and execute policy. If you can't always work "smarter and less hard," you should be able to let others do the work for you.

## NEXT STOP: REVIEW MARKETING PRINCIPLES

Okay, you have your personal house in order. You have learned to manage your time skillfully and to delegate with aplomb.

Yet before you can grow your business, we need to review a few fundamental marketing principles.

# CHAPTER 2

# Understanding Marketing

Purpose: *The purpose of chapter 2 is to review marketing fundamentals (including product differentiation, branding, promotion through logic or emotion), understand the buying process, and create brand loyalty.*

———◦———

**W**hat is this thing called marketing? My dictionary defines marketing as "the offering of something for sale." Sounds simple. Take something and sell it.

When academicians begin talking about marketing, they use phrases like "backward channeling," "quintile analysis," or "cluster forecasting." They seem to make the subject as mystifying as possible, as if only they understand it in all its complexity and subtle nuances.

Balderdash.

**Marketing is the satisfaction of needs and wants through the sale of your products or services.**

That's it. No corollaries. No fancy bric-a-brac. That definition works for all possible contingencies.

It is imperative, however, not to confuse needs and wants. The two are not the same, and therein lies a fundamental principle of marketing.

Consider the differences. Human needs are few: food, clothing, shelter, love, esteem, and maybe a good mutual fund.

Wants, on the other hand, are desires for specific goods that satisfy a need. A person needs food and wants a cheeseburger; needs clothing and wants an Armani suit; needs shelter and wants a home on the water.

He (or she) who can turn wants into needs reigns supreme. It's as simple as that. Nevertheless, it presents an unending challenge.

Marketers don't create needs. Needs have always existed. Good marketers create wants. They point out how their particular product satisfies a basic human need. They try to influence desires by making their products attractive, affordable, and easily available.

They suggest to consumers that their desire for esteem can be satisfied by a BMW—or their desire for safety by a Volvo. Or their desire for belonging can be satisfied by using public transportation.

Needs exist. Wants can be created. Marketing is simply the act of creating wants that satisfy needs.

Every company operates within a limited marketing budget. And every good marketing program needs a means of allocating those limited resources.

This starts with good planning.

# THE FOUR P'S

Marketing is a set of variables. These variables are frequently referred to as the **Four P's.**

1. **Product**
2. **Place**
3. **Price**
4. **Promotion**

## Product

How you manufacture your product to satisfy customer wants is a marketing variable. The name, features, options, sizes, packaging, and level of quality are each important in satisfying your customers' wants.

Changing your product can affect your sales. Higher quality, more options, or even a snazzy package will attract customers to your product over your competitors'.

All of these variables need to be considered as you develop your strategic marketing plan. Should I make my product available in different sizes, colors, or with different features?

The added benefits of these factors need to be weighed against the added costs.

## Place

Where you sell your product is also a marketing variable. The channels of distribution, transport, and locations will affect your sales. For instance, should you sell your line of exercise equipment through department stores, specialty stores, or directly to consumers? If selling direct, what sort of transport arrangements will be necessary? Standard ground transport? Next-day air?

When Avon began selling its line of cosmetics, they could have chosen to compete against Maybelline and Max Factor in department stores. Instead, they distributed their products directly to the home, and became a leader in the industry.

## Price

Your pricing policies will dramatically affect your sales results. Price, however, means more than just the price you charge for an item. Credit terms, warranties, discounts, and return policies can all be used to outshine the competition.

One retailer may charge you a little more for a new washing machine. But when that retailer says you don't have to pay for it for a year, it makes his offer very attractive.

## Promotion

This is what most people think of when they think of marketing. Promotion includes:

- Advertising
- Publicity
- Personal Selling
- Direct Marketing
- Sales Promotion

Those brochures you mail to prospects, the sales calls made by your sales team, the press release to your industry trade journal, the trade show you attended last year, coupons, bonus packs, ad specialties—all are forms of promotion.

There is a common misperception that "advertising" and "marketing" are interchangeable. But marketing is more than simply a few ads in the newspaper. Media advertising is but one form of promotion. And promotion is just one part of an overall marketing program.

The **Four P's** are the fundamental building blocks of your marketing program. Balance them wisely for maximum impact.

## ESTABLISH YOUR IMAGE

Perhaps nothing is more important than creating an image for your company or product. Called **branding**, it is the subject of numerous books and constant debate among marketing gurus.

Yet the principles of branding are really quite simple. Identify your product's unique characteristic, the thing or things that make it unique/different/better than anything else in the marketplace. In marketing, perception is nine-tenths of the sale. Creating a branded image of your product and its attributes is every bit as important as its efficacy.

This is more than a reiteration of the mission statement. This defines your place in the grand scheme of things, including your market niche (or niches), your fundamental market strategies, and your customers' perception of your company and its products.

 **Case Study** **FORRER BUSINESS INTERIORS**

### THE PROBLEM

FORRER Business Interiors, the largest purveyor of office furniture in Wisconsin, was asked to pitch an important piece of business: the complete design and furnishing of a large corporate accounting department.

The potential customer had a panel of three people who would make the purchase decision: the manager of accounts, the chief financial officer (CFO), and the facilities manager. Each had different motivations in the purchase decision.

How do you determine what your image should be? That depends:

• Upon your target customers
• Upon your competition
• Upon your costs

Often your brand image can be found within one of three categories:

**1. Quality**

**2. Service**

**3. Price**

Your product may have exceptional durability, or special features, colors, sizes, or models. These are all **quality**-related issues.

Your product may have the industry's best warranty, the fastest delivery time, or an outstanding service record if anything ever goes wrong. These are **service**-related issues.

**Price**-related differences include low price, multiple price points, credit terms, or quantity discounts. Hyundai's long-term warranty is a price characteristic.

Using Q, S, & P is a good way to begin to analyze your product or service. Common sense says you can only offer two out of three.

Think of it as a big equation: $Q + S = P$ where a large Q means better-than-average quality, a large S means better-than-average service, and a large P means lower-than-average price.

If your quality is high and your service is excellent, your price must be high, too (an unfavorable thing, a small p).

$$Q + S = p$$

If your quality is high, but your service is poor, your price should be lower:

$$Q + s = P$$

And if you sell second-quality goods, no matter how good your service, your price must reflect the quality of the merchandise:

$$q + S = P$$

For example, Chef Pierre's Café François features escargot and filet mignon and impeccable service. But Chef Pierre may cost you your credit limit. $(Q + S = p)$

McDonald's restaurant on the other hand offers quick service and a low price. But their food can't compare with Chef Pierre's. $(q + S = P)$

Now imagine if Chef Pierre tried to offer great quality, impeccable service, and match McDonald's prices, too: Surf & Turf (plus a free toy) for $3.99. His restaurant would be crowded with happy patrons, and he would lose money on every one. He would soon be out of business.

Likewise, think what would happen if McDonald's suddenly decided to compete with fancy restaurants like Chef Pierre's: Supersize McLobster for $3.99 (including a free toy!). McDonald's would be packed with seafood lovers, and the drive-thru would back up around the block. McDonald's would soon be out of business as well.

## Case Study | FORRER BUSINESS INTERIORS

### THE SOLUTION

FORRER designed a proposal that featured three distinct sections. The first emphasized quality and durability. Beautiful four-color photographs of the furniture were displayed to the accounts manager, the person most concerned with the quality of the product since his department would use it.

Another section featured the ease of servicing the modular workstations, the interchangeable parts, quick assembly, and reliability. This was of most interest to the facilities manager, whose job it was to move and adapt workstations as the need arose. She was also pleased to learn of FORRER's repair and replacement policies.

The CFO, naturally, was most concerned with cost containment. For him, FORRER demonstrated the value in using high-quality products over cheaper competition that might need replacement sooner. He was also presented payment options, including a leasing plan.

FORRER won the job by emphasizing the Q, S, & P to whom it most mattered. www.forrersbi.com

Chef Pierre doesn't advertise low prices. Nor does McDonald's pretend to have the best food in town. In the minds of their customers, neither tries to be something it is not. Yet both do very well simply by being the best at their two out of three.

There is an exception to every rule, and this rule is no exception. When you want to **buy market share**, you may need to offer all three.

If you do offer all three—quality, service, and price—you had better have confidence you can make up for any loss on that customer's next orders. Long term, you will need to charge more, substitute lower quality, or create lower service expectations to avoid losing money. (More on buying market share in chapter 4.)

By being flexible, some companies are able to create the perception that their customers receive all three. They can adapt their pricing, or service, or even the quality of their product according to their customers' needs. In effect, they simply choose the two that best suit the situation.

For example, a printing company is faced with a customer who orders a high-quality brochure and requires it immediately. The customer can expect to pay extra because the printer has to bump someone else's job from the production schedule to accommodate his rush order. Months later, that same customer asks the printer for another great-quality brochure, but his budget is dry and he needs a low-ball price. The printer can accommodate him by fitting the order at the end of the production schedule.

By choosing which two out of three to offer, the printing company has *created the perception* that he offers all three. His customer is happy and he makes a profit.

Any firm who offers only one of the three will soon be discovered by his customers. They probably won't be customers for very long. A low price will not make up for poor quality and lousy service both. Nor can the best product be sold at a high price if the service is lackluster.

## COMPETING ON PRICE

With little to differentiate one brand from another, commodity products compete primarily on price. To customers, your brand looks much the same as any other, so they simply buy what's cheapest.

Advertising genius David Ogilvy first realized the importance of product differentiation

### MICRO MARKETING

*The Q, S, & P formula can also be helpful when micromarketing, that is, targeting a specific customer.*

*Say, for instance, you want Zyde Company as a customer. ZydeCo currently buys from your competition.*

*Your salesperson does her homework and determines the competitor is providing great quality and low price, but little or no service.*

*Position your sales pitch around your superior service.*

back in the 1960s. He took a commodity product—gasoline—and managed to set his client, Shell Petroleum, apart from the competition by simply identifying an ingredient found in all gasoline and suggesting to the public that this ingredient was unique to Shell. His ad campaign for Shell, with Platformate, is legend.

Now truth be told, all gasoline back then contained Platformate. Yet Ogilvy recognized the importance of getting there first. His claim preempted the competition. And Shell became the bestselling gasoline in the U.S. It took years for the competition to dispel the idea that Platformate was unique to Shell.

Today, most consumers recognize gasoline is a true commodity. So petroleum retailers try to create product differences by offering additional services. Some offer Speed Pass convenience at the pump. Others have partnered with fast-food restaurants. Many have combined with convenience stores, selling milk, bread, and other household necessities. Anything to set themselves apart in a commodity marketplace.

Commodity markets offer few options for long-term profitability. The older the product category—whether gasoline or packaged goods, financial services or pharmaceuticals—the more likely they are to be perceived as commodities. It becomes increasingly difficult to eliminate sameness.

## Case Study ) McDONALD'S RESTAURANTS

### THE PROBLEM

McDonald's is the leading fast-food restaurant chain in Wisconsin, with more restaurants than any other.

They advertise heavily and work hard at maintaining clean stores and a pleasant experience for all their customers.

From time to time, other fast-food restaurant chains have tried to "out advertise" McDonald's in an effort to gain market share.

Modest product refinements get lost in a cluttered environment. Any improvement is quickly copied. Ultimately, competitors scrambling to convince skeptical consumers of their brand's unique benefits will lose, spending heavily while margins get thinner and thinner.

By augmenting the product, you can redefine what is being purchased. For instance, a B2B firm selling durables may add services: logistics, consulting, integrated Internet services. By adding value to the core product, a firm can set itself apart from competitors in the consumer's mind.

# BECAUSE I HEARD OF IT

Clearly, the first step in creating any perception at all for your product is to create awareness of it. The worst perception of all is complete ignorance of its existence. It is critical that your customers and prospects know who you are and what you stand for so that you are among their choices when it comes time to make a purchase.

Customers of all types—whether buying business-to-business or as consumers—often choose one particular brand over another simply because they are familiar with the name.

Research conducted in shopping malls and grocery stores suggests that the primary reason for purchase of a particular brand is based upon name recall. Asked why they bought a product, people invariably responded, "Because I heard of it."

That's name awareness.

How do you acquire name awareness? Repetition. Repeat the name of your company or product wherever and whenever you can. Put it on your purchase orders, invoices, and other mailings to suppliers and customers. Outfit your employees in T-shirts and jackets with your company name and logo on them. Get a sign for the side of your car. Sponsor a soccer team and be sure the team wears uniforms with your name on them.

Frequent advertising, conspicuous signage, regular mailings, and positive publicity in the newspaper or other media will translate into "Because I heard of it."

One of the best ways to assure name awareness: use a multitude of tactics across a variety of media simultaneously. Multiple media exposure creates name awareness and that all-important sense of credibility.

Radio listeners hear the announcer tout the benefits of your product. Then, they see your name on a billboard, read about your company in a newspaper article generated by your press release, and receive a brochure from you in the mail. When it comes time to make a purchase, they remember your name and, perhaps only subliminally, they remember that someone (the radio announcer?) said something good about you or your company or your product. They go out and buy your brand "Because I heard of it."

## Case Study: McDONALD'S RESTAURANTS

**THE SOLUTION**

McDonald's prides itself on being number one in its category. They conduct quarterly market research in which they ask consumers, "Can you name a fast-food restaurant?"

In the Milwaukee market, over 90 percent name McDonald's first when asked to name a fast-food restaurant.

If that number falls below 90 percent in any quarter, McDonald's is quick to beef up its advertising and promotion spending.

At McDonald's, they understand the importance of "top-of-mind" awareness. www.McDonalds.com

The secret is to make each ad work harder for you by supplementing it with other promotional tactics—newspaper ads, radio spots, publicity, brochures, newsletters, and direct mailings, all timed to your industry's biggest trade show.

Suddenly deluged by your company message, your customers and prospects begin to sense a leader in the marketplace. They will naturally be more apt to call on you rather than a competitor when it's time to buy.

## DIFFERENTIATING YOUR PRODUCT

It's a commodity world. Your research and development team may try to convince you that their new product idea is unique in the entire world. Try not to laugh at them.

This is not to say new product improvements or innovative processes are not important. They are (see chapter 7).

But true innovation is fleeting. When previously it took years for competitors to catch up, it now takes days. Minor product improvements—a better bell or new whistle—can be deengineered and duplicated almost instantaneously.

Satellite communications, global manufacturing, and Internet technology have all

> ## A COMMODITY WORLD
> ............................
> *Your product improvement introduced on Monday is known round the world by Tuesday, deengineered on Wednesday, copied by Thursday, and launched by your competitor on Friday.*

conspired to shorten the gap between innovation and commodity. Your novel product improvement introduced on Monday is known round the world by Tuesday, deengineered on Wednesday, copied by Thursday, and launched by your competitor on Friday.

Despite this lack of uniqueness, your product must be perceived as unique, positively unlike any competing brand. The key to strong brand image is differentiation. Differentiation sets you apart from the competition. It makes your product easier to remember when it comes time to purchase. Differentiation gives consumers a reason, *other than price,* to choose you over the competition.

It is no wonder everyone is looking for a way to differentiate his product from his competitors'.

Whether it's the bigger this, the faster that, or the longest-lasting other thing, finding that key point of difference, the unique characteristic that makes people want to buy your product over someone else's means the difference in winning or losing the sale.

With today's technology, most products have become "commoditized." So when you do develop a true product difference, it is imperative you exploit it—and fast.

Even if there is little or no difference between your product or service and your competitors', you still need to create a perception that it is distinctive.

Unilever's Dove hand soap competes in a mature category where consumers find little difference between brands. Yet Dove remains one of the category leaders. Its consistent message—"Made with one-quarter cleansing

# THE NEED TO DIFFERENTIATE
·····························

*Young & Rubicam, Inc., the global advertising agency, tracks thousands of brands and the ways consumers perceive them.*

*Among their findings:*

- *New brands enjoyed success when they were highly differentiated, even when their awareness levels and credibility were still low.*

- *Conversely, brands that lost market share had less differentiation in consumers' minds.*

Source: Y&R, Inc.

cream," sets it apart. It is perceived as a mild soap, the perfect facial cleanser, ideal for maintaining soft skin.

The secret is finding that unique product difference, because it is the thing that you must advertise, the primary strategy for promoting your business, and the hook where you hang your hat.

Here's a good way to identify your product's unique difference. Imagine that every product has three parts:

1. The **Actual Product**
2. The **Core Product**
3. The **Augmented Product**

The **actual product** is the specific thing you receive in exchange for money (or barter).

If you buy shampoo, it's the container and the liquid itself. If you buy a drill bit, it's the twisting piece of hardened steel. If you buy an airplane ticket on Midwest Airlines, it's simply the ticket itself, the piece of paper or email confirmation that promises a seat on board some future flight.

The **core product** is the primary product benefit you receive.

For shampoo, it's the clean hair. For the drill bit, it's the hole. And for the airline ticket, it's the seat from here to wherever.

The **augmented product** is the unique product difference, the characteristic that makes that product distinctive, better than anyone else's product.

For the shampoo, it's the shiny hair, the tangle-free hair, or the dandruff control. For the drill bit, it's the hardened carbon steel, or the carbide tip. For Midwest Airlines, it's the first-class-only seating, the in-flight champagne, and above all, the chocolate chip cookies baked in flight.

Good marketers promote more than simple product benefits. Any shampoo will get your hair clean. It's the extra shine, body, or dandruff control that makes that shampoo unique. That distinctive characteristic is what must be promoted.

Midwest Airlines doesn't promote the lowest fares, nor do they emphasize their vast route system. Theirs is "The Best Care in the Air" exemplified by their first-class service and delicious cookies.

# REASON VS. EMOTION (LEO BURNETT VS. BILL BERNBACH)

Once found, how do you communicate your augmented benefit to consumers?

There are two schools of thought on the subject. One suggests logic and reason, convincing buyers of the value of your product over the competition. The other proposes appealing to the emotions, making the customer feel good about purchasing your product.

Famous advertising executive Bill Bernbach said that the real giants in advertising were those who jumped from the realm of facts into imagination and ideas. Advertising must connect on an emotional level. Before an advertiser can be believed, he must first be liked. "Advertising is fundamentally persuasion, and persuasion happens to be not a science, but an art."

Leo Burnett, founder of the Chicago School of Advertising, stressed finding the inherent drama in a product and writing the ad out of the drama, rather than using mere cleverness. "Draw attention to the product, not the advertisement," Burnett often said. He believed that it was only creative if it sold product. "We want consumers to say, 'That's a hell of a product' instead of, 'That's a hell of an ad.'"

The Burnett way of thinking depends upon logical arguments in favor of the product. It focuses on problems or consumer wants, and how the product solves

## PRODUCT AUGMENTATION

*The Internet offers a vast array of product augmentation opportunities. Examples abound:*

*Proctor & Gamble's Tide detergent has a website, Tide Stain Detective (www.tide.com/stain detective), where consumers can learn how to remove virtually any stain. It provides credibility and differentiates the brand in a crowded commodity category.*

*Nickelodeon's website (www.nick.com) receives more than 1.5 million hits each week from kids who want to expand their TV-viewing experience.*

*Disposable diapers have matured into a commodity category. But P&G's Pampers uses its website (www.pampers.com) to maintain a point of difference, with online sweepstakes, toddler craft projects, and more.*

those problems or achieves the benefits sought. For example, comparison advertisements contrast product features against competitor features. They ask the prospect to follow the logic of buying their product over another.

I come from Leo Burnett's Chicago School and have always believed that, given a logical argument, consumers will prefer my product to my competition. But I have come to appreciate the benefits of appealing to buyer's emotions. This appeal to the heart, rather than the head, is growing in popularity among marketers. Product proliferation, information overload, and instant communication has consumers confounded and confused, at a total loss for differentiating products.

Emotional advertising goes straight to the heart of consumers. It appeals to their feelings, and their desires associated with a product or service. Fear, sex, joy, grief, enlightenment—all are evoked by emotional advertisements. Michelin sells tires based upon the premise, "So much is riding on your tires." They tug at our heartstrings, pull us into their emotional argument, and grab our wallets.

In the past, emotional messages were reserved for luxury goods, high fashion, and insurance. Promoters of perfume, liquor, and luxury automobiles, perhaps hard pressed to offer logical arguments to buy their products, appealed to our emotions. They associated their products with popular and attractive people having fun. Luxury products signify wealth, and the wearer/user/driver is therefore worthy of respect.

Luxury items—cars, watches, jewelry—in particular work well with emotional appeals. It is far easier to justify buying an expensive watch because it makes you look classy than because it keeps time any better. Emotional appeals also increase post-purchase satisfaction levels. Ultimately, there may be no logical reason to spend that much money on a specific brand. But as long as the item lives up to its emotional appeal (rather than more logical features/benefits), consumers will not experience the "buyer's remorse" often associated with buying luxury goods.

Commodity products can also sell better with an emotional appeal. Logical arguments are pointless when consumers cannot distinguish any difference from one product to another. Many everyday products have begun to find benefit in emotional advertising.

For instance, milk could be sold logically, based upon its nutritional value, its vitamins, calcium, niacin, potassium, and other nutrients it contains. But most people know that already. Instead, the Milk Marketing Association uses athletes, actors, and other role models to create an emotional bond with the product.

Emotional appeals can lift me-too products above the fray and position them as unique. Absolut Vodka effectively differentiates itself from other vodkas by focusing not on the spirits inside the bottle, but the bottle itself.

When selling services, credibility is essential. A prospect must feel a sense of trust before becoming a buyer. Service companies should use emotional branding whenever possible. Service providers (accountants, architects, software designers, and consultants) use speaking engagements and journal articles to build credibility. Insurance companies use testimonials in their advertising from victims of fire- and flood-damaged properties to build that sense of trust. If the insurer helped out those folks, they must be okay, and I can count on them helping me out if I get in a jam, too.

Business-to-business marketers also use emotional appeals in their messages. While companies may follow more logical decision-making patterns than consumers, the decision maker is only human, with human emotions, needs, and wants. It only stands to reason that appealing to the decision maker's emotional side while still building a logical case for the product is the best way to sell B2B.

# HUMOR ME

One of the best ways to create emotion in your advertisements is through humor. It also makes your ads more memorable. Victor Borge, the great Danish comedian, once said, "The shortest distance between two people is a laugh."

Humor has a way of cutting through formality, breaking down barriers, and allowing people to talk one on one. What better way to make friends? And customers!

Humor can be used effectively in the promotions you do for your company. Think about the advertisements you remember best. They tend to be the ones that made you smile. Playfulness sells.

Dear Mr. Smith:

Help! Please save my home life by reading the enclosed catalog.

My wife has been slaving over it night and day, working like a dog, and treating me like one in the process. If it's not a smashing success, can you imagine what it will be like to live with her?

So won't you please read Judy's catalog? It contains all sorts of new products designed to make your life easier (and mine, too).

Sincerely,

Joe Dokes (Judy's husband)

Sometimes it's the unexpected that makes for humor, as in this sales letter. The number of personal notes to Joe that showed up with orders attested to the effectiveness of this approach.

Two of the most common ways of instilling humor in advertising is the use of **critters** and **buzzwords** (or phrases).

## FIVE REASONS TO ADD HUMOR TO YOUR MARKETING EFFORTS

1. *Humor causes intimacy. It breaks down barriers and brings people together. Admit it. The people you like best are the ones who get your jokes.*

2. *Humor attracts attention. It can make your advertising stand out amid the clutter.*

3. *Humor is more memorable. Most everyone will remember a good joke and enjoy telling it to someone else.*

4. *Subtle humor flatters your intelligence. The best joke is the one that makes you laugh for five seconds, and think for ten minutes.*

5. *Humor is endearing. After all, we would all rather buy something from someone we like, from someone who makes us laugh.*

Remember "Where's the beef?" for Wendy's hamburgers? Or "Whassup?" for Budweiser? Buzzwords or phrases are memorable and help position the brand.

Finish this sentence: "Fly the friendly skies of _____ ." Or this one: "Nothing runs like a _____." How about: "Melts in your mouth, not in your _____."

Leo Burnett Company also uses critters to add an emotional message or humor to its clients' brands. Charlie the Tuna brings humor to an otherwise mundane product. Keebler elves make cookies even more fun. The Pillsbury Doughboy puts a giggle at the end of every commercial.

One of the easiest and most effective ways to create humor in your advertising is to take the primary benefit of your product or service and stretch it, exaggerate it to the point of absurdity.

For example, Dunkin' Donuts wanted to demonstrate their speedy service. So their television commercial shows a police chase from a helicopter's point of view. During the chase, the crook stops at a Dunkin' Donuts for a bagel and coffee (so does the police officer chasing him). They are both in and out quickly. The primary benefit (speedy service) exaggerated to the point of absurdity makes for a humorous TV spot.

By using humor, we create a bond, a sense of belonging together, a sense that, "Hey, this guy's funny. I think I'd enjoy working with him." In short, humor sells.

One final word on reason vs. emotion. Emotional messages help develop relationships, a bond between customer and brand.

But the emotional link must still be consistent with the logical reason to purchase. Understanding what is important to the customer remains paramount. Then, linking an emotional message to logical persuasion can effectively differentiate your brand.

Lastly, sometimes an emotional message can confuse. Not everyone relates to humor, fear, and desire in the same way. What one person finds hilarious may offend someone else. Without solid logic to persuade buyers, the emotional message can become muddled and lose its ability to convert shoppers to buyers.

Next, you need to understand exactly who it is that will buy your products, their likes and dislikes, their unique characteristics, their motivations. Who are these people? What do they have in common? What makes them tick?

# THE BUYING PROCESS

Advertisements entice us. Compelling packaging grabs our eye as we walk the shopping mall. Salespeople hawk their wares, constantly bombarding us with one sales pitch after another. Buy this! No, buy this!

But customers don't all respond in the same way. Sometimes we weigh each purchase carefully. Other times we buy on impulse or make rash decisions (which we may regret later).

However we make our purchase choice, that decision-making is an ongoing process. It is more than what happens at the moment we fork over the cash and receive a product or service in return. It is a series of steps that take us from the point at which we realize we have a need, beyond the purchase, to the experience we have with the product after it is purchased.

Both organizations (B2B) and consumers (B2C) buy in much the same way. There is a subtle pattern that occurs deep in the subconscious as it travels through the buying process. It's a predictable pattern, and it looks like this:

1. **Problem Recognition**
2. **Information Search**

3. **Evaluation of Alternatives**
4. **Purchase Choice**
5. **Post-Purchase Evaluation**

A customer experiences a need for something (**Problem Recognition**). Let's say the oil light on his car suddenly goes on. He's low on oil. He goes to his local garage and asks the mechanic about his options, the benefits of 10W-30 or 10W-40, regular or synthetic, one brand or another (**Information Search**).

He then weighs the benefits of each option (**Evaluation of Alternatives**) based upon performance, price, and any intangibles (he may have seen a TV commercial for a particular brand). Finally, he takes out his wallet, plunks down his money (**Purchase Choice**), the cash register goes "cha-ching," and he is on his way.

But that's not the end of it. He tells a friend about his brand choice and his friend concurs that he made a smart decision. The oil light goes off. The oil performs up to the buyer's expectations. He experiences positive reinforcement from his friend and feels satisfied with the performance of the product (**Post-Purchase Evaluation**).

Let's examine each step:

## Problem Recognition

Problem recognition occurs whenever someone feels there is something lacking in his life. He has a need, a problem he wishes to solve. It could be something small and simple (the toothpaste tube is empty). Or something larger or more complex (the outdated piece of equipment is causing higher costs).

Some marketers use promotion to induce a state of "need." A television commercial might suggest you would look great in a jazzy convertible and have a better chance of attracting envious stares, rather than the derisive laughs you receive now because of the old clunker you're driving. Oral-B makes a toothbrush with color embedded in the outer layers of the bristles. As the bristles become thinner with use, the color wears off, alerting the user it is time to buy a new one—built-in problem recognition!

## Information Search

This is the next step in the decision process, when you check your memory and begin noticing advertisements that pertain to your need. Past recommendations from friends ("Fred bought a new Mustang convertible and he really likes it. The girls are paying more attention to him now, too."), often called word-of-mouth, are the best form of advertising because they are often unsolicited testimonials made by actual users (rather than a paid advertising copywriter). Internet searches, TV ads, trade journals, advertising brochures, *Consumer Reports* magazine, and company sales representatives, or your next-door neighbor all offer means of conducting research before making a purchase.

## Evaluation of Alternatives

This begins during the information search. Price considerations quickly eliminate some alternatives. While you may dream of owning a red Mercedes convertible, reality sets in and you limit your search to more affordable cars—makes and models you may have heard about through friends or advertisements.

With higher-priced purchases, like an automobile, the next step is to evaluate based upon the criteria most important to you personally. Low mileage, low mpg, low price. Something sporty? Red or blue?

Disposable goods, like toothpaste or chewing gum, typically do not require a great deal of conscious evaluation. Their cost is less significant. And they often lack multiple criteria. Nonetheless, if two toothpastes offer cavity protection and whitening, you may still weigh the value of one brand versus another based upon price, taste, and perhaps the package.

Whether durables or disposables, as consumers, we prioritize these criteria and determine which are most closely met by each option. Perfectly logical.

Or so it would seem.

Often, consumers make decisions based purely upon impulse. Or for seemingly irrational reasons. For example, the Point-of-Purchase Advertising Institute claims that two-thirds of all retail buying decisions are made in the store. Impulse purchase. Bill Bernbach may have been right. Connecting with a customer emotionally may be as important (or more) as appealing to his sense of reason.

And that, too, is perfectly logical.

## Purchase Choice

Time to buy. Time to solve the problem, satisfy the need, the want. Time to fill the hole in your happiness. After agonizing over the options for weeks (or not), you take out your wallet and buy.

All that thinking about your decision has been driving you crazy. You immediately feel relieved. You have what you wanted. Your happiness has been sustained for another day.

Or has it?

## Post-Purchase Evaluation

Begins the moment you own it, whatever "it" is. Now you begin to evaluate just how good a choice you have made.

Everyone at some time or another has felt regret after making a purchase, just as we have all been pleased by something we have bought. Post-purchase evaluation results in an overall feeling about the purchase we made. We are either satisfied or dissatisfied.

Two factors contribute to our feelings of satisfaction/dissatisfaction: perception and empirical evidence. Perception is how we feel about ourselves as a result of our purchase. If your friends gawk in awe at your new car, this may add to your level of satisfaction. If the new car performs up to your expectations (smooth ride, good gas mileage, few repairs), this is the empirical evidence you need to feel satisfied.

Post-purchase evaluation is most important in higher-priced goods. You go to a bar, order a beer, and if it doesn't taste as good as your regular beer, you may not feel horribly dissatisfied. You just don't order that beer again. But if your new car is always in the shop and its poor design and dull color cause nobody to stare in envy, you are likely to feel highly dissatisfied.

Marketers of automobiles understand this principle. If you buy a new car, both the dealer and manufacturer will likely follow up within a few weeks with satisfaction surveys and incentives (free oil change, car wash, etc.) to enhance your feeling of satisfaction. Their television commercials almost always have a "reassurance" component. "Aren't the Hendersons smart for buying a Honda? Their neighbors paid much more for far less . . ."

---

### THE BUYING PROCESS

........................................

**Problem Recognition**
*"I'm thirsty."*

**Information Search**
*"Bartender, whadda ya got?"*

**Evaluation of Alternatives**
*"Wine, whiskey, or beer?"*

**Purchase Choice**
*"Gimme a Miller Lite."*

**Post-Purchase Evaluation**
*"Ah, that hit the spot."*

This process holds for consumers (B2C) as well as organizations (B2B). But selling B2B, nevertheless, has its unique challenges.

# ORGANIZATIONAL BUYING HABITS VS. CONSUMER BUYING HABITS

It's no secret. Organizations buy differently than individuals.

If you sell B2B, you already know this. Corporations have committees. They have policies, procedures, forms to fill out, and hoops to jump through.

Yet both individuals and corporations have one thing in common: they both follow the **buying process**.

For example, let's say the maintenance fore-man looks at his old lawnmowers—parts cobbled together, in constant need of repair—and he gets approval to buy half a dozen new lawn-mowers to cut the lawn at the company's twen-ty-acre complex (problem recognition). He calls his outdoor equipment supplier (you) from whom he has recently purchased several snow blowers, and requests a brochure on lawnmow-ers (information search). He does this with sev-eral competitors as well to compare models and prices (evaluation of alternatives).

> **THE BUYING PROCESS**
> ......................................
> *1. Problem Recognition*
>
> *2. Information Search*
>
> *3. Evaluation of Alternatives*
>
> *4. Purchase*
>
> *5. Post-Purchase Satisfaction*

Finally, he makes his decision. He buys all six mowers from you (purchase). Congratulations. You deliver the mowers, provide set-up and operating instruction, and offer a ninety-day warranty. He smiles and shakes your hand (post-purchase satisfaction).

How is that different from selling a lawnmower to a homeowner (besides the quantity)?

Organizations buy goods for three reasons:

**1. Goods as an end product**

The goods that, added together, make the products that the manufacturer sells. These include raw materials and manufactured parts that go into finished goods.

**2. Goods used to build end products**

The machinery, equipment, and tools used to manufacture or assemble the end products (but not those a part of the end product). These include capital

## DIRECT SALES TO ORGANIZATIONS VS. CONSUMERS

*When sending direct mail to organizations, use short copy with clearly defined specifications. Organizational buyers do not have time to read superfluous copy points.*

*Consumers purchasing the same item may be making a serious financial commitment. They take the time to read long copy because they have the time.*

*B2B, use bullet points of key benefits and product specifications.*

*B2C, use lots of facts, detailed explanations of features, and how the benefits apply to them.*

goods, accessories, computers (CAD, CAM, robotics, etc.).

**3. Goods *not* part of the end product**

Overhead, like office supplies, services, maintenance products, etc.

Organizations typically do not *consume*. They use purchases to produce things, or simply to resell.

They have more people involved in the purchase decision, too. The machinist may tell his foreman he needs a new machine. The foreman reviews a variety of options and makes a recommendation to the vice president of manufacturing, who reviews the budget and okays the requisition. The CFO reviews the requisition with the budget committee, which eventually signs off. The purchase order is authorized and the director of purchasing actually buys the machine.

Along the road from problem recognition to purchase are a variety of policies and procedures that must be followed, and paperwork—quotes, purchase orders, acknowledgements, etc.—that must be generated.

Generally, organizations have skilled negotiators, experts in product quality and prices because they have purchased these items hundreds of times in the past. Consumers, on the other hand, may make a major purchase of a particular item only seldom.

# BRAND LOYALTY

All customers (B2B and B2C) go through the buying process. But, with good marketing (and a good product), it is possible to short circuit the progression.

The ultimate objective of all promotion is to create **brand loyalty**. Someone who is loyal to a particular brand skips the **information search** and the **evaluation of alternatives**.

She perceives a need, goes out and buys her regular brand. No comparison-shopping; no consideration of alternatives.

She is brand loyal. (More about how to create brand loyalty in chapter 7.)

# MARKET MOTIVATION

Problem recognition is the first step in satisfying needs and wants. But how are needs created? Why do we have needs? And how can marketers turn needs into wants?

Once we have a need, we begin to seek out ways to satisfy the need. The stronger the need, the more powerful the motivation for satisfaction.

Psychologist Abraham Maslow developed a means to categorize motivation according to levels of importance. Human beings seek to satisfy basic needs before seeking to satisfy more complex needs. So Maslow developed a pyramid, a hierarchy of needs, with the most basic needs (food, water, warmth, sleep) on the bottom, and more complex needs as you move higher up the pyramid.

Remember the movie *Cast Away* with Tom Hanks? After the plane crash, Hanks's character, Chuck Noland, is washed up on the beach. The first thing he does, the very *first* thing, is fall asleep, exhausted. Sleep is one of the most fundamental of needs.

> ## BRAND LOYALTY
> ......................................
> ***Problem Recognition***
> *"I'm thirsty."*
>
> ~~*Information Search*~~
>
> ~~*Evaluation of Alternatives*~~
>
> ***Purchase Choice***
> *"Gimme a Miller Lite."*
>
> ***Post-Purchase Evaluation***
> *"Ah, that hit the spot."*

Next, Chuck begins searching for food (coconuts). He finds shelter from a storm in a cave. For companionship, he invents an imaginary friend from a volleyball, Wilson. As he achieves each level in the hierarchy, he begins to seek the next level. Chuck is never able to achieve status or ego. (In his frustration, he tries to kill himself, but even that effort goes awry.) Self-actualization and spiritual fulfillment, therefore, are unattainable.

Smart marketers understand the level of needs relevant to customers in their target markets. They tailor their products and messages to them.

Volvo is made in Sweden of the finest steel, able to withstand a 100 km/hr collision with a moose (which are as plentiful as deer in Wisconsin). Safety features throughout the car provide a sense of well-being to drivers and passengers alike. Volvo sells security.

Jaguar makes a luxury vehicle with a hand-finished walnut dashboard, 320-watt sound system, and impeccable styling. Jaguar sells status.

Finding your brand image may be as simple as choosing from Maslow's hierarchy.

Hobbies, travel, continuing education
(U.S. Army – "Be all you can be")

Self-Actualization
enrichment experiences

Lexus, Ferrari, country club, luxury goods
(Polo sportswear, Rolex watch)

Status/Ego
prestige and accomplishment

Social fraternities, clubs, clothing, grooming aids
(Pepsi – "Join the Pepsi generation")

Love/Belonging
friendship, acceptance

Car alarm, insurance, retirement plan
(Allstate Insurance – "You're in
good hands with Allstate)

Safety/Security
shelter, protection

Medicine, food staples, generics
(Quaker Oats – "It's the right thing to do")

Physiological Needs
water, sleep, food

**MASLOW'S HIERARCHY OF NEEDS**

# CHAPTER 3

# The Strategic Marketing Plan

*The purpose of chapter 3 is to demonstrate how to:*
- *Understand your industry and your place in it*
- *Identify demographic, psychographic, and benefit characteristics*
- *Choose ideal target customers*
- *Establish sales objectives*
- *Write a marketing plan*

———◦———

**Y**our company's strategic plan consists of three parts: the operations plan, the financial plan, and the marketing plan.

The marketing plan drives the other two. The marketing plan tells the operations people how much raw material, labor, and supplies will be needed. The marketing plan tells the financial people how many widgets you will sell at what price and how much revenue to expect.

What does a marketing plan look like? Despite myriad variations, every good plan has five basic parts:

1. Situation Analysis
2. Objectives
3. Strategies
4. Tactics
5. Budget

The **situation analysis** contains three elements:

1. **Sales Analysis:** An examination of recent sales and profit results, target market analysis, and sales estimates.
2. **Competitive Analysis:** Your company's strengths and weaknesses vs. key competitors and product substitutes.
3. **Environment Analysis:** An analysis of the environment in which you operate, including technology, government regulations, economic factors, supply chain analysis, and broad industry trends.

The **objectives** are where you want to be and when you want to get there.

• Is the purpose of your marketing plan to boost revenue from existing products? If so, one of your objectives might read: "Increase revenue 8 percent from our existing line of products over the next six months while maintaining current profit margins."

• Is the purpose of your marketing plan to launch a new product or line of products? Your objective might then read: "Achieve 10 percent market share within the first twelve months of product launch."

Notice that each objective is quantified and features a limited time frame. It makes your objectives quantifiable and measurable. This also lets everybody know how they are doing along the way.

If your objective is where you want your company to be, the **strategies** are the route you need to take to get there. There are five strategies, and only five strategies, that can build any business. These are the means for kicking your company to the next level. More on that later.

Strategies define direction, provide motive, and guide you along the path from here to there.

For example, if the objective is to increase sales revenue, your strategies might be:

• Target new customers among eighteen-to thirty-four-year-olds (Hunt).

• Focus promotional spending on higher-priced units (Buy Market Share).

---

**STRATEGIC MARKETING PLAN**

·····························

*–Outline–*

• *Executive Summary*

• *Situation Analysis*

  • *Sales Analysis*

  • *Competitive Analysis*

  • *Environment Analysis*

• *Objectives*

• *Strategies*

• *Tactics*

• *Budget*

• Increase sales of accessory items to existing customers (Farm).

**Tactics** are specific actions. A brochure is a tactic; an ad in the newspaper is a tactic; promotional pens or T-shirts with your name and logo on them are tactics. In other words, while strategies are conceptual visions, tactics are the tangible fulfillment of those visions.

The **budget** is the price of your tactics. Add up the cost of all the tactics you plan to use and you know what your budget must be to achieve your goals.

A strategic plan is the first step in growing your business, and the marketing plan is the first step in developing your strategic plan.

# THE SITUATION ANALYSIS

To understand where your organization should fit in the grand scheme of things, it's important to answer this:

Who am I and where am I going?

Let's imagine for a moment you are the coach of a National Football League team. You're sitting in your office, the videotapes are running, and all the players have gone home. Why are you working so late? What will the tapes reveal that can help you beat your opponents?

First, you review the tapes of your own team. You want to know your team's strengths and what opportunities they present for next Sunday's game. You also want to know your weaknesses so that you can compensate for them.

Next, you review tapes of your opponents. You want to know their strengths and weaknesses and what threats they pose.

Naturally, you already know everything you can about the game itself. Is it home or away? Grass or artificial turf? Who will be officiating and how will they call the game?

## SITUATION ANALYSIS
...............................................

*The Situation Analysis is the fundamental building block upon which all planning is constructed.*

*Every Situation Analysis consists of three parts:*

*1. Sales Analysis*

*2. Competitive Analysis*

*3. Environment Analysis*

  • *Technology*

  • *Governmental Regulations*

  • *Economic Factors*

  • *Labor and Raw Materials*

  • *Industry Trends*

A good coach will analyze his situation carefully so as to optimize the tools at his disposal.

In business, it's called the **situation analysis**, and it is the fundamental building block upon which all planning is constructed. When you develop a plan, you set objectives—where you want to be by this time next year, or five years from now.

But how can you decide where you want to go unless you know where you began? It's like trying to make travel arrangements to Poughkeepsie without knowing what city you're in right now.

The situation analysis has three basic parts:

1. **The Sales Analysis**
2. **The Competitive Analysis**
3. **The Environment Analysis**

# THE SALES ANALYSIS

How far can you reach? Could you triple your sales in five years?

You won't know how far you can reach unless you first analyze. To take your successful company to the next level, you must know your market and how your organization fits.

Begin with an assessment of your company's strengths and weaknesses (sometimes called SWOT Analysis for strength, weakness, opportunity, and threat). How do these compare to your competition? Where are you better? Where are you most vulnerable? How can you take advantage of your strengths and exploit your competitors' weaknesses?

## SWOT ANALYSIS

- **S**  Strengths
- **W**  Weaknesses
- **O**  Opportunities
- **T**  Threats

For instance, your company makes innovative products (**strength)** that offer clear advantages over the competition. Your costs are higher, so your prices are higher (**weakness**), and you often lose customers to lower-priced competitors.

This simple analysis helps you to create strategies that offset competitors' advantages—strategies that maximize your company's strengths and minimize your weaknesses.

Next, examine your organization's **opportunities**. Let's say your key competitor has just announced a price increase. You know the fallout from a price increase because you suffered through yours last year. You lost some business to the competitor in the process. So now, how do you take advantage of your competitor's situation? What opportunity does it offer?

Next, analyze your **sales history**. What are the trends, and why? What are the fundamental reasons behind your sales curve? Knowing why your sales have trended up or down is vital as you begin to set objectives for your marketing plan.

Let's say your sales built steadily for five years, but have been flat the last two years. Why? What happened? Maybe a key salesperson left and took several accounts with her. Maybe a competitor introduced a new product that significantly impacted your revenue.

The answers can lead to strategies that regain your momentum.

> *A few words about SWOT Analysis:*
>
> *•Strengths and weaknesses are typically internal issues, while opportunities and threats are external.*
>
> *• Strengths and weaknesses assess past performance. Opportunities and threats offer predictions for the future.*
>
> *• S, W, and O may explain why your sales have increased, decreased, or remained flat.*
>
> *• Only S, W, and T apply to your competitors (you don't care about their opportunities).*

# IDENTIFY TARGET MARKETS

After analyzing your past sales, the next step is to determine whom you will sell to in the future. You can't sell to everybody. That just doesn't work. Customers are too numerous and too different. They do not all have the same needs or wants.

By breaking the market into bite-size segments with similar characteristics and serving those whose needs match your product's features, you can maximize your sales and profits.

Targeting your market requires three steps:
1. Identify segments with similar characteristics (segmentation) using demographic, psychographic, and benefit analysis.
2. Select primary and secondary markets to enter (targeting).
3. Determine the best way to communicate benefits key to those target segments (positioning).

A **mass market** includes all buyers in a category. Wal-Mart sells to a broad spectrum of people. They identify similar needs held by a majority of people (low prices) and serve them. Their mass method of purchasing, distribution, and promotion creates lower costs. But while Wal-Mart (and others) has been successful at **mass marketing**, it can be the most difficult method of building sales.

Today, consumers have more ways to shop (malls, specialty stores, warehouse megastores, catalogs, online, etc.) and are bombarded with promotion messages through a wide variety of channels (TV, cable, radio, print, direct mail, outdoor, ad specialties, telemarketing, e-zines, webcasts, etc.). As it becomes increasingly difficult, and expensive, to reach a mass audience, more companies choose to separate the market into segments and promote their products to those segments. A **market segment** is a group of customers with a similar set of wants. Selling to a **market segment** allows a company to create a product, price it appropriately, and promote it as the solution to that segment's needs.

While a **market segment** may have similar demographics, it cannot necessarily be defined that way. For instance, a soft drink company targeting active teenagers may find active teenagers differ about what they want in their soft drinks. Some may want low calories; others want fruit flavoring; still others want only bottled water. The **market segment** is the group who prefer fruit-flavored drinks, regardless of age, gender, race, or income level (more on demographics in the next chapter).

A **niche market** is similar to a segment, only smaller and more narrowly defined. Customers in a **niche market** have a distinctive set of wants and will pay a premium price for the product that best satisfies those wants.

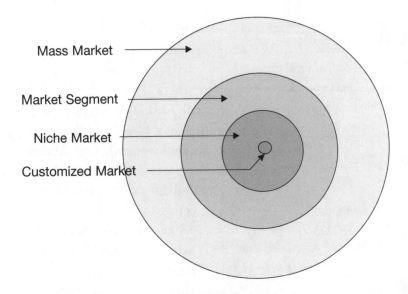

Mass Market
Market Segment
Niche Market
Customized Market

For instance, umbrellas are sold to a **segment** of the population who need protection in rainy climates. Oversize umbrellas are a separate **niche** within the umbrella segment. Becher, a German company, has carved out a profitable **niche**, with a 50 percent share of the world market for oversize umbrellas.

**Niche markets** can have significant economic advantages:

• Fewer competitors
• Lower costs due to specialization
• Premium pricing
• Higher margins, profits

If you are number one in your market, a majority of your sales will come from people who simply say, "Hey, I can't go wrong with the leading brand."

If you are not number one in your market, find a niche and fill it better than anyone. Become number one. For instance, you may not be the best deli in all of Chicago, but you could be number one in Reuben sandwiches. Once you are number one in your market niche, you have something to brag about. This can lead to greater sales,

## PROMOTING TO EACH MARKET SEGMENT

*Mass Market = Mass media (TV, radio, newspapers)*

*Market Segment = Directed Promotions (cable TV, event sponsorships)*

*Niche Market = Still More Focused Efforts (Direct mail, telemarketing)*

*Customized Market = Personal Selling (one-on-one)*

## NICHE MARKETS

*Low entry barriers for Internet start-ups have led to many small businesses aiming at more segmented niche markets.*

*Successful Web entrepreneurs choose hard-to-find products that consumers need not touch or see.*

*For example, www.ostrichesonline.com offers everything ostrich, from ostrich meat to feather boas, books, games, toys, coins, cosmetics, and cartoons. All ostrich-related.*

## SELF-SELECTION

*Proctor & Gamble's Cheer laundry detergent advertised its Cheer Free brand (the same Cheer detergent with no fragrance for those who have allergies to perfume additives) on television heavily, but briefly, a few years back. The pitch said to call a toll-free number if you wanted a free sample of Cheer Free.*

*P&G had no way of knowing who these allergy-sensitive users might be, but the advertising attracted potential users who identified themselves (or someone they knew) by responding. The company then was able to switch to a more targeted promotion method, direct mail.*

which allows you to use the resources to pursue other markets.

Large corporations also pursue **niche markets**. Hallmark segments the greeting card market into multiple niches, such as Shoebox Greetings (humorous), Fresh Ink (young women), and Mahogany (African Americans). The result: Hallmark enjoys a dominant share of the $8 billion worldwide greeting card market.

A **customized market** is a market of one. It is the ultimate level of segmentation, to focus on a single customer.

In past centuries, many sellers customized their products for each customer: the cobbler, the tailor, the builder. The industrial revolution ushered in a period of mass production and consumers were made to accept whatever products were available.

Some services are naturally customized. Doctors, lawyers, life insurance, financial planning, even your hairstylist or manicurist offers custom services designed especially for you.

More recently, custom-manufactured products have become more commonplace. **Mass-customization** is the ability of a company to customize a product to suit the customer's particular tastes.

The information revolution allows you to order customized products exactly suitable to your needs. Automobile companies tell you to pick your color, seat fabric, accessories, and options, and your new car will arrive in a few weeks, exactly as you have specified. Dell (www.dell.com) offers customized computers over the Internet. Both Dell and the car manufacturers modify a basic product to meet an individual's specifications.

Personalization is king. If it doesn't appeal to your particular peculiarities, they're not really marketing to *you*.

Several leading food companies have begun to customize your food and beverage choices. Go to Proctor & Gamble's www.personalblends.com and customize your coffee blend to suit your unique tastes. Answer a few questions about

> ## CUSTOMIZED TO YOUR TASTE
> ....................................
> *Ever had a hankerin' to try Asparagus-Anisette Ice Cream? Now's your chance.*
>
> *Ciao Bella Gelato will make you whatever flavor tickles your fancy [five gallon minimum].*
>
> *www.ciaobellagelato.com*

your ideal cup of java and your taste in certain foods, and receive a personal "taste print" for your perfect cup of coffee. A pound is ten dollars, plus shipping.

Market segmentation means picking the customers you want—those who most accurately fit the profile of the product you sell. It would stand to reason that, to serve the most customers, you need to make products that appeal to the largest segments. But not necessarily. If you choose your tiny little market niche wisely, you may serve fewer customers but make more money doing it. Instead of scattering your marketing efforts (a "shotgun" approach), focus on buyers you have the greatest chance of satisfying (the "rifle" approach).

Some tiny niche markets use self-selection as a means to promote their products. They operate on the principle, "If you want my product, raise your hand." Promotion invites those who are interested in a brand to respond by sending back a form, calling a toll-free number, visiting a website, or sending an email message.

# THE MARKET SHARE MATRIX

Does your company offer multiple product lines to satisfy many diverse market segments, some which are completely unrelated?

Each distinct target market is called a **Strategic Business Unit**, or **SBU**. Most companies operate several SBUs.

SBUs typically have three characteristics:

1. Separate and unique set of competitors.
2. Separate profit and loss with a manager responsible only for that unit.
3. Strategic plans separate from other SBUs in the company.

**The Market Share Matrix**

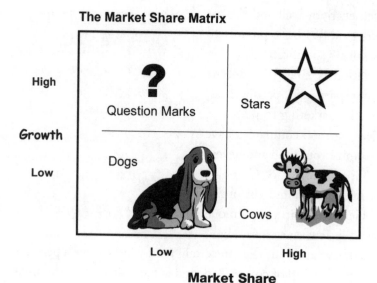

Separate SBUs offer a company diversity in its business. They help avoid seasonality or the cyclical nature inherent in many industries. If sales in one SBU falter, others can pick up the slack. For instance, a retailer of bicycles might sell snow ski equipment during the winter months, two separate SBUs that eliminate seasonality problems.

# D&S/DAVIANS

### THE PROBLEM

D&S Foods leases and services vending machines. Delivery trucks pick up food and beverages at 4:00 every morning, then drive all over southeastern Wisconsin to stock their customers' vending machines.

After many years of preparing fresh salads, sandwiches, and desserts (along with the usual candy bars and soft drinks), D&S Foods began offering onsite-catering services.

Demand proved so great, especially for large events, that D&S opened a 9,000-square-foot banquet and conference center in 1990.

The company requires separate analyses for each of its SBUs.

In order to plan, you need analytical tools to analyze the growth potential of each SBU. One such tool is the **Market Share Matrix** developed by the Boston Consulting Group.

**Stars** are the market leaders in high-growth markets. A star may or may not be a significant contributor to profit. Often, a lot of money must be spent on stars to keep up with the rapidly expanding market.

**Question marks** are SBUs that operate in high-growth markets but have a small market share. They eat cash. Companies must spend money to expand in the growth market and must promote heavily in an effort to overtake the market leader before the market growth slows.

**Cash cows** produce cash for a company. Market expansion has slowed and, because these are the leaders in their category, they enjoy economies of scale and are highly profitable. A company will use a cash cow to fund other SBUs in higher-growth markets.

**Dogs** are SBUs that have weak market share in slow-growth markets. Management must decide to either spend money to gain market share, or consider jettisoning these SBUs.

Typically, new markets begin with rapid growth. Those companies who have the leading share in these markets (stars) can make a lot of money. But maintaining that dominant share can be expensive, especially as the growth rate slows. And it always does.

If your company does not have a dominant share in a fast-growth market (question mark), you will need to spend money to gain share and for expansion of your infrastructure. The objective is to be a leader in your category when the growth rate declines—to end up with a cash cow. If you have a minor share when the growth rate declines (dog), you will need to either abandon the market or seek a specialty niche in order to remain profitable.

# QUINTILE ANALYSIS AND THE OLD "80/20" RULE

There is a general rule of thumb that says 80 percent of your sales come from 20 percent of customers. And while the rule doesn't always hold to an exact 80/20 relationship, it is surprising how accurate it remains in a wide variety of industries.

## THE 80/20 RULE

• *76 percent of all soft drinks are consumed by 30 percent of households.*

• *Coca-Cola has discovered that 84 percent of all Diet Coke is sold to just 8 percent of U.S. households.*

• *Just 16 percent of households account for 80 percent of all yogurt sales.*

• *At "family restaurants," a step up from fast food, 72 percent of sales come from 21 percent of households.*

• *For luxury cars, 4 percent of the population accounted for nearly 100 percent of all sales in 2000.*

And not just in the U.S. The same holds true throughout the world. More than 90 percent of Guinness, one of England's best-loved brands, is bought by just 2 percent of adults.

This 80/20 phenomenon is consistent from country to country, category to category, and brand to brand. A relatively few people exert enormous influence on the health and welfare of any brand or category.

The same holds true for profit. Your top customers are likely your most profitable. With so much potential in so few pockets, marketers cannot afford to be democratic. All consumers cannot be treated equally.

Time for some **quintile analysis,** a fancy marketing term that simply means dividing your customers into five distinct groups (hence, the Latin term *quint,* meaning five) and analyzing each for profitability.

# D&S/DAVIANS

### THE SOLUTION

D&S/Davians offers two distinct products: vending and catering.

Each product line has a separate set of competitors. Within each are several SBUs that the company analyzes in terms of dogs, stars, question marks, or cash cows.

D&S Food Services Division sells vending services, coffee services, and offers on-site cafeteria management.

Davians Catering Division provides on-site catering services, or at its Banquet and Conference Center. In addition, it provides table and room decorations, flower arrangements, and invitation and bridal registry services.

www.davians.com

In one study conducted by consultants Booz Allen Hamilton, it was discovered that 30 percent of customers represented as much as 200 percent of profits. About 50 percent were modestly profitable and the bottom 20 percent sucked cash in great gulps.

Use the 80/20 rule to build your profitability. It pays to take a hard look at your customers and determine which are worth keeping and which you want to encourage (gently) to take their business elsewhere. It may seem counterintuitive. Who wants to lose customers? But analyzing your individual customers' behavior and responding with strategies to maximize each one's profitability is essential to improving the bottom line.

Smart companies prune unprofitable products (see "dogs," above). Pruning unprofitable customers is no different.

How do you recognize a "bad" customer? Typically, bad customers have certain characteristics:

- They buy infrequently.
- They pay slowly (or not at all).
- They make unreasonable demands (quality, service, *and* low price).

Terminating a relationship, of course, is a last resort. Once lost, it is extremely difficult to get a customer back.

Every effort should be made to convert a bad customer into a good one. How? Remember the rules of Q, S, & P? You can't be expected to offer all three. You may have to change the rules to make bad customers profitable.

## QUINTILE ANALYSIS AT CAPITAL ONE

*In 1988, most retail banks charged the same price to all their credit card customers, despite major differences in their cost to the banks.*

*Along comes a small, relatively unknown bank called Capital One. They specifically target consumers who fit their profile of best customer, the top 20 percent, and woo them away from competitors with a balance-transfer approach.*

*They offer lower rates to anyone who transfers a balance from a competitor credit card. This attracts credit card users who typically do not pay off their balances each month, and to whom a lower APR is attractive (not coincidentally, these are also the most profitable customers to credit card companies).*

*Since 1992, Capital One has risen from $1.7 billion in loans to over $60 billion, and is one of the top ten credit card issuers in the country.*

Typically, this means premium pricing, or "up-charging" (smaller P). But it could also include changes in the service rendered (smaller S), or even changes in the product itself (smaller Q). For instance, customers who typically take an extra thirty or sixty days to pay are charged an additional holding fee or service charge equal to (or greater than) the time value of money.

All bad customers should be given an opportunity to become good ones, with the sales force given the responsibility of converting them. Granted, some will remain unprofitable no matter what steps you take, and those should be gently nudged into the street. If you don't focus on your most profitable customers, you take the chance that someone else will.

Here's a simple idea: Target good customers.

Use the 80/20 rule to build your business. Analyze your top 20 percent. What makes them good customers? What characteristics (demographics, psychographics, needs, and wants) do they share?

The lesson: If you cannot fire your unprofitable customers, you may end up spending time and resources on them while a competitor chases your top customers. Your growth plans could be in jeopardy. Better idea: Go after *their* best customers, the ones who have characteristics similar to your "Top 20."

The next step to understanding your customers is to figure out what those common characteristics are.

## DEMOGRAPHICS, PSYCHOGRAPHICS, AND BENEFITS

| Demographics | Psychographics |
|---|---|
| [Physical Attributes] | [Personality Attributes] |
| • age | • interests |
| • income | • opinions |
| • geography | • beliefs |
| • gender | • lifestyle |

When you identify your target markets (or when you analyze your current customer groups), you will find similar demographic, psychographic, and benefit characteristics.

The 80/20 rule says that the vast majority of your sales are derived from a relative few customers. These customers may have similarities.

Understanding the demographic, psychographic, and benefit characteristics will help you identify other prospective customers with like characteristics, and how to promote to them.

Demographics are the statistics that measure a population. They include:

|  | *B2C* | *B2B* |
|---|---|---|
| Size | Number in HH | Number of employees |
| Age | Personal age or age category | Number of years in business |
| Gender | Male or female | |
| Ethnicity | Hispanic, Asian, etc. | |
| Income | Personal or HH income | Total revenue |
| HH Make-Up | Married/single, children | Office workers vs. factory workers |
| Education | Highest level attained | |
| Occupation | Personal | Industry (SIC Code) |
| Location | Zip code or census tract | Zip code or census tract |

Predict the size of a potential market or pinpoint your best prospects (e.g., Hispanic women eighteen to forty-nine who live in dual-income households with income of $50,000 or more in five specific zip code areas). Analyzing your customer base over time helps you adjust your product line to allow for their changing needs.

You can gather data on your customers and prospects till the cows come home. But the most helpful information identifies those characteristics that most accurately separate potential customers from those not likely to buy. This helps you locate those areas with the highest concentration of potential buyers.

## FINDING DEMOGRAPHIC DATA

*Demographic information is available from a wide variety of sources, from your local Chamber of Commerce, the U.S. Census Bureau (www.census.gov), or any number of private marketing information companies.*

American Demographics *magazine (www.demographics.com) publishes a Directory of Marketing Information Companies, a comprehensive list of demographic information providers for all industries.*

## BRAND AND CATEGORY DEVELOPMENT INDICES (BDI AND CDI)

*Understanding how well your brand is doing in a market can help you determine strategy.*

*Let's say your product sells 120 million units in Illinois, including 30 million units to women in Chicago's Cook County. You analyze census data and discover that about 22 percent of all Illinois women live in Cook County. You know that about 20 percent of all sales in your product category are made to women in Cook County. How do you use this data?*

*To determine how well your brand is doing in this market, use the* **Brand Development Index (BDI)** *formula:*

$$BDI = \frac{\% \text{ of total brand sales}}{\% \text{ of population}} \times 100$$

$$BDI = \frac{\% \text{ of your sales to Cook County Women}}{\% \text{ of women living in Cook County}} \times 100$$

$$BDI = \frac{25\%}{22\%} \times 100 \qquad BDI = 114$$

(continued next page)

Who are your customers? How old are they? Where do they live? What are their interests, concerns, aspirations, values? Knowing the answers to these questions gives you insight into the best promotional approach, what message might best appeal to them, and which media to use.

Demographic information allows you to refine who your customer is, who it can or should be, and how it is likely to change over time. People have different needs at different stages in their lives. Divorce, cohabitation, out-of-wedlock births, and an increasing number of women in the workforce have changed the marketing landscape. The stereotypical family of the *Leave It to Beaver* era has been replaced by two harried, harassed, working parents with less time available.

The most significant demographic factor affecting buying habits is age.

# THE U.S. GROWS OLD

Demographers identify five age categories:

| Age Category | Born |
| --- | --- |
| 1. Silvers | 1930 |
| 2. Middlescents | 1930 to 1945 |
| 3. Baby Boomers | 1945 to 1965 |
| 4. Generation X | 1965 to 1980 |
| 5. Generation Y (Millennials) | 1980 to 2000 2000 + |

**Silvers** (sometimes called the GI Generation) suffered through the Great Depression and fought World War II. This group has about 22 million households, many of them single-person, but represents only 13 percent of total spending.

The Great Depression, ancient history to most marketers today, had a profound impact on their lives. For perspective, the S&P 400 lost 69 percent of its value between 1929 and 1932 and did not recover to its 1929 level again until 1953, twenty-four years later. Born in this environment, Silvers retain the scars of financial anxiety. As a group, they are frugal, deeply concerned about financial security, and, due to a rash of bank failures during the Depression, skeptical of many financial institutions.

Most Silvers live on a fixed income and, not surprisingly, spend more than twice the national average on health care (drugs, insurance, medical services). They spend much of their free time at home, so their spending also skews higher on home goods like groceries, stationery, and cleaning supplies.

They are unfamiliar with technology (a select few use email) and are skeptical of broadcast advertising. Reach them with print, or better yet, go to them directly. For instance, a financial planning seminar held at their church or assisted living facility will be better attended and serve to overcome their fears of financial skullduggery.

**Middlescents** are the smallest group, representing just 14 percent of households

(continued from previous)

*Your brand does 14 percent better than the number of potential customers would suggest. With such high penetration, your potential for growth in Cook County may be limited.*

*But how is your whole category doing? To find out, use the* **Category Development Index (CDI)** *formula:*

$$CDI = \frac{\% \text{ of total category sales}}{\% \text{ of total population}} \times 100$$

$$CDI = \frac{\% \text{ of category sold to CCW}}{\% \text{ of women living in Cook County}} \times 100$$

$$CDI = \frac{20\%}{22\%} \times 100 \qquad CDI = 91$$

*Your product does well in Cook County, but the rest of your category, as a whole, does not. Perhaps Chicago women know something about your product that women in the rest of Illinois have yet to discover. By all means, tell them. Set your sights on promoting to all the other women throughout Illinois. Avoid using expensive media in and around Chicago.*

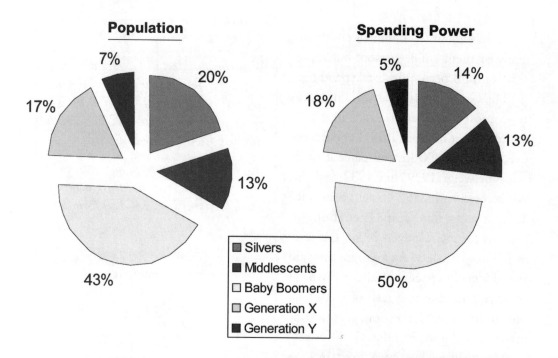

and 14 percent of the buying power. Individually, they have more disposable income than any other group, but little to spend it on. Their kids are gone, their mortgages are low or paid off, and their concerns about health care are well in the future.

What they buy are indulgences: the fancy ice cream, the extended vacation, the antique car, the second home. One of the hottest products sold to this group is toys. Grandparents buy more than 20 percent of all toys purchased at retail— anything for their grandkids.

Marketers have problems selling to this group. Young advertising copywriters do not understand the Middlescent mind-set. They picture them as "old," really old. Just like their own grandparents, who seem two steps from the grave to a twentysomething—codgers with walkers and wheelchairs.

Middlescents respond to print advertising better than broadcast, which they mistrust. Use healthy Middlescents in the ads, and lots of facts, facts, facts. Appeal to their sense of nostalgia, too, a throwback to the "good old days" of their youth. Use print. This group reads, and more important, they believe what they read. Forty-five percent of people fifty-five-plus trust advertisements they read, a much higher percent than any other age group.

**Baby boomers** have dominated U.S. buying habits since after World War II. They made *Dr. Spock's Infant and Child Rearing* the second bestselling book in the history of the world (after the Bible). They grew up on television's *Leave It to Beaver*, *Father Knows Best*, and (later) *The Partridge Family*. As kids, they bought hula hoops, Davy Crockett caps, and Superman comic books. As teens, they made Coca-Cola, McDonald's, and Motown into corporate giants.

Today, Boomers constitute 46 million households and make up over half of all domestic spending. They buy homes or improve the ones they're in. They cash in the used car for a new one, spend money on clothes and education for their kids and family entertainment (videos, pets, toys, play equipment, and driving vacations).

They spend less on health care than any other category. Why? Because "getting old is for other people." The generation that didn't trust anyone over thirty is now turning fifty at a rate of seven per minute. They're trying hard to stay young and feeding the skin cream, plastic surgery, health club, and hair-coloring industries (over half of female Boomers color their hair). These former hippies also have a strong endearment for organically grown food, homeopathic medicine, and all things environmental.

Find them watching television with their kids or attending sporting events or friends' children's weddings. Use family values to appeal to their emotional side.

**Generation X** (also called the Lost Generation) is the generation of latchkey kids, divorce, day care, and disillusionment. They tend to be conservative in nature, cynical of advertising, and resigned to a dual-income household to support even a meager lifestyle.

As a group, they are just beginning to face adulthood, forming households (20 million of them), becoming soccer moms and dads, and they represent 18 percent of total spending power, a number that is growing rapidly.

Theirs is the fast lane. Busy lifestyles require in-home services like house cleaning, lawn service, meal preparation, and an au pair. They spend less than any generation in history

> ## MORE BDI AND CDI
>
> *Sometimes, you may discover you have more than one set of customers. Low-fat frozen dinners are purchased by young women trying to stay slim, as well as by retired adults seeking a light meal.*
>
> *Use BDI and CDI for each set of customers to determine your penetration and where you should concentrate your promotional efforts.*

on cleaning supplies. They do, however, spend money on their kids (from the fanciest stroller to the newest toys) and are filling up family-style restaurants.

Generation X responds to sassy, irreverent, rebellious, self-mocking messages—which explains the popularity of *Beavis and Butthead*, *South Park*, and the *Simpsons*.

**Generation Y** (also known as Echo Boomers) is the group coveted by marketers as the next new wave of buyers. Though most have not formed households yet and their spending power is just 5 percent of the U.S. total, their sheer numbers (71 million of them) well exceed Generation X and are only slightly less than Boomers (78 million), their parents' generation.

It is an enormously powerful group that has the ability to transform every life stage it enters, just as their parents' generation did before them.

They do not remember the Cold War and have no recollection of Ronald Reagan as president. They never watched television without a remote, never saw a turntable or a house without a microwave oven. They have no concept of a busy signal or an unanswered telephone. The incident at Columbine High School is the greatest defining moment in their lives, followed by the war in Kosovo and the Oklahoma City bombing.

The way in which these events were handled, particularly Columbine and Oklahoma City, made teens skeptical of the news. A study conducted at Marquette University found Gen-Ys to be alienated from, and wary of, mainstream media in general. Most teens feel as if the media exploited these events and handled each as a media opportunity. Reality TV seems more credible to them than fantasy fictional TV shows.

Despite their skepticism, they will listen to personalized messages, particularly through interactive media. Not surprising. These are the children of the information age. They want instant information, instant answers, instant results. They buy clothes, cars, college educations, and electronic gear. The best way to reach them is with customized promotions through television, Internet, and CD-ROMs. Avoid print.

## THE RACE REPORT

After age, the most significant demographic affecting buyer choices is ethnicity. Nearly one-fourth of the U.S. population (nearly 70 million people) today identify themselves as something other than White alone (according to the latest U.S. Census Bureau data).

Immigrants pouring in from Latin America and Asia have increased the percentage of minorities from 20 percent in 1980 to over 25 percent today. A greater proportion of these are children due to higher fertility and cultural norms. Today, one third of all children in the U.S. are either Black, Hispanic, or Asian.

Where twenty years ago, garlic was the most exotic condiment on the grocer's shelves, now salsa (which outsells ketchup) is available next to the couscous and the kimchi. Minorities control over $900 billion in annual spending, more than double the amount in 1990, according to the Selig Center for Economic Growth at the University of Georgia.

Following is a snapshot of each ethnic group and how it could affect your marketing choices in the next few years.

## PEPSI CHANGES FOCUS

*No brand has focused on youth more than Pepsi with its Pepsi Generation commercials. Recognizing, however, that colas are the baby boomers' drink and more youths are turning to fruit flavors or non-carbonated drinks, Pepsi has begun to court older consumers.*

*A recent Pepsi commercial featured a teenage boy in a mosh pit at a rock concert, only to turn around and discover his father rocking out nearby.*

*The Pepsi Generation is multigenerational!*

### African Americans

This group is upwardly mobile and growing fast. While the total U.S. population grew 13 percent from 1990 to 2000, the African American population grew nearly 20 percent. And their household incomes also grew, from $18,676 in 1990 to $30,439 in 2000. More than half of married African Americans have annual income greater than $50,000. Ten percent have incomes of $100,000 or more.

Blacks are the most fashion conscious of all ethnic groups. Thirty-four percent say they like to keep up with changes in trends (vs. 28 percent of Asians, 27 percent of Hispanics, and 25 percent of Whites). Research suggests they have favorite stores and are willing to drive a long way to shop, especially if the price is right. More Blacks favor factory-outlet stores than any other group.

### Hispanic Americans

We are fast becoming bicultural as the growth of Hispanics has soared over the past decade. Fueled by immigration and high birth rates, the share of Hispanics in the U.S. doubled from 1980 to 2000. Now totaling nearly 40 million people, Hispanics have surpassed African Americans as the largest minority group in the nation.

"Hispanic" covers many nationalities. Over 60 percent are of Mexican heritage; 12 percent are of Puerto Rican descent; and the remainder includes Central Americans, Dominicans, South Americans, and Cubans. As expected, most (75 percent) of the Hispanic population is still concentrated in the South and West, but many are moving into the Midwest, where their numbers have doubled in the past decade. Minnesota alone saw its Hispanic population increase 165 percent, from 54,000 in 1990 to 144,000 today.

Many Hispanics have strong ties to their native land, relatives, and friends. They live here in clusters and Spanish-speaking neighborhoods, and among authentic restaurants and small businesses. They long for the familiar. Name brands do well with this group.

### Asian Americans

Also growing rapidly, the Asian American ethnic group doubled in size from 1990 to 2000. Most are located on the West Coast, with pockets in New York, Boston, and Chicago, but many have drifted to more rural settings in recent years.

Like Hispanics, Asian Americans are increasingly segmented. Marketers must resist lumping them all together in one subgroup, but recognize the cultural and linguistic differences among Chinese American, Japanese American, Filipino, Vietnamese, Hmong, Korean, Indian, and Pakistani markets. Finding commonalities among them is unlikely.

Asian American households are, on the average, far more affluent than all U.S. households. A whopping 39 percent have incomes topping $75,000, compared with just 27 percent of the total population. Marketers will be rewarded if they seek to sell to each subgroup individually.

### Native Americans

The smallest minority group has called America home longer than any other cultural group. About 4 million people claim Native American heritage.

## Case Study

# PROCTOR & GAMBLE

**THE PROBLEM**

Proctor & Gamble wanted to determine who was buying dishwashing soap.

Demographic analysis revealed women, men, and even kids bought dishwashing soap for one reason or another.

Psychographic analysis also offered little insight into their purchase behavior.

Historically plagued by poverty, their buying influence is growing as the success of their casino investments begin to pay off. Gambling on Indian reservations took in over $6 billion last year, and much of that wealth is then spread throughout the tribes, fostering a growing middle class. Native American–owned companies are also prospering, as investment in their companies outpaces national averages.

This cultural subgroup may be the easiest to reach by marketers, as they tend to cluster geographically. Many younger Native Americans (Gen-X and younger) are anxious to adapt non-tribal ways. But older Native Americans remain remarkably resistant to most mass media messages and prefer to live frugally, following many of the ancient tribal customs.

### Multiracials

A new minority is emerging. Labeled multiracials, these are members of more than one ethnic identity. Some 7 million Americans identify with two or more races, among them Tiger Woods, Halle Berry, Christina Aguilera, Mariah Carey, Derek Jeter, and Vin Diesel.

Though just 3 percent of the population, multiracials are a growing community of primarily young people (42 percent are under eighteen years old vs. 25 percent of the general population). These are the early adapters, the

## MULTIRACIALS

- *Mariah Carey, singer, has a Venezuelan/African American father and an Irish mother.*

- *Naomi Campbell, model, has a Black (Jamaican) mother and a father who is part Chinese.*

- *Tiger Woods, golfer, has a Thai/Chinese mother and a father of multiracial descent.*

## MUSICAL TASTE OFTEN DEFINES LIFESTYLE

*Radio may be the perfect medium to pinpoint your customers based upon their psychographics.*

*Radio offers a wide variety of music to suit every taste and every lifestyle—from jazz to rap, classical to country, and shock jocks to Christian Coalitions.*

*Think about the older, upper-crust, country-club type who drives a Buick. Is he more likely to listen to Shostakovich or G-Unit?*

*How about the bearded Lucky Strike smoker with the tattoo on his forearm and the three-bedroom bungalow in the suburbs? Wynton Marsalis or Garth Brooks?*

buying leaders whom marketers covet. Young, aggressive, savvy, and street smart, they follow no ethnic norms. Instead, they set their own.

They epitomize the Gen-Xers who grew up post-Civil Rights. No cultural boundaries. No preconceived notions of ethnic specificity.

Many marketers, in their never-ending effort to stay hip and trendy, court the multira-cials (and the multiracial wannabes). In the field of fashion, many of today's hottest models are of multiracial ancestry. Clothiers see an opportunity to appeal to all cultures by offering up models of ambiguous heritage.

Acculturation among ethnic groups has cre-ated a homogenous society best characterized by the multiracials. Marketers after elusive Gen-X-ers would do well to court this pacesetting group.

## PSYCHOGRAPHIC SEGMENTATION

While demographics are the statistics that measure a population, **psychographics** measure psychological, sociological, and anthropological factors. These include values, beliefs, hobbies, habits, and lifestyle.

While demographic information is useful, it does not always tell you enough about your customers. Demographics may tell you, for instance, that female college students wear sandals. But do they prefer them for comfort or for fashion? Or for sex appeal?

Psychographic data helps us understand reasons *why* people purchase.

Psychographics can also be used to segment product usage. Some marketers prefer to sell to heavy users; others want to target light users or non-users.

You may choose to develop your own psychographic categories to classify your clients. But many companies opt to purchase the information from infor-mation service providers who specialize in psychographic information.

## PROCTOR & GAMBLE

### THE SOLUTION

Proctor & Gamble conducted research to determine the primary benefits sought by consumers of dishwashing liquid. They found three benefits consumers wanted most:

1. Take away grease.
2. Soft on hands.
3. Make dishes shine.

Rather than sell dishwashing liquids based upon demographic or psychographic characteristics, P&G developed three different products—Dawn, Ivory, and Joy—one for each benefit.

All three are among the top sellers in the category.

www.pg.com

The most well known of these services is VALS™ (Values and Lifestyles) and PRIZM. VALS segments consumers by three value systems: Principle Orientation, Status Orientation, and Action Orientation. It identifies people who are most likely to be interested in certain products based upon their lifestyles. For example, Isuzu marketed its Rodeo sport utility vehicle to thrill seekers, part of the VALS Action Orientation module.

## BENEFIT SEGMENTATION

Your products serve customer needs and wants. Yet these same customers may not fall neatly into any specific demographic or psychographic category.

Purchasers of dishwashing liquid, for example, may include single moms, African American males, kids who need to wash the dog, or small business operators with coffee cups to scrub. Some buyers buy based upon the benefit provided. They may have identical demographics and psychographics, yet completely different purchase habits.

Demographic and psychographic characteristics may tell only part of the story. Benefit analysis may be necessary to determine your customers' true buying motivations.

## SEGMENTING FOR THE NEXT TWENTY-FIVE YEARS

By the year 2030, baby boomers will be retired, many in their late seventies and early eighties. The over-sixty-five set will dominate the nation. This graying population means that marketers will have to find ways to attract older consumers without alienating younger ones. Companies formerly focused on youth will need to rethink their strategies.

People define themselves by activities they're involved in more than by their age. College students can be ages twenty, thirty, or sixty. Although grandparents can be forty-five, sixty-five, or eighty-five, they all want to buy gifts for their grandchildren. People cycle in and out of different lifestyles at different ages. Their purchases will be based more upon their interests rather than traditional demographic characteristics.

By 2030, the term "minority" as we use it today will be obsolete. Non-Hispanic Whites will still be the majority, but only barely, with just 55 percent of the population (vs. 70 percent today). In a nation no longer dominated by Whites, business will be marketing to a patchwork of racial and ethnic identities. Companies must wake up and smell the kimchi tacos. Those who embrace multiracial marketing today will be far better accepted than those who wait.

Now that you have a thorough understanding of your sales history, your organization's strengths and weaknesses, and who your customers are, it's time to evaluate the external factors that affect your industry.

## THE COMPETITIVE ANALYSIS

The second part of the **situation analysis** is the **competitive analysis**. Just as you analyzed your firm's strengths, weaknesses, and opportunities, so too should you examine your key competitors' strengths, weaknesses, and threats.

Analyze your top three or four competitors thoroughly. Take note of their strengths and weaknesses and how you can minimize the former and take advantage of the latter. What threats do they pose? Do they have a new product in the works? A new promotion campaign that might lure away your customers?

Next, review any alternative choices your customers could have. For example, at McDonald's, we looked at Burger King, Wendy's, and Hardee's as our primary competitors in the hamburger marketplace. But we also wanted to know about any threats from other fast-food restaurants, including KFC, Pizza Hut, Taco Bell, and others.

Identify both similarities and significant differences between your organization and your competition. What do you both offer customers? What do you offer that they do not? What do they offer that you do not? Should you offer what they offer?

When you win sales from your customers, what are the reasons? Likewise, when you lose sales, what are the reasons? Competitive information can come from industry trade journals, magazine reps, or trade shows.

Good competitive analysis has three purposes:

- Understand the differences so that you can better position your organization and its products.
- Identify areas where customers perceive you to be weaker.
- Create awareness of new products, services, or processes to avoid being blindsided.

This is not an exercise to mimic your strongest competitors. Rather, it is best used to develop a unique position in the marketplace that can be exploited, one that differentiates you from your competitors, and one that can be promoted to your customers.

### Case Study    BRIESS MALT

#### THE PROBLEM

Briess Malt & Ingredients Company supplies malt to a majority of the breweries in the U.S., as well as a dozen foreign countries. But beer sales have remained relatively flat for decades, hampering the company's growth opportunities.

The company developed products for new markets, including home-brewing, snacks, and pet food. But by 1998, less than 20 percent of sales were derived from food products.

# THE ENVIRONMENT ANALYSIS

The third section examines the environment in which you operate. This can best be broken down into five areas:

1. Technology
2. Government Rules and Regulations
3. Economic Factors
4. Raw Materials and Labor Availability
5. Industry Trends

## Technology

What effect will changes in technology have on your business? Can you increase your productivity if you update your equipment? Have robotics changed the labor cost/unit ratio? Have electronic scanners made the use of cash in your industry obsolete? Has technology changed your business, and that of your competitors, so as to change your marketing strategies?

## FIVE PARTS OF THE ENVIRONMENT ANALYSIS

......................

1. *Technology*—*Changes that could make your product, pricing, or distribution obsolete.*

2. *Government*—*Regulations that could affect your operations.*

3. *Economy*—*How economic factors will affect your business.*

4. *Raw Materials and Labor*—*Supply-chain problems that could affect your industry.*

5. *Industry Trends*—*Cultural issues that could change your customers' buying habits.*

## Government Regulations

What new government regulations will affect your business? Governmental or other regulatory bodies closely scrutinize companies in the financial services, public utilities, pharmaceutical, and transportation industries.

Regulatory measures can affect any industry. If the government suddenly slaps a tariff on imports in your supply chain, that will likely change how you market your products.

## Economic Factors

Changes in interest rates (the cost of borrowing money) may affect your expansion plans. Inflation, unemployment rates, inventory levels, and credit terms are all factors that need to be considered when developing your marketing plan.

## BRIESS MALT

### THE SOLUTION

When severe flooding in some of the major sugar-exporting countries of Central America caused sugar prices to skyrocket, Briess began marketing malt extract to the health food industry as an all-natural alternative to sugar.

Its rich, flavorful malt proved ideal as a natural sweetener in cereals, granola bars, and healthy diet snacks.

Sales took off and now represent nearly half of total revenue.

www.briess.com

## Raw Materials and Labor Availability

Your industry may suffer shortages of raw materials or skilled labor. A sharp rise in the cost of supplies may allow competitors using substitutes to woo away your customers.

During the Y2K scare back in 1999, no one could find qualified IT professionals. Engineering firms had to put many projects on hold until the labor situation became more favorable. Your marketing plan could bring in new sales opportunities, but if you cannot find the labor to fill the orders, you could disappoint your customers.

## Industry Trends

What are your industry's trends? Is the demand for your product category growing or shrinking? Do fads or fashion affect your sales?

Industry trade associations and salespersons at trade journals can provide insight into industry developments that signal trends.

Knowing where you begin your journey is as important as determining where you want to go. The situation analysis tells you. Properly written, it may also lend insight as to how you will get to there.

Here is a quick quiz (hey, after all, I'm a teacher) that may help you understand the difference between the three parts of the situation analysis.

# SITUATION ANALYSIS QUIZ

Imagine you operate the Amalgamated Widget Company (AWC). The following list of factors will affect your marketing efforts over the course of the next year and need to be considered as you develop your sales estimates. Which issues belong to which part of the Situation Analysis? Place the correct letter next to the corresponding issue. Answers below.

**A** = Sales Trend     **B** = Competition     **C** = Environment

1. Aging population is causing a decrease in demand for widgets, a slowdown in overall industry sales.
2. United Widget reduces prices to encourage new sales.
3. Factions within AWC hurt overall sales efforts, causing poor relationship with customers.
4. New government regulations require widget digit protector, a product available through AWC.
5. *Wall Street Journal* exposes corruption in widget industry.
6. New ad campaign planned by Acme Gizmo & Widget Co.
7. Interest rates climb, hurting new equipment purchases in the industry.
8. AWC offered popular training courses last year resulting in positive feedback among customers.
9. Successful industry lobbying efforts in Washington receive positive press.
10. New computer program increases efficiency of AWC manufacturing process.
11. Scandal in Argentina widget market causes restrictive regulations in U.S.
12. New AWC website attracts new customers.
13. Industry trade magazine announces new "Widget Wacker" may make widgets obsolete.
14. Layoffs at several large corporations may mean recession is imminent.

# SITUATION ANALYSIS QUIZ ANSWERS

1. C    This is an issue affecting the environment in which your industry operates.
2. B    Your competitor has reduced prices, which may cause you to lose customers.
3. A    Your company's (AWC) sales were off because of internal problems.
4. C    Government regulations may affect your company in a positive way.

5. C   Negative industry publicity, though not about AWC specifically, could still hurt sales.

6. B   Your competitor is launching a new ad campaign that could hurt your sales.

7. C   Economic factors affect your industry.

8. A   Positive customer feedback could have positive affect on your company's sales.

9. C   Lobbying efforts affect the entire industry.

10. A   New computer system could decrease delivery times, increase customer satisfaction, and lead to more sales.

11. C   Overseas scandal adversely affects the entire industry.

12. A   Your new website has helped increase sales.

13. C   Bad news for your industry if an industry innovation makes your company's and your competitors' products obsolete.

14. C   Economic indicators are down, which could portend bad news for your industry.

To take your successful company to the next level, you must know your market and how your organization fits in it. The **situation analysis**, including an analysis of your sales, your competition, and your environment, is crucial if you want to grow exponentially. With your Situation Analysis complete, it is time to set our sites on objectives—where it is you are taking your company.

# SETTING SALES OBJECTIVES

There is no successful company that does not set goals. Without goals, you are a rudderless boat; no course, no direction, and simply sailing to oblivion.

Whether sales goals, financial goals, or debt-to-equity ratio goals, the more clearly defined your objectives, the more motivation your employees will have, and the more successful your organization will be.

While there are no sure-fire schemes that will guarantee your objectives are achieved, here are five steps to ensure a better chance for success:

> *"Give me a stock clerk with a goal and I will give you a man who can change the world. Give me a man without a goal, and I will give you a stock clerk."*
>
> —J. C. Penney

## 1. Begin with sales estimates

The process begins with sales goals. They are the first objectives your organization should be setting.

Allow the salespeople to set their own goals. This is important. They are more likely to achieve goals they set themselves. This is not always true when somebody dictates goals they deem unrealistic. No one should set someone else's goals. To be truly successful, we must set our own.

### OBJECTIVES
. . . . . . . . . . . . . . . . . . . . . . . . . . . . .
*Make sure yours are:*

• *Quantifiable*

• *Measurable*

• *Attainable*

Allow your salespeople to establish their own objectives (as long as they are consistent with your company objectives). That way, they know exactly what you expect from them, and they'll work that much harder to achieve it.

Ask each to give detailed explanations of how each individual goal will be achieved. For instance, if she states: "I will acquire $1,000,000 in new customers over the next three years," ask her to specify where those new customers will come from, how she will identify them, when she will be calling upon them, what promotional aids she will require, what assistance if any she may need from others in the organization, etc.

Do not set only long-term goals (annual sales goals for instance). Just as organizations need to set long-term and near-term goals, so too do you with your sales force. Establish some intermediate goals to measure their progress and encourage them along the way.

### LONG TERM?
. . . . . . . . . . . . . . . . . . . . . . . . . . . . .
*Note: The **10–5–1 Rule** is not inflexible, as it may be more appropriate for your company to use a **5–3–1 Rule**.*

*If your industry is changing rapidly (software, stem-cell research, nanotechnology), you may need to take a shorter-term "long-term" view.*

### 2. Clearly define your goals

The better defined they are, the more likely they will be achieved. Make them quantifiable, measurable, and attainable. None of this "Increase sales and profits" stuff. Rather, "Increase sales by 12 percent during the next eighteen-month period while maintaining current gross margins."

• Not "Increase market share," but "Increase market share 9 percent over the next twelve months."

• Not "Increase revenue 100 percent," but "Increase revenue an average of 12 percent annually over the next five years."

This quantifies the objectives and makes them measurable. Whether or not the goal is attainable depends upon the research you have conducted for your situation analysis.

Some objectives may not be about sales or profits, but are equally specific. For example, one of the most frequent objectives of small- and medium-sized businesses is to allow the owner or principal to spend more time on management and planning, less on day-to-day operations. Or to simply reduce the number of hours the owner/principal needs to spend at the office. These are specific objectives, measurable and attainable.

### 3. Set intermediate goals

When setting your objectives, think long-term, but allow for short-term goals, too. Entrepreneurs tend to be impatient. They want to see sales results from promotional efforts immediately. But to install the machinery and the methods necessary to produce the efficient, smooth-running operation they desire takes time.

Instead, set up short-term goals, measurements along the way so that you can see that you're headed in the right direction. Many managers tend to set only long-term goals. Too often, they aim for touchdowns. But just as most touchdowns require a few first downs along the way, some intermediate goals need to be established.

## ESTIMATING SALES

*A step-by-step process for establishing sales goals.*

**Step #1**
*Record last year's sales.*

**Step #2**
*Subtract any sales aberrations. Include one-shot customers you do not expect to return as well as one-time sales from current customers you do not expect to be repeated.*

**Step #3**
*Subtract some percentage (5 to 10 percent) for attrition, i.e., customers who have moved away, gone bankrupt, or died. Include some percentage for customers lured away by competitors, too.*

**Step #4**
*Examine your Situation Analysis and make adjustments for industry trends, changes in the supply chain, technology, government regulations, and economic factors, and how they might affect your overall industry's sales.*

**Step #5**
*Add some percent increase for the positive effect of your promotion campaign.*

**Step #6**
*Account for additional sales to your current customers (farming).*

(continued next page)

(continued from previous)

### Step #7
*Account for additional sales to new customers (hunting). See chapter 6.*

### Step #8
*If you are introducing any new products or services, add these to your sales estimates. See chapter 8.*

### Step #9
*Considering merging or acquiring any other businesses? Add for that, too. See chapter 9.*

### Step #10
*Add them all up for an estimate of your total sales.*

*This is your most likely case scenario. For budgeting purposes, it would be prudent to refigure each step for a worst-case scenario. You may wish to plan a best-case scenario as well. (Note: Finish reading this book before attempting to set sales goals. The five strategies will give you greater insight into your company's sales potential.)*

Short-term objectives offer several advantages. When you achieve these shorter-term goals, you begin to build confidence in your plan and in its implementation. Progress is easier to measure, and intermediate targets keep us from being discouraged by that goal line so far away.

### 4. Have a plan
Setting objectives is just a beginning. To get from store clerk to someone who can change the world, you need an action plan, a blueprint for achieving your success. Without a plan, you cannot achieve the goal, even by accident (outside of, perhaps, winning the lottery).

If you set a goal, but lack a plan to achieve it, it is only a wish. Like, "I intend to be rich," it is only a dim hope, one likely doomed to failure without a plan. Failing to achieve a goal discourages us from setting other goals. "Why bother?" we ask. "I'll only fail at that one, too."

To set your company's objectives, start with the **10–5–1 Rule**. Imagine your company ten years from now. Where do you want to be? What are your sales goals? What are your profit goals? What share of market do you want to have? What image do you want to have in the marketplace? What kind of reputation do you want to have in your industry? What kind of image in your community do you want to have?

Once you have a vision of where you want your company to be in ten years, ask yourself, "Where do we have to be in five years? What do we need to accomplish so that we are well along that path?"

Define your objectives for the long term first, the specific issues that need to be addressed. Then, describe the tasks that need to be accomplished along the way. What do you need to accomplish by next year at this time? Remember, be specific. Your objectives must be quantifiable, measurable, and attainable.

### 5. Follow the plan

No point in having one otherwise.

Once you have your sales estimates, you are ready to execute the 5 Kick-Ass Strategies.

# CHAPTER 4

# The 5 Kick-Ass Strategies

Purpose: *The purpose of chapter 4 is to introduce the 5 Kick-Ass Strategies and show you how you can use them to grow exponentially. Chapters 5, 6, 7, 8, and 9 examine each of the 5 Kick-Ass Strategies in detail.*

————◦————

**Y**ou have done your homework, researched your industry, analyzed your competitors, and established objectives—where you want to be in ten years, where you need to be in five years, and therefore, where you have to be by next year.

You're feeling pretty good about it, too. So you sit back, relax, and congratulate yourself. It was a lot of work, and you learned a lot. You take pride in the work, and in the knowledge.

What now?

The next step in developing your marketing plan is the five strategies. These are the means to the ends defined by those objectives, the conceptual blueprints for your company's success.

It is at this point that many entrepreneurs find themselves stumped. They have a thorough knowledge of their industry. They have defined their target markets and written their sales objectives. They just aren't sure how to reach the lofty goals they have set.

There are, however, only five strategies for growing your business, only five ways to increase your sales. These are:

1. Sell more of the same stuff to the same people (buy market share).
2. Sell more of the same stuff to different people (hunt).
3. Sell different stuff to the same people (farm).
4. Invent and introduce new stuff (new products).
5. Merge with or acquire another company (merge or acquire).

---

### THE 5 KICK-ASS STRATEGIES
············
*There are five and only five ways to build your business.*

*1. Buy Market Share*

*2. Hunt*

*3. Farm*

*4. New Products*

*5. Merge or Acquire*

---

# 1. BUY MARKET SHARE

Selling more of the same products or services to your current target market is often called **buying market share**—and for good reason. To sell more stuff to the same people, you need to buy customers from your competition.

This can be costly. It may require you to drop your price, offering all three, Q, S, *and* P. Or you may need to devote resources to advertising or promotions that induce more people to abandon their current loyalties and try your brand.

# 2. HUNT

Selling more of your products or services to different markets can also be expensive. Any time you **hunt** new customers, you need to create awareness and credibility for your company and your products in the new market.

If you are currently offering your services in North Dakota but want to start selling in South Dakota, too, you will need to let all those South Dakotans know who you are, what you stand for, and the features and benefits of your product line. You will need to educate them about the myriad reasons why all your North Dakota customers are so smart that they have made you the leading brand in the state.

# 3. FARM

This is the easiest and most cost-effective strategy.

While hunting new customers is important to maintaining a healthy sales picture long term, **farming** your existing customers is more efficient.

Statistics show that the cost of selling to new customers is more than twelve times as expensive as selling to current customers. Your current customers already know you. You don't need to create awareness and credibility with them. They already trust you.

There are many ways to harvest sales from existing customers:
- Rotation farming
- Suggestive selling
- Selling accessories
- Incentive selling
- Trading up

Rotation farming is selling to the customer who buys periodically, at regular intervals. For example, a florist might contact his customers and request their wedding anniversaries and spouses' birthdays. He keeps the dates in his database and reviews them periodically. Then shortly before each date, he calls and suggests a floral arrangement appropriate for the occasion.

Suggestive selling is perhaps the easiest sale. I call this the You-Want-Fries-With-That-Order? strategy. Your customers are already in a buying mood. You're simply suggesting they spend a little extra to enhance the quality of their purchase.

Sell accessories. If you sell a desk, suggest a matching chair or floor lamp. If a customer buys a gizmo machine, suggest he purchase the special gizmo machine lubricant to make it work better.

Incentive selling works, too. Free gifts, premiums, and discounts are all effective ways to build more sales from your existing customer base. For instance, buy these new cosmetics and get a free tote bag. Or buy one hamburger and get the second one for half price.

Trade up customers. Last year, your customer bought the standard model from you. This year, sell him the deluxe model. And sell him an extended service warranty, too.

## 4. NEW PRODUCTS

**New products** are absolutely necessary for the health of your company. They replace your products that are in decline, they provide fresh revenue from new markets, and they position your firm as an innovator in the industry.

But they can be risky. Statistics indicate more than 10,000 new products are introduced every year. A majority fail in the first year, more than 80 percent in the first three.

## 5. MERGE OR ACQUIRE

A **merger or acquisition** may offer a multitude of opportunities to increase your revenue. By merging or acquiring another company, you actually may carry out all of the other strategies at once.

Acquiring a competitor may indeed gain you market share, selling more of the same stuff to the same people. It may allow you to expand your markets, selling more of the same stuff to different people. Or it could be an opportunity to sell different products to your existing customers.

Once your vision for your company has crystallized in your list of objectives and you need to figure out how to achieve those goals, you now have the tools.

Let's examine each more closely in the next five chapters.

# CHAPTER 5

# Kick-Ass Strategy #1: Buy Market Share

Purpose: *The purpose of chapter 5 is to demonstrate how to gain market share within a mature market using a variety of discounting methods and promotion options, and the best way to establish your promotion budget.*

———◦———

**T**he big gorilla in the forest rules his domain. The same is true in any market. If you can dominate your particular industry, you can enjoy a variety of advantages.

So how do you become the market leader? You need to spend money. That's why it's called "buy market share." To buy market share, it will cost you in one of two ways:

1. **Discount heavily**
2. **Promote heavily**

Remember the Q, S, & P principle? Imagine that you offer great service and great quality. By definition, you have to charge a premium price or lose money.

Now imagine you still offer great service and great quality, but you drop your price. Yes, you will lose money, but you will gain many new customers. Bingo! You just "bought" market share.

Or instead, you strengthen the warranty on your product from one year to three years. This appeals to potential customers, and you are able to lure them away from your competition. But it, too, will cost you in the long run. Again, you just "bought" market share.

Any form of discount, whether it be a drop in price, stronger warranty, rebate, or better credit terms, is a means of "buying" market share.

### Case Study  D&S/DAVIANS

#### THE PROBLEM

D&S/Davians is a vending company founded by Dave and Vivian Kwarciany nearly fifty years ago. The company, now operated by their children, supplies vending machines to companies throughout southeastern Wisconsin.

Drivers arrive at 4:00 a.m., fill their trucks with the day's orders of soda, sandwiches, and candy bars, and then travel their routes to fill their customers' machines.

D&S/Davians is the leading provider of vending services, with about 20 percent market share.

When a large national chain decided to enter the market, D&S/Davians prepared for a market share battle. The national chain offered the same candy bars and soda (Q) and provided the same level of service (S) as D&S/Davians. But their two-year contracts were about 10 percent below the market price (P).

In short, the national chain offered customers all three: Q, S, & P.

Now imagine you increase your promotion spending dramatically. You develop a publicity campaign that runs in your industry trade journal. You start running ads every other month coupled with a series of direct mailings, and you follow up with a telemarketing campaign.

Suddenly, you're hot. Customers who hadn't considered using you before are now clamoring for your attention. Guess what? You just "bought" market share.

Yours sales increased dramatically. But at what cost? All that promotion lost you your profit margins.

Relax. It's only temporary. In the long run, it may be well worth doing.

While buying market share can be costly, the market leader often enjoys myriad advantages. The firm with the largest market share typically accumulates greater operating experience and has lower overall costs relative to competitors with smaller market shares due to economies of scale. The leader enjoys a strong reputation in the marketplace, frequently sets the market price, has the least difficulty finding distribution coverage, and can pick and choose new markets to enter.

Studies prove that market share leadership leads to profitability. Lower costs, combined with greater sales leads to higher profits. The leading brand in a category typically generates twice the profit of a weaker "also-ran."

This suggests that being a big gorilla in a smaller forest is more profitable. But while a larger market share has its advantages, the life of a market leader is not all joy and rapture. Leaders must maintain constant vigilance in the face of a variety of perils.

---

## BE A BIG GORILLA

*To achieve higher financial returns, dominate several smaller market segments rather than competing as a relatively minor player in a large segment.*

*One study found a 32 percent return on investment (ROI) for firms with market shares above 40 percent.*

*In contrast, for firms with market share between 20 and 40 percent, ROI decreases to 24 percent.*

*A market share of less than 10 percent generates just 13 percent ROI, on average.*

*This relationship also applies to firms' individual products.*

Source: Marketing Science Institute

---

The big gorilla is under constant attack by competition, like swarms of bees, each one stinging and biting and the gorilla responding as quickly as it can. Hazards include product innovation (e.g., Nokia and Ericsson's digital cell phone technology replaced Motorola's analog dominance), industry trends (Levi's baby boomer image lost share to trendier brands like Tommy Hilfiger and Calvin Klein), or simple misjudgment of the competition (Sears's underestimation of discounters Kmart and Wal-Mart).

Often, the first product in a new market will generate the most interest, and will often lead to market domination. But what if you're not the first in the market?

The most effective way to gain share in a mature market is to offer all three: Q, S, & P. That often means discounting your price.

## Case Study    D&S/DAVIANS

**THE SOLUTION**

The big national chain achieved a peak of 6 percent market share in the competitive Southeastern Wisconsin vending market. Their lower prices, combined with comparable quality and service, attracted customers. D&S/Davians share fell three points to 17 percent.

Two years later, as the big national chain's contracts began to expire, they tried to renegotiate at higher prices in order to begin making money on the customers they had acquired.

D&S/Davians conducted an aggressive campaign emphasizing their service and the fact that they were the "local alternative." Market share increased to 22 percent (two points higher than when the chain first came to town).

Meanwhile, the big national chain lost share. And while their market share eventually leveled out around 4 percent, that was 4 percent more than when they began. Their ability to withstand two years of losses gave them a foothold in the market, and their aggressive promotion techniques made them a player in SE Wisconsin.

www.davians.com

Discounts can occur in several forms:
- Price reductions (e.g., a sale)
- Incentives (e.g., premiums)
- Discounts (e.g., coupon, rebate)
- Warranties and Guarantees (e.g., ten-year, 100,000 miles vs. four-year, 50,000-mile industry standard)
- Credit terms (e.g., no payments till next year)

## HOLD A SALE

A sale is among the top traffic builders for retailers. But it is also an effective tool for any business, whether consumer or B2B, durable products or customized services. A sale brings in customers, moves merchandise, and helps cash flow.

Competition has made the sale an even more significant factor in gaining market share. Customers are more price-conscious and sales-oriented as sellers take a more aggressive approach to reducing inventories and generating revenue.

Sales are particularly effective if:

### 1. Competitors are having a sale.

This creates a "sales mentality" among customers. If a number of firms in your industry are having sales and you're not, potential customers may ask, "Why not?" You are perceived as "full-priced." They may feel reluctant to buy from you until you have a sale.

### 2. You are willing to accept lower profit margins and make it up in volume.

Sometimes, market share is more important than profit margin. If you can capture new customers with your sale, you may sell enough merchandise to pay for the promotion and still have some left over for yourself. This is a case where you may be able to get help from suppliers. Purchasing in larger quantities may afford you a discount, which you can pass along to your customers during the sale.

### 3. You want to reduce inventories and build business during slow selling periods.

Your shelves are full. The stockroom is jammed. And you've just ordered a new supply of goods. Here's when you want to get rid of bloated inventories. Discount deep enough (at least 10 percent, but 20 or 30 percent is even better) to make it move. It's costing you a lot to keep those goods in stock. You have all that money tied up in goods that could be used to buy more, faster-turning inventory.

### 4. You are trying to attract new customers.

Here's your real chance to build market share. A sale can grab attention, make prospects aware of your products, and maybe interest potential customers who might not otherwise

---

*When holding a sale or offering a deep discount:*

*1. Be sure to have plenty of stock on hand of whatever is on sale. Offer a rain check to customers if you run short.*

*2. A sale must be heavily promoted so as to attract non-customers. You don't simply want to give a discount to the folks who would regularly buy from you anyway. The sale should attract new customers in order to build share.*

*3. Every sale must have a reason. Simply having a sale doesn't create the perception in the minds of your customers that they are getting a bargain. Rather, they will simply believe that you are overpriced the remainder of the time.*

have considered buying from you. The sale advertising and promotions are one more way to put your name in front of customers. And name awareness is the number one reason people buy products.

# FIVE REASONS TO HAVE A SALE

To build market share, discounting of merchandise or services offers a significant reason for prospects to switch from their present supplier to you. But no matter how clever your advertising, and no matter how many customers inquire, a sale is not successful unless it moves merchandise.

The product has got to go out the door or your promotional money is wasted. And product will not move unless your customers perceive they are getting a bargain. So when you hold a sale, it must have a plausible reason, one that convinces your prospects that this is a rare opportunity, one that motivates them to buy from you over a competitor, and one that makes them buy now.

Here are five reasons for a sale that retailers can use to bring in customers and move out merchandise. But the principles can also be applied for non-retail businesses, too.

## 1. Truckload Sale

Here's a retail idea that can also work for B2B companies. Conduct this sale in cooperation with one of your major suppliers. Park a big truck in your lot and stack a few pallets and boxes around it with the name of your supplier on them. Offer product demonstrations in your store. When a customer buys a product, you can even have him walk out to the truck to pick it up.

Use a big sign to keep a running tally of the number left of each product. Promote the sale through media advertising, mailings, and lots of display signs. You could rent a trailer sign and park it near the street.

The customer perceives you got a good price on the product because you bought a whole truckload, and you are passing along the savings to him.

## 2. Downtime Sale

Every company has slow periods, times when customers just don't seem to be around, times when you think you might be better off not even opening the doors. Maybe it's Thursdays, or even slow seasons, like the entire summer for instance.

Run a special during those slow periods. Your "Thursday Sale" or "Summer Sale" could offer specials on specific products or a straight percentage discount on everything you sell.

Promote your "Thursday Sale" with window displays and in-store signs, mailings to senior citizen centers, PTAs, and other groups whose members may have time to shop during these off hours.

A "Summer Sale" may encourage early buyers to lay in a supply before prices go up. This moves merchandise during a slow period, and helps improve cash flow.

### 3. Your Birthday Sale

Here's another retail idea: offer a discount (say 10 percent) to any customer on his or her birthday (or even during the birthday week). This sale creates goodwill among customers as well as moving products out the door.

Promote the sale using in-store signs, a flier stuffed into the bag with every purchase, and even in your advertising.

A twist on this idea is the "Birthday Club." Customers fill out a form listing their birthday. Then a week or so before the date, you send them an invitation to stop by for a free product or special discount, just for them.

Free publicity: Get a local newspaper columnist signed up and have him do a story on how he celebrated his birthday at your store with a free gift. You could also do a story about which birthday had the most customers.

### 4. Product of the Week/Month Sale

Every week or every month, feature a different product at a special price. Be sure to offer deep discounts on exciting products that will lure customers back week after week or month after month.

This can be a tremendous traffic builder. Naturally, they'll spend plenty on other products besides the sale item.

Promote this sale heavily. Be sure to feature each week's/month's special item and its deep discount price in your advertisements or direct mail.

### 5. Senior Sale Days

Want to focus on an affluent, oft-overlooked target market? Seniors are often more flexible with their time. They are perfect for drawing into your store during otherwise slow periods. Offer a senior discount at traditionally slow times, say one morning each week.

Promote this program through seniors clubs, senior citizens centers, and senior newsletters. During May (Senior Citizens Month), ask your local paper to do a story about your busy Senior Sale Days as a "human interest" feature.

Discounting the price is one way to buy market share. But there may be times when you do not want to reduce your price. You still want to increase your market share, right? Then you still have to offer those customers some reason to leave your competitors and buy from you.

## AD SPECIALTIES

Called gimcracks, gewgaws, doo-dads, or chotchkies, they're the pens, notebooks, key fobs, coffee mugs, and sports accessories brandishing your organization's name and logo.

Ad specialties are different than premiums only in that premiums require a purchase. Ad specialties are given away free.

# INCENTIVES

Everyone likes to get something for nothing.

Incentives offer that feeling to consumers, dealers, salespeople, or anyone else to whom the seller wants to create a motivation to purchase *now*. They create a reason to purchase over and above the obvious benefits of the product itself.

Because you are offering that additional something for nothing, incentives are a form of discount. "Buy one, get one free" is really just an inducement for you to purchase two of something. If you do, you'll receive each at half price. A discount.

Incentives (often called **sales promotions**) offer a direct inducement, an extra incentive to create an immediate sale. Smart marketers use them as an alternative to mass media advertising. As target markets become more fragmented, incentives offer a means of creating a connection with consumers, dealers, or your own sales staff.

Incentives are the fastest-growing form of promotion, faster than publicity, advertising, or direct marketing. There are a variety of reasons for this.

First, the consumer market is increasingly fragmented. Incentive promotion offers a way to segment the market and offer a highly targeted approach.

Secondly, it is more accountable than media advertising. Retailers using scanner technology can track sales promotions results quickly and accurately. Manufacturers especially like incentive promotion at the retail level because of the growing proliferation of brands (20,000 new consumer products are introduced each year) and the declining influence of media advertising.

Sales incentives and sales promotions have been around for centuries in every industry from appliances to zithers. The first premium incentive had its roots in failure. Benjamin Babbitt, a soap manufacturer, decided to wrap his soap, Bab-O, in paper. (Prior to that time, soap had been sold unwrapped, the grocer simply lopped off a piece from a larger bar.) But women didn't want anything to do with this nonsense. They weren't interested in buying paper, and the wrapped soap didn't sell.

So Babbitt decided to create value in the paper as well as the soap. He offered to redeem twenty-five of the wrappers for an attractive color lithograph. Sales took off. Later, he began requiring users to send an additional sum of money that by itself covered the cost of the prize.

## CROSS-PROMOTE

*Team up with a non-competing brand to promote one or both brands.*

*For example, pay for printing tickets to a local sporting event. On the back of the tickets, place your offer ("Bring in ticket for a free gimcrack!" or "Go to our website and win a prize!").*

## EXAMPLES OF INCENTIVE MARKETING

| To Consumers: | To the Trade: |
|---|---|
| *Samples* | *Samples* |
| *Coupons* | *Trade Shows* |
| *Premiums* | *Trade Allowances* |
| *Contests/Sweepstakes* | *Contests* |
| *Rebates* | *Rebates* |
| *Bonus Packs* | *POP Displays* |
| *Training/Seminars* | *Training/Seminars* |
| *Ad Specialties* | *Ad Specialties* |

## SOFTEN A PRICE BOOST
..............................
*Increase the price of a product but include a premium for a limited time. Then, discontinue the premium offer, and your price increase remains.*

## POINT-OF-PURCHASE DISPLAYS
..............................
*Manufacturers give away the POP if a retailer will use it in the store.*

*Knowing floor space was at a premium, Hanes designed a free-standing POP display to hold L'eggs panty hose, the first time panty hose was ever sold in grocery stores. Displays were set near the checkout counters for impulse purchase.*

*L'eggs became a hit with working women on the go who had little time to seek out the panty hose counter at local department stores. The higher sales volume per square foot of space also pleased the grocers.*

During the late nineteenth century, picture cards of everything from tall ships to opera singers served as incentives to promote purchase. Coupons began to dominate the incentive market in the early twentieth century, and are still used heavily today by advertisers large and small. Beginning in the 1950s, grocers began offering trading stamps as a way to build market share and retain customer loyalty. During the 1960s, savings and loans expanded the use of premiums to encourage new depositors.

Today, you can find examples of sales promotions everywhere. Companies offer sales promotions in conjunction with every other form of promotion. Mass media advertisements may contain a coupon or rebate offer. A direct mail program may include a free sample. Ad specialties are given away freely at trade shows. Premiums dot the shelves at grocery stores.

Proctor & Gamble used an incentive program on the Internet to relaunch Pert Plus shampoo. P&G developed a new website (www.pertplus.com) to create awareness, give-away free samples, and learn more about website users. Within two months, over 170,000 consumers visited the site with 83,000 requesting free samples.

Motion pictures are famous for sales promotion tie-ins. Toys and video games are coupled with characters from hit movies. Walt Disney's animated film, *Monsters, Inc.,* attracted over $80 million in promotional tie-ins from McDonald's, PepsiCo, and Kellogg.

Despite the myriad benefits of sales promotions and incentives, they cannot take the place of other forms of promotion. In fact, they are most often used as support for other media. The reason is that sales promotion and incentives almost always result in temporary short-term gains. Whereas advertising, direct marketing, and personal selling build awareness and credibility for the long-term benefit of a product or service, incentive promotions offer reasons to buy *now*. They are designed to give your company an instant sales boost.

The chart below illustrates the long-term effect of sales promotions.

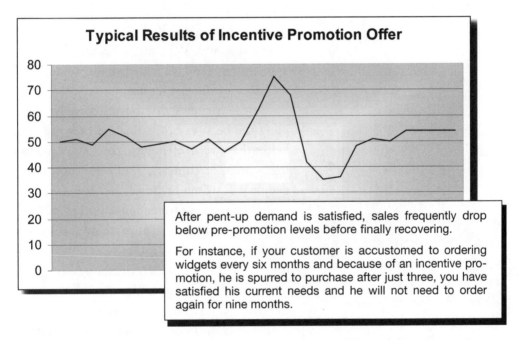

**Typical Results of Incentive Promotion Offer**

After pent-up demand is satisfied, sales frequently drop below pre-promotion levels before finally recovering.

For instance, if your customer is accustomed to ordering widgets every six months and because of an incentive promotion, he is spurred to purchase after just three, you have satisfied his current needs and he will not need to order again for nine months.

The short-term effect is an immediate bump in sales. But many of those sales come from customers who would have bought anyway. They simply decided to take advantage of the promotion offer and buy sooner. As a result, they need not buy again for some time. Sales drop below prepromotion levels.

Your one hope is that the promotion offer will attract new users, too. They will then convert to regular customers. In the example above, sales hovered at fifty units/period, then shot up to seventy-five units as a result of the sales promotion, only to sink below prepromotion levels after the promotion ended. Eventually, customers returned and sales settled slightly higher, at fifty-five units/period, as new users were converted.

# SAMPLING

Sampling is one of the premier ways to generate interest in your product and gain market share.

Sampling puts product directly in the hands of the people you most want to reach. It's a powerful way to create awareness for your product. And it's an ideal way of demonstrating all its benefits to the user.

## SAMPLER'S GUILT

*Everybody likes to get something for nothing. But surprisingly, most of us feel guilty about it.*

*Subliminally, we feel an obligation to buy if we have been given something for free. We receive a free sample and we are compelled to buy the product so as to reciprocate.*

*Think about the last time you were at the grocery store and received a free sample of some food item. It tasted good, the lady who gave it to you was nice, so you bought the product. You may not have wanted it, or it may not have been your regular brand. But you received a free sample, so it was really the polite thing to do.*

Marketers know that if we bestow a free sample of our product upon our target customers, they are far more likely to purchase the product than if we simply advertise it or even offer a discount. Why not? A sample is instant gratification. And it's a no-risk way to decide if we like a product or service.

Research shows that buyers consider sampling the best way to evaluate a new product, better than word-of-mouth, coupons, advertising, games, or contests. And seven out of ten people will switch brands if they like a sample.

Samples create tremendous credibility for a product. Customers realize that a company would not give it away if they were not 100 percent behind the product. Sampling says: "We have a product. It's darned good. We want you to try it and see how good it is, too."

Many companies use samples to introduce a new product. Proctor & Gamble won't launch a new product without first sampling it in test markets. But new products are not the only time to use samples. Here are five other times you should consider sampling:

### 1. Sample when you need to reach a new audience

For years, high-energy snack bars were a food staple among backpackers and athletes. But when companies began aggressively sampling, snack bars found their way from health food stores to the supermarket shelves.

## Case Study: McDONALD'S

**THE PROBLEM**

When Wendy's launched its now famous "Where's the beef?" campaign, the impact was felt at McDonald's. The clever advertising campaign increased Wendy's business dramatically, while McDonald's sales dropped.

But McDonald's had 100 percent all-beef hamburgers, too. Store managers needed a way to counteract the perception that Wendy's had the beef.

### 2. Sample when you need to change customer perceptions

A free sample may be necessary when you face an indifferent, incredulous, or even hostile audience. Use a sample to create awareness of your product as an alternative to what customers may think they know about it.

New in the market? Let your prospects try a sample to help overcome any skepticism. Can't give away your product because it's too costly? Let the prospect try it for thirty days. I was still considering the purchase of a new mattress when the store manager agreed to deliver it to me free of charge. No obligation. After a week, I realized two things: I really needed a new mattress, and this new one was too soft. No problem. The store exchanged it for a firmer model. A week later, I bought the new mattress.

> **SAMPLING WORKS**
> ·····························
> *Samples generate excitement. After all, nothing works better than "FREE!"*
>
> *1. Sample when you need to reach a new audience*
>
> *2. Sample when you need to change customer perceptions*
>
> *3. Sample to build traffic*
>
> *4. Sample to showcase a new use for your product*
>
> *5. Use samples to encourage trading up*

### 3. Sample to build traffic

Often, the best way to sample a product is when the customer is already in a buying mood. Your suppliers may be willing to provide sample products for distribution through you because they know they are more likely to turn the customers' sense of reciprocation into sales.

Contact some of your suppliers and ask about offering their products as samples. It's a low-cost way to increase your customer reach without discounting your regular merchandise. And it's an easy way to attract new users and build market share.

### 4. Sample to showcase a new use for your product

When Mrs. Dash, a salt substitute, wanted to encourage the product's use as a pizza topping, it was offered free with Boboli pizza crust purchases. Consumers had an opportunity to try the product on their pizzas, and both product awareness and sales soared.

## McDONALD'S

**THE SOLUTION**

McDonald's wanted customers to see just how good their 100 percent pure beef hamburgers really were. So we cooked up a batch of burgers, chopped them into bite-size pieces, put some toothpicks in them, and offered them free to customers.

Later, research showed a dramatic jump in quality perceptions and consumer satisfaction levels. While Wendy's was asking, "Where's the beef?" McDonald's was delivering.

www.mcdonalds.com

### 5. Sample to encourage trading up

"Now that you have your free starter set, would you like to purchase this deluxe set, or maybe this handy carrying case?" The Lego Toy Company often gives away simple starter sets of its connectable toys. They hope that, after you use a basic set for awhile, you will want to trade up to one of their more elaborate assembly toys (at an elaborate price, of course).

If you sample to draw new customers, be sure to advertise the offer. No sense giving stuff just to the folks who were already going to buy from you anyway. While it's nice to reward regular customers, the objective is to draw new customers.

# GUARANTEES AND WARRANTIES

One way to create credibility in the marketplace is to offer a money-back guarantee if the customer is not satisfied, or a warranty if the product does not perform as promised. These are explicit or implied promises made by you, the seller, that your customer will be happy with the product's performance or you will either fix the problem or refund the purchase price.

Guarantees typically have a limited time frame. "Five years or 50,000 miles" is a typical new-car warranty. If anything should go wrong with the vehicle in that five-year period or before 50,000 miles (whichever occurs first), the manufacturer promises to fix the problem at no charge.

When Hyundai introduced their vehicles to the U.S. market, consumers were initially doubtful of the quality of cars made in Korea. To overcome their skepticism, Hyundai offered an unprecedented ten-year 100,000-mile warranty. Hyundai sales took off and, while many cars had to be repaired under warranty in those first few years, Hyundai honored the warranty and gained the trust of many satisfied owners.

> ## "IT'S GUARANTEED"
> *Guarantees provide a sense of security to customers.*
>
> *In the event something goes wrong, they know they can get their money refunded.*

Guaranties and warranties offer customers protection against product failure. They provide a sense of security to the user that, in the event something goes wrong, he can get his money (or some part of it) refunded. This can be helpful in convincing skeptical buyers, but it can also be costly to your company if the product fails too frequently.

Warranties have an added benefit: customer information and feedback. The buyer typically fills out a warranty card and returns it to the manufacturer. Cards may ask where the product was purchased, the price, questions related to the brand, usage habits, and demographic and psychographic information. Smart marketers then use this information to better serve their customers.

For instance, Gates Energy Products offered a $20 rebate to encourage return of warranty cards when the company introduced their new rechargeable batteries. This information was then used to market its products directly to consumers, bypassing retailers. The result: lower prices for buyers, and an increase in market share.

# REBATES

Any price reduction after purchase is called a rebate. The buyer sends a specified "proof of purchase" to the manufacturer who refunds part of the purchase price by mail.

So why doesn't the retailer reduce the price by the same amount? Typically, the retailer has no control over a rebate. He doesn't want to reduce his price at his store for fear of creating a false sense of value. Rather, the manufacturer uses the rebate to clear out overstock product or to speed the sales of an older model before introducing a new model.

While rebates have been around for decades, they have been highly visible in the car industry in recent years. After September 11, 2001, when uncertainty prevailed, automobile manufacturers wanted to maintain the economic momentum that they had at the time. So they offered rebates. Every major manufacturer participated. As a result, used-car prices dropped dramatically because it became cheaper to buy a new car.

New-car sales continued strong until early the following year when pent-up demand had been sated. Despite many of the manufacturers retaining their rebate offers, sales of automobiles plummeted. Demand had been met. Anyone who wanted a car, new or used, had taken advantage of the rebate wars. The deep recession that followed was led by soft car sales.

# CREDIT TERMS

Credit terms use the time value of money to gain share. If the value of a dollar is greater today than one year from now, it makes sense to take as long as possible to pay for something.

Businesses take advantage of credit terms all the time. Cash flow managers will tell you just stretching payment from thirty days to sixty days can help bolster your company's bottom line dramatically.

For many consumers (and companies), favorable credit terms may be more important than a price discount of less value. Consumers in particular frequently have difficulty managing cash flow. "No payment for twelve months" may be more attractive than a 10 percent discount (even though the cost of money—the prime rate—may be 8 percent).

Favorable credit terms are one more tool in your marketing toolbox that can help your company build revenue. If you perceive cash flow may be an issue with a particular customer, offer flexible credit terms, rather than dropping your price. This allows you to maintain the perceived value of your product. Pricing integrity is important so that customers do not begin to expect a lower price all the time.

Guarantees, warranties, rebates, favorable credit terms, premiums, contests, samples, or sales—they are all forms of discounting. They are all simply ways to entice buyers to switch from a competitor to your brand. All are used by marketers to sell more of their same stuff to the same group of people, to **buy market share**.

> ## CREDIT TERMS
> *Many suppliers offer "Two percent, net ten"—i.e., pay your bill in ten days and take a 2 percent discount.*
>
> *If your bill is usually due in thirty days, by paying twenty days early, you benefit from the equivalent of a 36.5 percent discount (2 percent is to twenty days as 36.5 percent is to one year).*
>
> *Not bad for helping out your vendor's cash flow.*

# PROMOTION

The other way to buy market share, rather than discounting price, is to increase your promotion spending. The fact is, the more people who know about your company and its products, the greater your sales potential.

If you spend more than your competitors, the marketplace begins to take notice of your message. Ultimately, you become "top of mind." **Top of Mind** is the all-important measurement that assures you customers will remember your name *first* when it comes time to make a purchase decision.

At McDonald's, we wanted a top-of-mind rating of 90 percent or higher. That is, when our telephone survey people called, we wanted nine out of ten people to say McDonald's *first* when asked to name a fast-food restaurant.

Remember the **buying process**? Increasing your spending puts you first among your prospects when they begin their **information search**. They will compare all others against you as they evaluate alternatives.

Increasing your share of voice among your target market leads to higher market share. Higher market share leads to lower costs. Lower costs lead to higher profits. Spend more to make more.

There are five promotion categories:

1. Mass Media Advertising
2. Publicity/PR

3. Incentives (see p. 104)
4. Direct Marketing
5. Personal Selling (see chapter 5)

# MASS MEDIA ADVERTISING

How should you spend your promotion dollars? Most people think mass media when it comes to creating greater visibility. Media advertising makes your company name recognizable and remembered. It gives credibility to your products and paves the way for your sales force or direct mailings.

## THE BUYING PROCESS

1. *Need Recognition*

2. *Information Search*

3. *Evaluation of Alternatives*

4. *Purchase*

5. *Post-Purchase Satisfaction*

Mass Media Advertising is comprised of print media (newspapers and magazines) and broadcast media (radio and television). Print media offer one major benefit over broadcast media. With print, you can offer far more detailed information about your product or service. Radio and TV spots are here and gone in sixty seconds or less. Print stays with us. It may lie around the office or the house for long periods. It may be read more than one time and by more than one person.

Magazines are the most specialized of all media. There are magazines covering virtually every market you or I can think of: magazines for gourmets, chess players, and dollhouse collectors. There are magazines for short people, tall people, and even twins.

Magazine ads have better recall than television ads. Readers are involved with their magazines. By taking the time to read it, they feel a commitment to the magazine. And most magazines offer outstanding reproductive capabilities, so your food photography actually looks delicious on the page.

## MAGAZINES

*Magazines are the most specialized of all media.*

*There are magazines for every pursuit, profession, or perversion.*

Magazines do, however, have their limitations. They have limited reach. Even *TV Guide*, one of the world's largest-circulation magazines, reaches only 13 percent of U.S. households. In addition, magazines have long lead times. You need to have your advertisement at the magazine at least forty-five days prior to publication. Most require seventy-five days lead time.

Newspapers are one of the most frequently used advertising media. And for good reason: penetration. More than 70 percent of all households read at least one newspaper.

Newspapers offer great geographic selectivity. There are national, regional, and local newspapers; daily, weekly, and special audience editions; as well as magazine inserts.

Display advertising represents about 70 percent of all newspaper ads. The balance is made up of classifieds (20 percent) and specialty ads and inserts.

Short lead times make newspapers extremely useful if your ad message changes frequently. Classifieds can often be modified with as little as twenty-four hours advance notice. Display ads often with just forty-eight hours notice.

Newspapers have high credibility. "It must be true. I read it in this morning's paper," is a common phrase.

Unfortunately, newspapers also have a short lifespan. There is nothing as old as yesterday's newspaper. Also, newsprint offers poor reproduction quality. The newsprint absorbs ink and causes "bleed," and some photography can look slightly blurred or downright awful—unfortunate if your product has eye appeal (e.g., food or cars).

Newspapers also suffer from "clutter." Because about 65 percent of an average daily newspaper is made up of advertising, your ad must compete with dozens, often hundreds of

## PARTIAL LIST OF PROMOTION METHODS

- *Brochures*
- *Business Cards and Stationery*
- *Newsletters*
- *Direct Mail Pieces*
- *Telemarketing*
- *Print and Broadcast Advertising*
- *Advertising Production*
- *Mass Media*
- *Personal Selling Expenses (Including Training)*
- *Trade Shows*
- *Point of Purchase (POP)*
- *Sales Promotions*
- *Yellow Pages*
- *Ad Specialties*
- *Database Marketing Systems*
- *Catalogs*
- *Publicity and Public Relations*
- *Website Development and Operating Costs*
- *Membership Dues (Trade Assoc, Chamber of Commerce, etc.)*

(continued next page)

(continued from previous)

- *Subscriptions (Trade Journals, Advisory Reports, etc.)*
- *Customer Questionnaires and Response Cards*
- *Charitable Donations*
- *Sports Team Sponsorships*
- *Golf Outings*
- *Uniforms*

others. For that reason, use plenty of white space to set your ad apart, and be sure it has plenty of visual impact.

Newspapers and magazines are passive media. Advertising in them assumes readers have an inherent interest in your product. Busy readers, however, frequently pass by an ad if they don't know they need the product.

For that, you need more intrusive media: radio or television.

Broadcast media's misunderstood stepchild is radio. Radio lacks the visual impact of TV, but it offers a multitude of opportunities for the creative mind. Garrison Keillor creates a whole town with vivid prose and a few sound effects.

Radio can also be targeted at specific audiences. Each radio station appeals to a very select group of listeners (see chapter 2, psychographics). And ratings companies monitor exactly who is listening when.

But radio has its limitations, too. Most people don't "listen" to radio; they simply "hear" it. It serves as background noise while they work, or while they drive.

So unless your radio spot is extremely unique, and can grab the "hearers" and make them "listeners," use radio cautiously.

The most intrusive medium is television. You watch a program, and suddenly the program is interrupted by a commercial. So, you watch it, too.

Oh, sure. There are "zappers" out there who use their remote control to switch channels. Or they simply press mute. But still, TV offers the best opportunity to create awareness for your product or service in the minds of your customers.

This is particularly true if you are introducing a new product, or have a product or service your customers may not know they need. TV commercials are best remembered if you can afford heavy repetition, or if you use memorable slogans and jingles.

Yellow pages advertising is a directional media. That is, it is not useful for creating awareness, but it can be used to point people interested in your product category to your specific address or telephone number. There are

## BROADCAST MEDIA
...........................................
*Radio can reach very specific groups of listeners.*

*But television is more intrusive.*

over 6,500 books throughout the U.S. and the number is growing. New, competing books are creating a fragmented market for yellow pages advertising.

Out-of-home media, like transit, sports stadiums, and outdoor posters offer both advantages and disadvantages. Advantages include targeted reach, good frequency (imagine your ad on the side of a bus being seen over and over again as it rolls through the city), lower cost versus many traditional media, and opportunities for creativity.

Disadvantages include wasted coverage (that same bus may be seen by quite a few non-prospective customers), limited message space, wear out, and poor image.

# MAKING THE MOST OF MEDIA

Media repetition helps your prospects remember. If you place a big ad in a newspaper or magazine, get reprints. Mail them to all your customers and potential customers. Enlarge them and display them in your booth at trade shows. Hang them up in your place of business.

Repeat your media message in your direct mailings. By itself, your brochure or company literature may lack the impact of media advertising. But when you feature the same ad that your customers have seen in the media, it further enhances your company's credibility and adds to that all-important frequency. The more often your customers see your ads, the better the ads sell.

So just because you are tired of seeing the same ads for your products doesn't mean your customers are. They haven't seen them nearly as often as you have. Don't be afraid to run your ads over and over again. And then, when you're so tired of them you could scream, run them again.

Whichever media you use, you can stretch your budget by flighting, or staggering, your use of media.

> ## R × F = GRPs
>
> *All media works on the basis of reach and frequency.*
>
> **Reach** *is the percent of the audience that sees (or hears) your advertisement.*
>
> **Frequency** *is the number of times, on average, they see it.*
>
> **General rule of thumb:** *Reach creates awareness. Frequency sells.*
>
> *When comparing different media, use the formula:*
>
> *Reach × Frequency = Gross Ratings Points*
>
> $R \times F = GRPs$
>
> *This is the standard for measuring media.*

## MEDIA REPETITION

*If you don't keep your name around constantly, it's forgotten as quickly as last year's Super Bowl champion.*

For example, let's say you can afford twenty radio spots a week for twelve weeks (a total of 240 spots). Rather than run twenty spots each week, consider running forty every other week. You'll achieve more impact by creating the illusion you're around all the time. Listeners won't know you're not on the air during the off week. They'll simply assume they just weren't listening when your ads were running.

Another effective media-buying maneuver is called front loading—heavily saturating your audience with your message in the first few weeks of your campaign, and then tapering off.

For example, try running one hundred radio spots during the first few weeks and two during each of the next eight weeks. Or try using full-page ads in the first two months, and quarter-page ads for the next six months. It gives your message more impact.

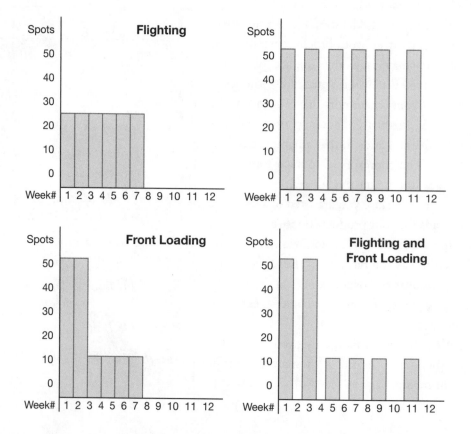

# PUBLICITY AND PUBLIC RELATIONS

Editors and columnists depend upon information from industry to keep them apprised of the latest innovations. You can provide a vital service by submitting that information in the form of a press release.

For the best chance of getting published, make life easy for the editor. Put all the salient points (who, what, where, why, when) up front. The less the editor has to edit, the greater the chance she will use your material.

Always put "For Immediate Release" or "For Release" (and remember to include the date the story will be current) at the top of the page. Summarize the important points with a headline.

Because the editor depends upon your veracity, it must be accurate. And it must not smack of advertising. Leave out your company's promotion adjectives or endorsements. Skip the superlatives; they won't print those either. The editor knows it has been prepared to benefit your company, but it also must benefit her readers.

At the beginning of the release, be sure to include your name and telephone number. The editor may want to check certain details for accuracy. Or she may want to expand on your story.

Send along a color photograph (5 × 7 is best) with the press release. According to a Gallup Poll, a story with a picture is read about eight times more often than one without. Hint: when quoting a person mentioned by name, include the age.

What should be publicized? If you have something of interest happening at your company, send your industry's trade journals a press release.

What's the first thing you looked at on this page? Articles with pictures are read about eight times more often than articles without.

- Most trade journals have a new products/services section. It provides information that may be important to readers.
- If you have a new machine that vastly improves the quality or delivery time of your products, you actually provide a vital service by submitting that information to your trade journal editors so they in turn can publish it for their readers.
- The grand opening, the new addition or remodeling also makes for good publicity. Any time you expand quarters, send out a press release. Mention

the greater convenience, additional elbow room, and how it will benefit the readers of the article, your potential customers.

• Adding a new person warrants a press release. A new executive's first responsibility should be to submit a brief autobiography and have his picture taken (good items to have in the employee files anyway). The release should include who he is, what he will be doing, what he is expected to accomplish (here's where you slip in the commercial about specific areas of expertise), and details about his education, experience, associations, and family.

• When you sign a big new account, send a press release (with the account's permission, of course). Let everyone know. It's one more opportunity to put your name before the public. It also gives you credibility in your industry. People in related businesses will think that you must be experts in that field, or else Harry at XYZ Company wouldn't be buying from you.

When nothing else is happening, *make* news.

The industry "prediction" is always good. For example, "Joe Dokes, president of Okey Doke Computer Supplies, predicts a paperless office by the year 2010. 'The world will communicate via fax and modem,' says Dokes. 'Computers will operate our homes, run our hospitals, etc.'"

The secret of this technique is to make a statement that is intriguing, maybe even fantastic, but never unbelievable. This approach endows the quoted person with instant expertise. He has made a publicized prediction; therefore he must be a respected sage. Everyone wants to work with a company headed by such a renowned and revered seer.

## PUBLICITY

*However limited your budget, good publicity can stretch it further than you might think.*

*It's free. And because it is presented in the press as a story, it has more credibility with readers than paid advertising.*

Another device you can use to break into the media is a statement about the condition of the economy: it's good, but it could get worse; it's bad, but it will get better. Back it up with a few accurate statistics and the implications to your industry, and you have yourself an interesting news release.

Remember, unlike advertising, there is no guarantee your story will run. You may work for weeks, even months, preparing an article and putting it before the proper magazine and newspaper editors. But reasons beyond your control may prevent your story from appearing within the time frame you desire.

Be patient. It's worth the effort. Because of its credibility, editorial publicity is generally considered to be worth more than ten times the same amount of space in paid advertising. And that print space or broadcast time costs you nothing. Sweet.

# DIRECT MARKETING

Telemarketing, direct mail, infomercials, QVC, Amazon.com—all are forms of direct marketing.

When you want to make direct contact with customers and prospects without intermediaries—no distributors, no retailers, just you and the customer—you use direct response marketing. Using a database of names and addresses, direct response marketing employs a creative message to create demand for a product or service, and a fulfillment service to deliver the product or service.

Ever since Montgomery-Ward started the mail-order business in 1872, it has been a prime method of targeting specific customers without the inherent waste of mass media advertising. In addition, advertising is designed to shape attitudes and perceptions. Not direct marketing. Direct marketing causes a specific action or behavior. "Call this toll-free number." "Send in this coupon." "Buy now!"

There are four basic components of direct marketing:

1. **The Offer**
2. **The List**
3. **The Response**
4. **Fulfillment**

The Offer is the promise you make in exchange for money or a specific customer behavior. It takes the prospect through all the decision steps—attention, desire, desire, action—and frequently is good for a limited period of time to create a sense of immediacy.

Often, especially in B2B direct marketing, the offer may require a second-step behavior: "Send for a free demonstration video and receive a free gizmo," or "Come to our trade

## DIRECT MARKETING
...........
*Over two-thirds of U.S. adults order products by mail, telephone, and/or the Internet each year, representing about 6 percent of all domestic sales.*

Source: Direct Marketing Assoc.

## DIRECT MARKETING EFFECTIVENESS

*Here is an example of the effectiveness of direct marketing in the telecommunications industry.*

*A manufacturer decided to test two campaigns. Campaign A used predominantly media advertising, while Campaign B used predominantly direct mail and telemarketing. Each campaign cost $125,000, but Campaign B generated significantly more leads and had significantly less cost per sale.*

### Budget Allocation ($000)

|              | Campaign A | | Campaign B | |
|--------------|------|-------|------|-------|
| Advertising  | 70%  | $ 90  | 10%  | $12   |
| Direct Mail  | 30%  | $ 35  | 25%  | $32   |
| Telemarketing| —    | —     | 65%  | $81   |
| Total Budget | 100% | $125  | 100% | $125  |

### Results by Medium

| | | | | |
|--------------|-------|------|-------|------|
| Advertising  | 219   | 35%  | 188   | 10%  |
| Direct Mail  | 406   | 65%  | 375   | 20%  |
| Telemarketing| —     | —    | 1,312 | 70%  |
| Total Leads  | 625   | 100% | 1,875 | 100% |

(continued next page)

show booth and enter to win a new car," or "Try this product for thirty days and receive a discount on your next order."

Use an offer that the prospect can't resist. "FREE!" always works well. Regardless, be sure to put the primary benefit in your headline.

The List is vitally important to the success of any direct marketing campaign. You can either compile your own list using database software, or purchase a list that matches your prospect demographic and psychographic characteristics.

Lists are sold based upon the cost per thousand (CPM) names. The more defined the list, the more costly. For example, a list of all women in the U.S. eighteen to thirty-four might cost $20 per thousand names. A list of all single women eighteen to thirty-four in a specific zip code who also use a credit card and subscribe to at least two women's fashion magazines might cost $100 CPM.

The quality of any list is measured by recency, frequency, and monetary value (RFM). The more recently a customer has purchased via direct mail or another direct marketing method, the more likely that person is to purchase again. The more frequently a person purchases via direct marketing, the more likely that person is to purchase again soon. And the more money that person spends, the more he or she is likely to spend on future purchases. If the RFM is strong, you are likely to pay more for the list.

The Response can take many forms: Call a toll-free number, go to a website, become a member, donate to a charity or cause, visit a trade show booth, or a variety of other behaviors.

But be prepared for the response. You do not want to put a caller, a prospective customer, on hold. You should have any product you're pushing in stock (the traditional allowance of four to six weeks for delivery is no longer the accepted norm). And you should have knowledgeable people available to answer any questions.

The last step is Fulfillment, delivering the product, brochure, information, etc. in a timely manner. Fulfillment is big business. Fulfillment operations dot the country, offering services to companies not equipped to handle outbound delivery of product, literature, or information. While in-house fulfillment offers control over the services provided, outsourcing to a fulfillment house can be far more cost effective.

Most direct marketing efforts employ a one-step approach. They are used directly to obtain an order. "Call 1-800-123-4567 to order your gizmo today!"

But some companies use a two-step approach to sell goods. The first contact may be used to screen prospects or to alert them of an impending contact from a company spokesperson, for instance, a phone call to determine interest followed by a salesperson visit. Publisher's Clearinghouse advertises heavily simply to create awareness for their future mailing ("Watch for your Publisher's Clearinghouse Sweepstakes entry form in the mail!").

Direct marketing offers one huge advantage over most all other methods of promotion: It is measurable.

---

(continued from previous)

*Mass media advertising often produce lower-quality leads because of the limited information they can carry. A direct mail piece or telemarketer can provide far more information because they are not limited by time (e.g., :60 or :30 in broadcast media) or space (e.g., quarter-page, half-page, or full-page) requirements.*

## CATALOG SALES
......................................

*Some retailers rely solely on direct marketing methods. They have no bricks-and-mortar presence (Lands' End, 800-CEO-READ).*

*Others use direct mail catalogs or online catalogs as their primary sales vehicles (L.L. Bean, Dell Computers).*

*Still others use direct mail and Internet marketing as a supplement to their store sales (Nieman-Marcus, Eddie Bauer).*

Response Rate = Number of Offers Mailed ÷ Number of Responses

If a mailing of 100,000 generates 10,000 responses, that is a 10 percent response rate.

In a one-step approach campaign, simply add up the cost of the mailing and subtract the profit from orders to determine whether or not the mailing was a success.

In a two-step approach campaign, you must convert responses into orders. An inquiry alone is of little value unless it can be converted into a sale. Of those 10,000 responses, let's say 2,000 are converted to sales (a 20 percent conversion rate), then the numbers change significantly.

Sales Rate = Number of Offers Mailed ÷ Number of Orders

Direct marketing is most-often effective when used in conjunction with other promotion methods. Media advertising can create awareness so that when your catalog or brochure falls on your prospect's desk, she opens it rather than tosses it.

Direct marketing is best suited to retaining and growing current customers. Database technologies make it possible to track customer behavior, including product preferences, purchase rates, and spending patterns. It also makes it easier to determine the profitability of each customer.

Best of all is its accountability. A marketer can know within days the attractiveness of an offer, the creativity of the execution, and the quality of the list because the response is its own measurement device. Furthermore, each variable can be tested separately, which can increase the cost-effectiveness of the effort. Lastly, because

## ADVERTISING VS. PROMOTION

*Research conducted by Information Resources, Inc. (IRI) follows the effectiveness of advertising vs. sales incentives in developing increases in consumer spending on specific brands.*

*IRI studies the effects of various incentives (including store displays, coupon programs, premium giveaways, contests, sweepstakes, bonus packs, and packaging) versus advertising. A review of nearly 400 research studies showed that advertising had profound long-term effects on sales, while incentive effects were almost always short-term.*

*Other research corroborates the IRI findings. In one study, marginal advertising increases of $1.00 increased sales only $0.50 in the short term. But the long-term marginal sales return was three times as large, or $1.50. Advertising's long-term effects seem to justify the expenditures.*

the lists are targeted to those most likely to respond, you eliminate a lot of media waste.

One drawback is the high cost per prospect reached. Direct mail efforts, for instance, may have costs of up to $300 CPM vs. just $20 to $30 CPM for media advertising. Clutter can also be a problem. Consumers especially are deluged with junk mail, inundated with spam, and bored senseless by infomercials and cable shopping channels.

If the desire is to deal directly with customers—no distributor or retailer static to garble your message—direct response marketing provides a wealth of opportunity. Imagine if your message is water, mass media is a hose that gets everyone wet. Direct marketing is a water pistol that wets only those whom you choose to target.

All your promotion efforts (advertising, incentives, direct marketing, public relations, and personal selling—more on selling in the next chapter) cost money. How much? To know the answer, you need to understand the many ways a promotion budget is established.

> ## SPENDING AS A PERCENT OF SALES
> ..........................................
> *While different industries vary in the amount of money they budget for promotion as a percent of sales, spending generally follows a prescribed pattern.*
>
> *Manufacturers = 2% to 4%*
>
> *Distributors = 4% to 8%*
>
> *Retailers = 8% to 12%*
>
> *Manufacturers have fewer customers so they need not spend as much on promotion.*
>
> *Retailers have a vast array of customers from a wide variety of target groups. They need to spend far more of their budgets as a percent of sales on promotion.*

# SETTING YOUR PROMOTION BUDGET

How much should you spend on promoting your business? It's an oft-asked question.

The correct answer of course is: *enough.*

But how much is enough? That depends on your competition and what it is you wish to accomplish. In general, there are four methods to determine your budget:

1. **Affordable**
2. **Percent-of-Sales**
3. **Objective-Task**
4. **Share-of-Voice**

More than half of all companies use the **affordable** method. That means they look at whatever is in the checkbook and decide what they can afford. The next media sales rep through the door with a glib tongue and an attractive offer gets the company's promotion dollars that month.

No plan. No strategy. No kidding. They simply spend whatever they can afford. Extremely inefficient. And extremely ineffective.

In every industry in every category, marketers promote their products by spending some percentage of their annual sales. Year to year, a company may compare the amount spent and determine next year's budget based upon what they have spent in the past. This method of budgeting for promotion is called **percent-of-sales**.

Most industry trade associations publish average promotion and advertising expenditures as a percent of sales. For example, many manufacturing businesses spend as little as 2 to 4 percent of sales on advertising. Wholesalers and distributorships typically spend 4 to 8 percent.

Retail firms have far more customers to reach. So they spend far more, as much as 10 to 12 percent of sales. McDonald's restaurants spends up to 16 percent of gross sales on combined national and regional advertising and promotion.

These percentages are not carved in stone. An industry that is extremely status- or style-conscious may spend far more. For example, a fashionable jeans manufacturer might spend as much as 25 percent of sales on advertising. A perfume company might set its promotion budget at 50 percent of sales or more. Athletic shoe companies spend 20 percent plus.

When companies use the percent-of-sales method, their budget is based upon future sales. For instance, let's say your company has $2 million in sales now, but your industry is growing dramatically and you think you can be a $3 million company within the next year or so. If your industry spends 5 percent of sales on advertising, budget 5 percent of $3 million (or $150,000 for promotion), not 5 percent of $2 million (or $100,000). This will allow you to achieve your sales goal of $3 million while spending 5 percent of sales on promotion.

To maintain your share of the market, you will likely have to spend the same percent of sales as your major competitors. To increase, or buy market share, you may have to spend far more than the normal industry percent-of-sales in promoting your product.

If you want to develop business in a new geographic area, you can't simply budget a percent of sales. For this new region, there are no sales yet. In this case, estimate what you think you can reasonably sell to this new area in a year and budget a percentage of that figure.

Or if you want to introduce a new product or service, you can't simply budget a percent of sales. There are none yet. In that case, it's important to examine the total market for your new product or service and establish a reasonable goal for your share of that market. Then, use the percent-of-sales method to determine your base advertising and promotion budget.

> ## OBJECTIVE-TASK METHOD
> ......................................
> *One big drawback of the objective-task method is that it requires far more skill, judgment, and research in analyzing promotion options than the simpler percent-of-sales method. The time and talent may be in short supply.*

But that is only a base. When introducing a new product, remember that no one has heard of it yet. You will need to spend a significant premium (typically 50 percent) in order to create awareness for your new product.

Frankly, anyone can use percent-of-sales to determine his promotion budget. Objective-task (or zero-base budgeting) takes a bit more know-how. The objective-task method is widely used and favored by academicians and major companies. It is the method taught in this book.

First, establish your sales goals. Then, determine the tasks necessary to achieve those goals (hence the name objective-task). Each promotional tool must be identified and costs determined separately, then combined with others to find the total budget necessary to achieve your objectives.

For instance, suppose a retail business with $10 million in sales has a goal of increasing sales by 10 percent. It is agreed that, to achieve this objective, the company must increase awareness of its location to residents in a new area not currently served by the store.

The store reviews its past advertising and promotion budget and decides to focus on publicity and direct mail in the new area. Tasks can then be set and a budget determined as follows:

| | |
|---|---:|
| • Media Advertising | $800,000 |
| • Production Costs | 65,000 |
| • Direct Mail (*new*) | 76,000 |
| • Localized Publicity (*new*) | 42,000 |
| • Research | 43,000 |
| • 10 Percent Reserve for Contingencies | 114,000 |
| **Total** | **$1,140,000** |

| Brand | Annual Promotion Spending | Share of Voice |
|-------|---------------------------|----------------|
| Alpha | $1,200 | 30 percent |
| Beta | 1,200 | 30 percent |
| Gamma | 800 | 20 percent |
| Delta | 500 | 12.5 percent |
| Epsilon | 300 | 7.5 percent |
| Total Category Spending | $4,000 | 100.0 percent |

The budget increased by the cost of direct mail and publicity (total: $118,000) to the new area, or approximately 10 percent additional promotion spending to achieve the 10 percent increase in sales.

A company's share of advertising expenditures creates a **share of voice** in the marketplace. Share of voice is the percentage of media spending in a particular category that comes from one brand. A thirty-five share of voice means that, of all the promotion dollars spent in the category during a specified time period, 35 percent came from that brand.

For example, consider the following:

Brand Beta has a 30 percent share of voice in the market. If the product manager for Brand Beta wanted to increase its share of market (buy market share), she might consider increasing the share of voice by increasing the brand's promotion budget.

Share of voice pits your company directly against the competition. It is the most-often used method of gaining market share. The objective is to create a stronger presence in a market than your direct competitor, a greater share of voice in the media.

Whichever method you use to determine your budget, allow for contingencies and cost overruns with a contingency fund. Some opportunity may arise during the year that you just shouldn't pass up. Don't. Use your contingency

## SHARE OF VOICE
. . . . . . . . . . . . . . . . . . . . . . . . . . .

*Pepsi may decide to target the Minneapolis market, for instance, and increase its spending to 70 percent of the city's promotion share of voice in the soft drink category. Coca-Cola stands to lose market share unless it responds accordingly.*

*Political candidates are especially conscious of share of voice. They try to raise as much money as possible so they have greater message frequency than their opponent.*

fund for the big opportunity. A contingency fund should be 7 to 10 percent of your total budget.

The contingency fund also has other uses. Monitor the effectiveness of your promotions throughout the year to see if your objectives are being met. If not, you may need to tap into the contingency budget.

You may also wish to use the fund to meet special circumstances. A change in customer demand, or to counter a competitor's promotion, or simply to implement a new marketing tactic.

## WAR GAMES

One unique way of increasing your market share that does not fit neatly into either price reduction or increased promotion is called a war game. Nothing to do with problems in the Middle East, it is so named because the forecast methodology is similar to that used by the military.

And why not? Companies have territories and missions; they formulate strategies and tactics. They conduct forays into enemy territories and engage in blitzes to capture more market share. Managers map out campaigns and issue orders. Subordinates carry them out. They use guerrilla-marketing tactics. They soften up the beaches with advertising and promotion before they send in their troops of sales representatives.

Sounds like war.

We do use a surprising number of metaphors for war in business. Perhaps that is why the war game has become such an effective

### HOW TO CONDUCT A WAR GAME

........................................

*Company A enjoyed a 40 percent market share in Wisconsin when it heard that Company B from another state was about to introduce a new product in Wisconsin. Company A decided to simulate a war game to help determine the best defense.*

*They divided into two teams (including employees, advisors, and family members familiar with the company). Task Force One represented Company B. Task Force Two was to dream up countermeasures to combat the enemy/competitor advances.*

*Task Force One attacked with a superb ad campaign based on the claim that more customers in Company B's home state bought their product than any other product of its type. After careful review, Task Force Two decided this strategy might quickly destroy their market share.*

*As a countermeasure, Task Force Two devised a response that deflated Company B's claim. They chose the strategy of a "preemptive*

(continued next page)

(continued from previous)

strike." *Their ad campaign stated, "More customers in Wisconsin buy our product than any other."*

*Company A immediately began using this campaign strategy in its advertising, and subsequently Company B's product bombed in Wisconsin. Company A later learned from a media sales representative that Company B had originally decided to use exactly the advertising strategy the war game had predicted.*

strategic planning tool. It is especially effective for gaining market share and preventing others from encroaching upon your share.

War games allow managers to assess consumer and competitor activities and prepare a suitable counterstrike. They allow you to test alternative scenarios against alternative responses. Like a crystal ball, war games can give you hindsight in advance.

Larger companies use sophisticated computer models to simulate changes in market share based upon advertising spending or customer responses to changes in pricing, etc. But computer-generated simulations are expensive, ranging from a few thousand dollars to upwards of $30,000. For a smaller company, a more moderate non-computerized approach may better fit your budget.

Begin by defining the problem as narrowly as possible. "I'm not happy with our level of profit" is vague; "A competitor is invading our market with a new product" is more specific.

Next, assemble your teams carefully. Choose right-brain creative types and left-brain analysts for each team. Provide team members with all the facts, from spending limits to market share, production capacity, and distribution techniques.

Simulate the necessary scenarios and encourage your managers to think in fresh and unexpected ways. Dropped into a strange new world, your teams might just arrive at strange new solutions. Bring the collective imaginations of your best and brightest thinkers to bear on your most critical problems.

Used correctly, war games have remarkable predictive power. They are ideal for defending your market share, or for taking market share from others. They get you to think differently and help you develop and test alternative strategies to rapidly changing markets.

Best of all, they give you the courage to face the future.

As a kick-ass strategy, buy market share requires patience and a deep pocket. Offering all three—Q, S, and P—simultaneously can be expensive. Reducing price may lure customers away from your competitors. And increasing your promotion spending makes more customers aware of the benefits of your products. But be prepared to spend money.

Is it worth it? Perhaps. Being the industry leader has advantages. By leading a market, you enjoy greater clout with suppliers and distributors, economies of scale, higher profit margins, and long-term stability.

Before digging deep to buy market share, be sure to analyze the long-term gains against the cost.

# CHAPTER 6

## Kick-Ass Strategy #2: Hunt

Purpose: *The purpose of chapter 6 is to demonstrate how to hunt new business by developing the skills of your sales team, and by using alternative methods of building awareness to attract new customers.*

———◇———

**H**unting new business is essential to the health of your company. Despite all the best efforts at satisfying your existing clients to grow your business, you must hunt. Your existing customers will eventually desert you. For price, for a new technology, for other less logical reasons (to be able to work with a golfing buddy or fellow deacon at the local church), or simply because they go out of business, move away, or die.

Every customer eventually leaves. So, every business must hunt.

Hunting, in the traditional sense, meant seeking out and capturing meat to feed a family. Ancient man would wander far from his base in search of prey, using stealth and cunning.

## B2C DEMOGRAPHIC CRITERIA

Age

Ethnicity

Education

Number in HH

Gender

HH income

Location

In marketing, it is much the same. We seek out new markets and capture customers, customers formerly served by other suppliers, in order to feed the company coffers.

Choose new markets to hunt using demographic criteria. If your company sells gewgaws to women in Des Moines, consider selling gewgaws to women in Cedar Rapids (location).

Likewise, you could consider selling gewgaws to men in Des Moines (gender). Both location and gender represent separate demographic criteria. Hunting new customers using any of the demographic criteria will do.

At Proctor & Gamble, management sought new markets for its Pampers disposable diapers. Their primary market, young mothers, was saturated, and P&G found itself engaged in a costly market share war with Kimberly-Clark's Huggies, the other leading brand.

P&G opted to pursue a completely different demographic: older adults. The company made some modest design changes and renamed the product "Depends" for sale to incontinent older adults.

It works the same B2B. If you have been selling doodads to smaller architectural firms, you might consider targeting larger architectural firms. Or engineering firms. Selling chrome widgets to the boating industry? Try selling them to the snowmobile industry. The ATV market, too.

When hunting, use demographic criteria to pick off underserved market segments. Analyze the segment (us, them, the environment) for profitability, and promote your product differences based upon that analysis.

## B2B DEMOGRAPHIC CRITERIA

# Employees

Total Revenue

# Years in Business

Type (mfg, svc, retail, etc.)

Location

Industry

When entering a new market, avoid asking, "How can we help you?" An open-ended question like that tells them you don't know the market. Instead, try, "What specific problems are you facing?" This line of questioning is more likely to result in a problem for which your company has a solution.

<table>
<tr><td>Case Study</td><td>D&S/DAVIANS</td></tr>
</table>

**THE PROBLEM**

D&S/Davians is really two companies.

D&S Food Service maintains vending machines throughout southeastern Wisconsin.

Davians offers catering services in its 9,000-square-foot conference center, or in your home, your office, your meeting room, or any outdoor venue. Their food receives rave reviews from critics and is considered among the finest dining experiences in the region.

Despite their success, few vending customers knew that their vending provider was also a catering service. And catering customers had no idea the company also provided vending services.

A little market research can reveal untold opportunities for new markets, provide a wealth of knowledge about your competitors, and help you better understand your customers' needs and wants. Then it's simply up to you to satisfy those needs and wants, and turn them into sales.

# PERSONAL SELLING

Good hunting starts with good hunters. Because it is easier to continue selling to your existing customers, many salespeople will simply devolve into order-takers, revisiting the same customer over and over again to collect their commissions and seldom venturing into the rejection-filled world of cold calling.

Hunting new business may require a new approach. Options include:
- **Use Independent Sales Representatives**
- **Hire Hunters**
- **Train and Motivate Your Existing Staff**

## Use Independent Sales Representatives

Many small businesses cannot afford to hire experienced salespeople to help open new markets. Consider the independent sales representative.

## FOUR WAYS TO BE A GOOD CUSTOMER TO YOUR REP FIRM

### 1. Pick a Winner

*Find a list of independent sales representative firms in the Directory of Manufacturers' Sales Agencies at www.manaonline.org. Pick a few and send them a letter asking if they would be interested in selling your line. For those who respond, ask for references and call a few of their better customers. Most important, meet face-to-face to get a feel for their personality to see if they will be good representatives of your company.*

### 2. Share Information

*Be sure the rep understands your business, your products, what makes your company unique, what sells well, and what doesn't.*

### 3. A Partner in Your Planning

*Most reps will see more of your customers in a week than you may see in a year or more. Learn your customers' needs and wants through their eyes and ears.*

(continued next page)

A good independent sales rep is like a partner. He (or she) works for himself. He represents many different companies just like yours (though none that compete directly) to customers that you might never get a chance to see.

If, for instance, you sell gizmos in Wyoming and decide you want to hunt new business in Colorado, you might hire a few salespeople, pay them while they learn your business, and then spend a fortune on travel and entertainment while they cold call prospects in this new territory to try and convince them to switch to your product.

Or you could hire a rep firm, an individual, or group of individuals who are already known and trusted by your prospective customers, to simply add your line of gizmos to their bag of goodies they already peddle in Colorado.

Good reps can serve as your eyes and ears in the marketplace. They know your new territory, the customers, and the major players. You, in effect, become a customer of the rep firm. You buy their expertise and their trusted name in exchange for a commission on sales (10 percent commission is not untypical, more on specialty goods).

You, as a customer, have to know how to tell the good sales reps from the bad ones. Some reps are out for the quick sale and see-you-later. The best sales reps form a partnership with their customers.

Partnering with independent sales reps can pay off in numerous ways. They're a fountain of industry information, a good source for strategic ideas, and can help you hunt new customers in unfamiliar territories.

## Hire Hunters

Some salespeople become complacent over time. They reach a plateau, a comfort level, selling enough each year to earn a comfortable living. They have developed comfortable relationships with their best customers, who in turn are equally comfortable with them. They're old dogs no longer interested in the hunt who see no reason to rock the Barcalounger by calling on new customers.

Nonsense, you say. Cut their territories! Take away their comfortable customers! Change the commission schedule!

Whoa! Don't mess with their money.

Remember, these are the salespeople who got your company to where it is. They are the reason those comfortable customers are so comfortable with your company and its products in the first place. The last thing you want is for your star salespeople to quit, taking those comfortable customers with them.

(continued from previous)

### 4. Show Your Appreciation

*Drop them a note unexpectedly once in awhile. "Saw this article about our competition and thought you might find it of interest . . ."*

*Every summer my father held a picnic at our house and entertained the sales reps for his small company.*

*It was his way of demonstrating his appreciation for their help throughout the year. And they all had a chance to hobnob with the other reps, my father's way of letting them know they had competition, too.*

---

 **Case Study** **D&S/DAVIANS**

### THE SOLUTION

Deciding the growth opportunity was in catering, D&S/Davians developed a newsletter, brochures, and a variety of other promotional mailings that they began distributing to their vending customers to create awareness for the catering capabilities. Key corporate executives were targeted at all D&S Food Service vending customers for receipt of direct mailings for catering services.

This "crossover" selling opened a new market for Davians and catering sales began to soar.

www.davians.com

## Case Study

# FORRER BUSINESS INTERIORS

### THE PROBLEM

Salespeople at FORRER Business Interiors had painstakingly nurtured relationships with their biggest customers over the years. These customers were among the largest companies in the state, important business to FORRER.

But these major companies were not growing, and few needed new office furniture very often. The major growth in the economy came from younger, smaller businesses. And competitors catering to these small- and medium-size businesses were beating FORRER in the marketplace.

FORRER's salespeople were well compensated and reluctant to call on new customers for fear they would not be available when long-time big-name customers needed them. What to do?

There are better solutions. You could go the independent sales representative route (see previous). But that could prove troublesome if you are planning to expand in your same geographic area.

Better idea: There are salespeople who thrive on cold calling. It takes a certain personality to accept rejection after rejection. But some people can live with that for that adrenal rush they feel when finally the prospect says, "Yes."

Finding good hunters may not be as difficult as it would seem. Consider former telemarketers. Experienced telemarketers are ideal for hunting new business. And nationwide No Call Lists have put many competent telephone salespeople out of work. A recent want ad in Milwaukee for an inside sales representative drew over one hundred responses from former telemarketers.

Whomever you hire, be careful. You might have the best products, at the best prices, offer the industry's best service warranties, and sell them at the best locations in the country. But you can fall flat on your face if you have lousy sales help.

Your customers must not only feel comfortable with your salespeople, they must feel confident that the salespeople know the products they are selling. Your sales staff must be ready and able to appear in your place, to know as much about

## FORRER BUSINESS INTERIORS

### THE SOLUTION

FORRER hired new salespeople and a new sales manager dedicated solely to new business development. In addition, they adapted a new product line of lower-priced office furniture especially suited to small- and medium-size businesses.

The results were profound. While the old sales group maintained the big, profitable accounts, the new sales group focused on smaller businesses. Sales increased nearly 20 percent for three straight years, with almost all the company's growth coming from new business.

www.forrersbi.com

your product line as you do, and to be able sell as convincingly as you would. Your ability to transfer your product knowledge to your sales staff can mean the difference between a lost sale and a long-term repeat customer.

Selling is not a science. There are no cut-and-dried factors that make for good salespeople. It's an art, yes. But it is an art that has received enormous study and attention because of its critical importance to the success of businesses everywhere. These studies have shown that there are four factors in creating a good sales staff:

1. Hire Smart
2. Train
3. Motivate
4. Support

## Hire Smart

It's not an easy job. Many successful executives admit to hiring the wrong people. You can improve your odds by asking yourself a few basic questions:

Q: Does he or she like to sell? Seems simple enough, but surprisingly few sales managers even consider this.

Q: Is she dependable? Will she show up for work every day, on time, well groomed?

Q: Does he genuinely enjoy helping others, both customers and his fellow employees?

Q: Is she ambitious? Does she hope someday to have your job? Or her own company?

(More on hiring in chapter 12.)

## MOTIVATIONAL REWARDS

*Different salespeople respond to different types of rewards. Given the right motivation, you may be surprised to learn one of your otherwise mediocre salespersons could be a star.*

*Try offering a reward (color TV, savings bond, restaurant gift certificate, etc.) for the most sales on a specific product for a limited time. This will help you determine the real capabilities of your staff.*

*Add-on sales can be big profit boosters for your business. Motivate your staff for accessory sales by offering incentives on those items with a higher markup.*

## Train, Motivate, and Support Your Sales Staff

Training falls into two categories, product training and sales training. Each is equally important.

To begin the former, immerse the salesperson in product information. Ask the manufacturers (or their distributors) to provide videos, handbooks, or other sales training tools. One handy technique: ask your other salespeople to conduct a class for each product line. This helps motivate your staff and builds a sense of teamwork. And it assures everyone is an expert in at least one thing.

Next, assign your new salesperson to a senior staff member, or take charge yourself. Familiarize him with your company's products, past promotions, and standard operating procedures. Allow the new hire to observe the trainer's sales techniques. After a few successful sales, let the new salesperson try it solo. Have the trainer close by to provide product information as needed. Offer encouragement, but never criticize the employee in front of others.

Motivation is a necessary ingredient in managing the successful sales team. The problem is, what works for one may not work for others.

Money may seem to be the one motivating factor common to all salespeople, but sometimes a pat on the back is just as important, or even more. Some salespeople respond to gifts; others seek awards. You will need to decide what is going to work for your staff members.

If you offer rewards, you have several options:
• Individual rewards
• Team rewards
• Companywide rewards

Peer pressure often makes the latter two methods work best. But seeing one's fellow salesperson receive an award can be the best motivator of all. How to choose? Certainly, the salesperson with the largest total sales would seem logical. But you might also consider inviting customers to nominate a "Salesperson of the Month" and loudly promote the company's "Salesperson of the Year" award.

Offering sales incentives can encourage the sale of specific items, like high-margin accessories. Offer rewards for meeting sales goals within a specified period. For example, the most sales of gizmos in October wins a free trip to Cancun.

Get your sales staff to respond to customer needs. Recognize and praise any employee whenever he goes that extra mile for a customer (stayed late at a customer's request to show a product, or personally delivered and set up the customer's new product in his home or place of business).

Your salespeople can often make or break your company's success. They are the linchpins of your marketing program.

Hire smart. Train them well. Praise them profusely. Reward them for achieving their goals. After all, their success is your success, too.

## MYSTERY SHOPPER

*Try a "mystery shopper" program. Ask friends and relatives to contact your company with specific product questions you want asked (along with the correct answers). Have them report back to you with the results.*

*Without identifying the "shoppers," let your staff know of the program. It's up to them to be ready anytime for possible "mystery" visits.*

## SALESPEOPLE NEED LOVE, TOO

Salespeople like money. It's what motivates most of them to sell, and to excel.

But they also need love.

**Case Study** **STANDARD ELECTRIC SUPPLY**

### THE PROBLEM

Standard Electric Supply Company is a Milwaukee-based distributor of electrical and automation products. For more than eighty-five years, SESCO has been a leader in providing electrical applications and solutions to customers throughout Wisconsin.

This highly competitive industry is subject to rapid technological changes. Rigorous product training keeps the sales force current. They go to regular seminars, read industry technology reports, and attend classes.

After a particularly lengthy season of continuing education, Director of Marketing Pat Lawler needed a way to demonstrate the company's respect and support for the team that served as its lifeblood.

They spend their days amid rejection and complaints, courting the favor of petulant purchasing agents and belligerent buyers. They are often away from the comforts of house and laundry for long periods of time.

Along with the commission check, they need the ego gratification of management recognition, a symbolic pat on the back for a job well done. And that recognition should be visible to their peers.

One of the prime purposes of a sales meeting is to publicly acknowledge the salespeople's importance. They need to know that, while they're out there doing battle with the hostiles, somebody back home really does care about what they think, feel, and need.

Sales meetings furnish the salespeople with a feeling of belonging, of being a part of the team. And the fact is, it's good business.

Sales meetings should be held frequently. At least quarterly, if not monthly. Morning meetings are best. Get them while they're fresh. And keep it short, not more than an hour and a half. You want your salespeople to be out selling, right?

Once a year, plan a big bash (banquet, golf outing, or field trip to a supplier, for example) with awards and some form of entertainment. If you have lots of extra money floating around (which most small companies don't), hold your sales meeting in some exotic locale. Spend a week at a tropical resort. Or charter a boat. But for a small company on a budget, the two most practical ways of holding a sales meeting are to fly everybody to your company's hometown or meet at the annual trade convention.

The sales meeting at your company has several advantages. Your home staff gets a chance to meet and greet the folks in the field. And the folks in the field get a chance to tour the factory, see the products being assembled, talk to the production department about delivery schedules, review office procedures, and build coalitions with the various department heads one-on-one.

Salespeople in the field tend to think only of their customers and their commissions. But given a clearer understanding of the headquarters systems and challenges, they develop an appreciation for why orders cannot always be shipped when and how they want them.

Meeting at the annual trade show saves money. Most salespeople have to attend the show anyway, so why not get them all together there for your own annual meeting? Trade shows offer opportunities for guest speakers, industry experts already in attendance that could add insight to your meeting.

Consider inviting one or two suppliers or industry gurus to address your sales staff. While most will be happy to oblige without compensation, be sure to reward them for their time with a token gift, nicely packaged. It shows you and your company's appreciation.

Speaking of gifts, it's also a good idea to leave some with your sales force. Some token of appreciation, even a T-shirt or corporate coffee mug, reminds them that they're loved.

## LISTEN TO YOUR SALES STAFF

*Your sales staff can be a tremendous source of ideas for new products and services, suggesting better ways to serve your clients. And better ways for them to fill their sales quotas.*

*One sharp saleswoman I know noticed that the three-ring binders she was selling to office supply centers were also being bought by a local photo studio.*

*She investigated and discovered the photo studio was selling the binders as photo albums.*

*We promptly dummied up some literature aimed at the photo supply business and suddenly a whole new market was born.*

## Case Study · STANDARD ELECTRIC SUPPLY

**THE SOLUTION**

At SESCO, the electrical engineers are second to none in providing expert technical advice to their customers.

But the company's focus is on the sales force. Management's attitude of "Love thy sales force as thyself and they shall go forth and hustle for thee" is reflected in their sales meetings.

After several grueling weeks of product training and technology instruction, Lawler hired a troop of entertainers to teach communication skills. Billed as a three-ring circus of fun—with a message, the troop had the sales staff perform impromptu skits, improvise mock sales calls, and tell stories using just hand signals and body language.

All agreed the learning experience was a welcome break from the long hours of product training.

However, these tokens are not a substitute for annual or quarterly sales awards. These should be significant items, earnest expressions of corporate appreciation for a job well done.

## The Sales Meeting

Every sales meeting should have a planned agenda.

Start the meeting with a brief (that's brief) speech by the president ("Hi-glad-to-see-you-all-here-we've-had-a-great-year-and-let's-all-look-forward-to-a-great-future-now-here's-Joanne."), followed by the sales manager.

The sales manager is like the coach of a football or basketball team—part teacher, part cheerleader, part confessor, but mostly motivator. Her speech should be upbeat, inspiring, action-packed, and full of promise for a bright future.

However, if the past year has indeed been a poor one, face up to it honestly, explain how the problems are being addressed, and that you can all look forward to a bright, action-packed future full of promise.

Pace, pace, pace. Don't give anyone time to develop that glassy-eyed stare so common among aggressive type A salespeople bored with a program. Keep the meeting moving.

Agenda topics should include new products or services now being offered by the company, production problems and delivery schedules, and new advertising or other sales support. Here's when you explain the rules for your latest sales contest and awards program.

Allow time for "new business." Let your salespeople tell you what their customers are asking for. After all, they're the ones who see them every day. Your sales staff can be a tremendous source of ideas for new products and services, suggesting better ways to serve the clients. And better ways for you to fill your sales quotas.

> ## REWARD YOUR SALES STAFF
> ·······································
> *Tangible items (TV, VCR, trip for two to some vacation resort, etc.) often work better than simple cash awards.*
>
> *The tangible item serves as a long-term reminder of the company's appreciation, while cash may go to pay for the dry cleaning and the utility bills.*

Invite outside speakers to your meeting as often as possible. How about a key vendor, industry guru, top-notch motivational speaker, or even a clothing salesperson to talk about good grooming habits? Or what about an English teacher to help polish your staff's sales letters and presentations? Your salespeople can benefit from their expertise. And it shows that you acknowledge your staff's importance.

Part of every sales meeting should include some form of entertainment. A softball game, a golf outing, or simply tickets to a local show are all ways to cement the team spirit needed for your financial success. And most important, it tells them somebody back home really does care about what they think, feel, and need.

It tells them they're loved.

Following are two illustrations of kick-ass **hunting** opportunities that may serve as thought-starters for your sales staff.

## ANYTHING FOR YOU, PRECIOUS

Here is a great example of a missed opportunity for hunting new business: grandparents.

Few manufacturers and retailers are marketing themselves effectively to the burgeoning grandparent market. And it's their loss.

> ## SUCCESSFUL SALES MEETINGS
> ·······································
> *1. Have an agenda*
>
> *2. Invite an outside expert*
>
> *3. Allow time for new business*
>
> *4. Pace, pace, pace*
>
> *5. Provide entertainment*
>
> *6. Recognition awards*

## GRANDPARENTS: A MISSED OPPORTUNITY

• *One in three American adults is a grandparent.*

• *They spent $600/year on their grandchildren (up from $320 in 1992).*

• *55 percent purchased a gift for a grandchild in the past month.*

• *They buy one of every four toys sold in the U.S.*

Source: Roper Starch Poll

Grandparents are a huge market, a market growing bigger daily as the population ages. There are 78 million baby boomers out there, the oldest of whom are becoming grandparents at the rate of over 10,000 every day, nearly 4 million a year.

Grandparents today are taking on a bigger role in their grandchildren's lives. The increase in single-parent homes means children have less and less adult influence in their lives. It's the grandparents who are picking up the slack. Some grandparents are even becoming the main providers of such staples as food and clothing.

Grandparents are living longer; most have significant disposable income; most of them have time; all of them adore their grandchildren. And with today's blended families, a typical kid might have as many as six or more grandparents.

Imagine you are a toy manufacturer playing with the fickle desires of children. You advertise (along with every other manufacturer) on Saturday morning television, pay huge licensing fees to some Hollywood hotshots in hopes that their blockbuster movie translates to toy sales, and sit back and wait. And hope.

You just missed an opportunity to hunt a new (virtually untapped) market. Did you know that grandparents buy 25 percent of all toys sold in the U.S.? Who is advertising to them? Ad spending on toys, games, and hobbies topped $1 billion recently, according to Competitive Media Reporting in New York City. But little if any of the ad spending was directed at seniors.

We're not just talking about toys, either. Grandparents are buying travel, computers, recreation, financial services, and entertainment for their grandkids. They have the wherewithal financially—more so than their children—to spend money and travel and do all those things the parents can't do.

Not all companies are missing out on this mega-market opportunity. Recently, several firms have begun recognizing the potential of the grandparent. Disney advertises a limited edition *Peter Pan* video with a headline that reads: "The Quickest Way to Get Your Grandkids to Fly Right Over." *The Lawrence*

*Welk Show* in Branson, Missouri, advertises its programs with billboards that say: "Bring Your Kids . . . Heck, Bring Their Kids."

Catalog company Genesis Direct offers hobbies and games through its "Gifts for Grandkids" catalog. Their marketing strategy includes quarterly newsletters and a grandkids birthday club that works like a personal shopper.

Grandtravel travel agency offers nineteen worldwide destinations with tours specifically designed for grandparents and their grandkids. Many are educational; all are meticulously planned. Alaska is the number one destination, followed by Kenya.

Toys "R" Us recently instituted a program aimed at seniors: Grandparents "R" Us includes a splashy website that recommends popular toys, including many perennial favorites, such as model trains, Play-Doh, and Monopoly.

The number of companies that take the time to talk to grandparents is growing. Those that advertise effectively to them will reap the benefits of this burgeoning market. If you have a product that appeals to children, consider hunting up a new market segment—promote it to their grandparents.

## THE INDUSTRY WHITE PAPER

Having trouble reaching the decision-makers at prospective customers? Looking to build credibility for your company in a new industry?

Here's a unique method for scoring points with prospects and projecting an image of expertise. It's one of the most compelling tactics you can use in your arsenal when hunting new business.

 **Case Study** **WADE TAYLOR & ASSOC.**

### THE PROBLEM

When his former boss decided to get out of the health care design business, Wade Taylor decided to found his own architectural firm, Wade Taylor & Associates. The firm specializes in hospital and clinic design.

Unfortunately, the firm was not well-known among decision-makers in the highly competitive field of design/build for ambulatory surgery centers.

## EXAMPLES OF INDUSTRY WHITE PAPERS

*1. An accounting firm offers a free analysis of the rapidly changing health care industry for distribution to hospitals, nursing homes, or managed health care organizations in the hope of attracting new clients.*

*2. An office furniture distributor offers a free analysis of OSHA's rules on workplace ergonomics as a service to facilities managers at prospective customers.*

*3. A brokerage firm offers free investment advice on the controversial inheritance tax debate in an effort to attract older, well-heeled investors.*

*4. A home improvement center offers data on energy conservation in the home. This information, provided free to consumers, motivates homeowners to install new windows or doors in an effort to weatherize their homes. Naturally, they call the provider of the free information for an estimate.*

It's called the industry report, or white paper. It's applicable to most any industry, and it serves as an ideal entrée to prospective customers.

Here's how it works: the objective is to write a comprehensive paper on the state of the _____ (fill in the blank) industry (the industry of your prospective customers). You want to provide fresh information and some quotes from respected industry leaders. Include new insights. Load it with statistics. Make it inclusive, maybe even controversial.

Above all, be objective. Key to the successful white paper is its objectivity. This is not a shameless sales piece. Your firm may not even be mentioned in the report, except as its sponsor.

Position your company as a knowledgeable source of information in the industry. Recipients of your informative report perceive your company as the industry authority. Of course, everyone wants to do business with an expert.

Your white paper need not be anything elaborate.

A simple, ten to fifteen pages of well-written text with a few charts or graphs and a nice cover works best. Use secondary research (from the library, Internet, or published resources) combined with relevant quotes from a few acknowledged scholars in the industry.

How do you get quotes from acknowledged scholars? Here's your chance to speak to those key prospects and decision-makers.

Call and ask them for an interview. This is not the time for a sales pitch. Rather, ask for their perspective on industry growth trends, new product innovations, pending legislation, or other issues affecting their industry for inclusion in this important study.

Almost every executive is flattered to be sought out as a revered seer, an opinion leader in his or her industry. Most will be pleased to contribute. Their participation will add objectivity and credibility to your report. And they will naturally be avid readers of your white paper when it is finished, searching doggedly for their contributions, and those of their colleagues.

When the report is complete, distribute it so as to maximize the benefits to your firm.

**First**, send a copy with a press release to all your local business publications, newspapers, and small-town weeklies. Announce the availability of your informative report to anyone requesting one. Then send anyone who responds a copy along with your promotional material. Be sure to record the name and address for your database.

> ### CUSTOMER CONTACTS
> ............................................
> *A white paper offers four opportunities to contact prospective customers:*
>
> *1. The request for the prospective customer's comments to be included in the report.*
>
> *2. The announcement of the availability of the report to prospective customers.*
>
> *3. The sending of the report to prospective customers.*
>
> *4. The follow-up with prospects after the report has been sent.*

**Next**, mail a notice (with a return card and SASE) to all your prospective customers in that industry. Send along a cover letter extolling the benefits to your customer of the report. Include a summary of the key findings, enough to cause them to peruse the report.

**Finally**, send your report to all the industry trade magazines for publication. Most trade magazines are hungry for well-researched, well-written articles on their industry. Publication in an industry journal will further bolster your company's reputation.

Publishing an industry white paper has many benefits. It creates awareness of your company in the industry. It establishes you and your firm as experts in the field. And it puts you in contact with key customers on your prospect list.

One more weapon to have in your arsenal when you go hunting.

The most difficult aspect of **hunting** new business is the lack of awareness for your company and products. The new market may not know anything about you, or at least may not have considered you for their needs.

Case
Study    **WADE TAYLOR & ASSOC.**

**THE SOLUTION**

The firm sent out questionnaires and conducted interviews with industry leaders, compiled an industry white paper on Ambulatory Surgery Centers, and offered it free to doctors, health care consultants, and hospital administrators throughout the U.S.

They created awareness and credibility for their firm among key decision-makers.

www.wadetaylor.com

Combining modern technology and some basic human psychology, you can create a name for yourself (your company and your products) in a new market.

# MODERN MARVELS IN MARKETING

What's the best form of advertising there is? Word-of-mouth.

There are hundreds of occasions when people ask others—friends, relatives, business associates—for a recommendation for a doctor, a plumber, a hotel, a restaurant, or a movie.

If we trust the person making the recommendation, we often act upon the referral. And some lucky business gets one more customer without having to spend a nickel on advertising or promotion.

Word-of-mouth is the only method of promotion that is of the consumer, by the consumer, and for the consumer. Every business owner dreams of having loyal, satisfied customers who brag about his business to others. Not only are they repeat purchasers, but they become walking billboards for his company.

Best of all, it's low-cost, one of the lowest-cost forms of promotion there is. Keeping in touch with satisfied customers and encouraging them to talk up your business costs relatively little. Yet, those satisfied customers can help you hunt new customers effectively and efficiently.

Many entrepreneurs recognize the value of word-of-mouth advertising, but feel helpless to generate it on their own. They simply sit back and hope against hope that their satisfied customers will tell all their friends. And sometimes that works too (see box, "Good Buzz at Amazon.com").

But there are ways you can help the process along. Here are five word-of-mouth marketing tips that can help you build a network of referral sources and grow your customer base:

### 1. Get your customers involved

Encourage your customers to become involved in the process of making or delivering your product or service. This personal experience creates a sense of camaraderie and positive feelings that lead them to talk about your business to their friends.

Solvang, California, a popular tourist destination, is the home of at least a dozen candy and fudge shops. One of the most successful has the big marble slab where they mix all the ingredients right in the window, where passersby can't miss the display. Many stores put their mixing table in the window.

But what makes this store unique is who mixes the ingredients: kids. Children roll up their sleeves, put on plastic mitts, and start mixing and folding the rich chocolate, creamy caramel, and chopped walnuts, all spread on a well-buttered table. Guess which fudge shop gets good word-of-mouth (pun intended) advertising?

### 2. You scratch my back, I'll scratch yours

If your business receives referrals from another business, reciprocate. Refer business to the referrer. Or at the very least, offer the referrer a discount price.

My piano tuner gives me 50 percent off my next tune if I refer business to him. It's a good deal. I keep the piano in tune for a reasonable price. My friends get their pianos accurately tuned by a professional. He gets additional business from my piano-playing circle of friends.

---

## GOOD BUZZ AT AMAZON.COM

*Jeff Bezos, founder of Amazon.com, had no money for advertising when he launched his business.*

*Trusting that good service would win customers through word-of-mouth, he became obsessed with customer service.*

*According to Bezos, if you make a customer unhappy he may tell five friends, but if you disappoint a customer on the Internet, he may tell 5,000 or 50,000 people.*

*At Amazon.com, customer service became his number one priority.*

## HUNT NEW BUSINESS THROUGH REFERRALS
..............................

*Encourage referrals by offering a small gift or gift certificate.*

*A successful dry cleaning service sends out gift certificates to a clothing store for referrals, an appropriate gift since those new clothes may later end up in his store for cleaning.*

### 3. Tell stories

Stories illustrate a specific idea or selling point. They are an effective vehicle for spreading reputations because they communicate on an emotional level. If you have a company newsletter or brochure, include a story or two about your company that readers can pass along.

Nordstrom's reputation for good service is legend. In her book *Fabled Service*, Betsy Sanders, a former Nordstrom vice president, recounts the story of a woman in torn and filthy clothes who walked into a store one day. The sharp contrast between the disheveled itinerant and the bodacious abundance of the store drew the attention of a local minister who was shopping nearby.

When the bag lady entered the pricey Special Occasions Department, rather than being asked politely to leave the store as the preacher expected, she was greeted warmly and allowed to try on gown after gown. The salesperson exhibited infinite patience as she offered comments on which evening dress was most appropriate, which was most flattering. The old woman left the department store with her head held high, a spring in her step.

The minister was so impressed, she told the story to her congregation. Later, word of the minister's sermon, "The Gospel According to Nordstrom," was mentioned in the *New York Times*. It became so popular, her church eventually sold audiotape copies.

### 4. Teach your customers

Some companies have found that by educating their customers, they can boost their reputation and customer loyalty. Pick a topic relevant to your best customers and make yourself the source of credible, current information about that topic.

One paralegal services firm uses this technique effectively. In every newsletter, the firm includes a column on legislation, either pending or passed, that may affect the legal community.

Research discovered it was the most-often read portion of the newsletter.

Lawyers, the firm's primary customers, looked forward to the "news bites" on legislation in their field. It was a great way for the lawyers to remain current, and a great way to keep the paralegal services firm's name in front of their primary target market.

### 5. Fix problems fast

Nothing grates more than the slow resolution of a problem. Speedy response is vital to prevent negative word-of-mouth from spreading. Negative feelings about a product or service may linger for years.

Think about a restaurant where the food was awful or you received exceptionally poor service. You probably wouldn't recommend the place to friends. More likely, you might tell them to avoid it, even years later, because of the problems you had.

> ## WORD-OF-MOUTH TRAVELS FAST
> 
> *Research shows that for every good experience, we tell, on average, just three people.*
> 
> *While for every bad experience, we tell five or more friends, and this number is increasing with the use of email.*
> 
> *When faced with a complaint, the response of your employees should be, "How can I send this person away happy?"*

The best form of advertising is word-of-mouth. And certainly the best way to get positive word-of-mouth is by providing a quality product or service that meets the needs of your customers.

But there are ways to encourage your happy customers to spread the good word.

## WHAT'S THE BUZZ?

Entrepreneurs who compete in a crowded or cluttered category often find it is better—and cheaper—to let customers discover their product through positive testimonials from others. Positive word-of-mouth for a specific product or service can be implanted in the marketplace, and encouraged through adroit planning and subtle tactics. The result is a strong "buzz" for your product, one that spreads like wildfire among your prospective customers.

There are several hip and trendy terms to describe this marketing phenomenon. **Guerrilla Marketing** typically applies to edgy, unconventional campaigns that generate positive comments about a product. **Viral Marketing** uses the

## BUZZ MARKETING WITH LINKIN PARK

*Buzz marketing can be an effective way to introduce a new product.*

*When Mike Shinoda and his buddies started a band back in 1998, they weren't attracting a lot of notice. But they logged onto the Internet, got into the chat rooms of some hot bands like Korn and Limp Bizkit, and started hyping their sound ("There's this cool new group—here, check out their MP3 file") pretending they were fans of the band.*

*When interested kids emailed asking for more, the group sent back multiple music samples and instructions to pass them along to anyone with ears.*

*By the time the group finally signed with Warner Bros. in late 1999, Shinoda and his band, Linkin Park, had fans all over the world. They also had several thousand unpaid promoters creating a buzz about their music.*

*In 2002, they sold more CDs than any other band.* ,

Internet to spread the word about a product because of the way communication spreads on the Net like a virus.

But when SONY-Ericsson, the joint venture between two electronics giants, first introduced a new cell phone that incorporated a digital camera for sending photos via email, they used a unique promotion method, what has come to be known as **Buzz Marketing**.

SONY-Ericsson hired two models, a twentysomething couple, clean cut and attractive, and had them pose as tourists in Times Square, New York City. Periodically, the couple would ask people in the target market (eighteen to thirty-nine) to take their picture.

While the unsuspecting target would take the couple's picture, they were subjected to a low-key promotional pitch about the product and how cool it was. The trustful rube would then become excited about the product and, so the theory goes, begin telling all his or her friends.

Why didn't SONY-Ericsson use traditional forms of mass media, like newspapers or TV? For a number of reasons.

First, the cost of mass media has skyrocketed. Over the past decade (1990 to 2000, the latest period for which figures are available), television costs have increased over 340 percent. Newspapers are not far behind at 288 percent.

Second, this particular target market is hard to reach. In the past, you could reach over two-thirds of the country using the three big TV networks. Today, with more networks and cable alternatives, it's less than 30 percent.

The numbers get worse for the eighteen-to-thirty-nine-target group. Generations X and Y have so many media choices their numbers become fragmented.

Creating a buzz can also be more cost effective. SONY-Ericsson's cost of hiring two models was far cheaper than spot TV buys in New York City.

Buzz marketing has been around for decades, though the use of the Internet has increased its effectiveness. Cabbage Patch dolls, mood rings, Pokémon, Beanie Babies, Rubik's Cube, and the motion picture *Blair Witch Project* all benefited from buzz.

## FAST FACTS

*Buzz marketing* creates positive word-of-mouth about a product or service.

*Guerrilla marketing* uses edgy, unconventional promotion methods to generate buzz about a product.

*Viral marketing* uses the power of the Internet to spread the buzz, like a virus.

Why does buzz marketing work? One reason is the Internet. It helps spread the word. It's much easier to stay in touch with acquaintances and professional peers today than ever before.

In the past, we might correspond with friends as seldom as once a year during the holidays. With email, we send messages or forward jokes and pictures clear across the world with the touch of a button.

How can you create a buzz in your business? Your product need not be edgy or appeal to the counterculture to benefit from buzz. Even if your target market does not include twentysomethings, you can still use buzz marketing to create positive word-of-mouth about your product or service.

Let's say you have a gasoline additive that helps increase mileage, particularly in diesel-fueled engines. Your target is truckers and large trucking companies. You would think that driving a truck would be a lonely existence, with little opportunity for word-of-mouth.

But lunch counters and CB radios are the perfect incubators for viral marketing. Just a few drivers talking up the product at major truck stops and on their CBs, and your product is known throughout the country in a matter of days.

It works for business-to-business, too. Trade shows are ideal for creating buzz and nurturing interest in a product. Pick a few key industry leaders. Provide them with information about your new product. Then sit back and wait till someone

## THE POWER OF THE BUZZ

*In a European study, seven thousand consumers in six countries were asked who most influenced their purchase decision, a salesperson, an expert, or a family member or friend.*

*Over 60 percent claimed they were influenced most by family and friends. This was particularly true with products that were expensive, risky, seldom purchased, or suggested something about a buyer's status or taste.*

nudges you and asks if you've heard about that phenomenal new product and all its wonderful benefits.

Word-of-mouth is a powerful promotional tool because of its credibility. Research suggests word-of-mouth is hundreds of times as effective as television or newspaper advertising. Who wouldn't prefer to buy a product based upon the unsolicited recommendation of a trusted friend rather than some paid shill on television?

Experts agree, buzz marketing works. And it doesn't take a cutting-edge technology or something that appeals to Gen-Xers to be effective.

Here's how to generate good buzz for your business:

### • Seed a Vanguard Group

College campuses are favorite places for smart marketers to begin their buzz campaign. Many of our nation's trends seem to begin among college students. And every campus has a group of people whom others seek out for advice, trendsetters, leaders, and early adapters of the latest and greatest products.

### • Ration Supply to Create a False Sense of Demand

When Beanie Babies were hot, they were made hotter by the company's decision to hold back supply.

### • Use Celebrities or Trendsetters

When Palm Pilot published a photograph of Bill Gates, founder of Microsoft, on the Internet using an early model, sales exploded. Who wouldn't want to have the latest gizmo used by a man who could afford anything?

### • Be Wary of Advertising

Many people think that buzz works best when used in conjunction with media advertising. Usually, the opposite is true. When used either too early or too much, advertising can smother buzz before it ignites.

As you begin your hunt, the Internet can make it possible to create awareness for your products for less money than traditional media advertising. But many companies have been slow to adopt this technology. Others fail to recognize the shifting needs and wants of their customers.

# ADAPTING TO CHANGE

In order to be successful hunting new business, you need to predict where trends are headed, where your customers will likely be when you go in search of them, and why they will want your product over their current supplier.

Some marketers have an uncanny ability to predict the future of their industry and where their target customers' tastes and preferences are heading. I worship their artifice. The rest of us mere mortals must use painstaking research and good common sense.

Let me just say this: I am not a soothsayer. I do not predict the future. I have no crystal ball, and I don't read tea leaves. I have never met Shirley MacLaine. I have never even been Shirley MacLaine.

But like any good marketer, I do scan the horizon for technological changes that may affect my client's business.

What new product is our competition hatching? What innovation could make our product obsolete? What technology will change the way we work? What creative idea can we harness to sell more product?

Understanding the changing environment in which you operate is critical to your long-term success. And vital to being a good hunter of new customers.

A good hunter learns to connect things—ideas, people, technologies—to arrive at "possibilities," ways in which the future might affect his business, influence buying habits, or change the way he does business.

Today's consumer suffers from **attention deficit economics**. Inundated with advertising messages, our attention is constantly in demand.

As marketers, we use posters, labels, door hangers, jingles, contests, dinnertime sales calls, and pop-up ads on computers. I sink a putt on the eleventh hole and when I go to

## CONNECT THE TECHNOLOGIES

*Question:* Can you imagine grocery stores before electronic scanners, shopping before credit cards, or life before email? Now connect those ideas, those technologies.

*Answer:* A vending machine where you swipe your credit card to receive a ready-to-cook meal, and where that purchase information is then sent via the Internet to the vending company so they can track inventory and replenish the machine.

The technology exists. The vending industry is currently experimenting with machines that do exactly that.

## ATTENTION DEFICIT ECONOMICS

*The most valuable commodity of all is not time, but attention.*

*Increasingly, our attention can be bought, sold, or traded.*

retrieve my ball, an ad printed on the bottom of the cup says "Drink Pepsi."

Everything is fair game. Anything to grab a moment of your attention.

Teenagers are probably best at multitasking, and even though we think it's an ability that needs to be treated with Ritalin, it's really the exact response for the world we've given them: ten thousand things happening all at once, each one demanding that they pay attention.

Imagine how you might apply that thinking to your relationships with your clients. How can you control, or even manage, their attention?

Creating awareness for your product or service is only the first step. Getting them to pay attention to your message acknowledges that they are providing you with that most valuable resource, their attention.

Perhaps most frightening of all, technology is making location unimportant. Where you are doesn't matter. You have instant access to anybody, anywhere, through cell phones and cyberspace. You are no longer defined by your location.

Borders become muddled (think euros or NAFTA). We are no longer a culture of many. We are fast becoming a culture of one. A global culture. Your local supplier's customer service center is in Singapore. Your website designer lives in Caracas. Your car was made in Indiana, India, and Indonesia.

You need to begin thinking as a global hunter. Could any of what you sell be of value to someone in Toledo? Toronto? Timbuktu? In this new order of the future, everything is for sale (think eBay). Anything can be bought, sold, or exchanged anywhere in the world. The old corner store is just around the planet.

The future is overrated. Ultimately, it will not come unexpectedly. It is, after all, an evolutionary process.

We will still need food, clothing, and shelter, love, status, and self-actualization—the fundamental needs in Maslow's hierarchy. We will still seek employment, advancement, enlightenment. We will forever face the same mundane, everyday problems we face today.

Digital doesn't mean better. It simply means that problems may seem overwhelming and unfamiliar. Answers will not come from where they might be expected. We seldom learn from things we already know. And not all change is progress. Learn to combine technology and innovation with the best traditions of the past, and change becomes easier to accept.

The future may be overrated, but it's the only one we've got.

## HUNTING AHEAD OF THE CURVE

In order to continue turning a profit, you must stay abreast of technological changes affecting your industry. Likewise, smart marketers must stay alert for changes occurring in the marketing arena. Over the past several decades, the marketing function has undergone evolutionary change.

During the 1950s and 1960s, marketing was fairly simple. There were fewer product categories and fewer products. There were few media vehicles: television was just coming of age, there were only two dozen major weekly magazines, and FM radio had yet to be heard.

In the 1970s, alternative radio, UHF television, special-interest magazines, and the growing sophistication of direct mail brought greater diversity to the marketing mix. Marketers began to focus on niche markets. Successful products spawned product extensions. New categories developed almost overnight as consumers demanding social change also sought more diversity and uniqueness in their lives.

The 1980s saw the conglomeration of the marketing industry with the advent of mega-agencies such as McCann Worldwide and Darcy McManus Benton and Bowles. As a result, many skilled executives who were downsized formed "boutique" agencies and began specializing in their particular promotional forte. Niche marketing became more focused.

### EVERYONE'S AN EXPERT

*This age of information makes experts of everyone. We can all be an authority. This can be dangerous, because facts, manipulated to our own devices, can misrepresent anything.*

*For example, did you know that dihydrogen monoxide is a dangerous chemical found in most every home that causes thousands of deaths each year? It's highly corrosive and especially hazardous to small children!*

*Sounds dangerous, huh? Oops, it's only water.*

*The facts are accurate, but the message is biased. The problem again is time. Despite the availability of information, we don't always have the time to check the facts.*

## MARKETING TIMELINE

·····················

**1950s** *Commercial TV (VHF), AM radio, local newspapers*

**1960s** *UHF TV, FM radio, specialty catalogs, supermarkets*

**1970s** *Growth of direct mail, special-interest magazines, niche marketing*

**1980s** *Mega-markets, cable TV, explosive growth of sales promotion*

**1990s** *World Wide Web, email, growth of product extensions*

**2000s** *Blogs, satellite radio, viral marketing*

The 1990s offered an even more perplexing set of marketing and promotional options: hundreds of cable television channels; radio stations featuring shock jocks and Christian Coalitions; magazines for every pursuit, profession, or perversion. And most startling of all, the Internet!

Today, the challenge to marketers is: How do you go from hunting new customers because you want to, to hunting new customers because they want to be hunted?

This represents a fundamental shift in the way you look at your customers. And it represents a fundamental shift in the way the media must view their readers, listeners, or viewers.

For instance, it might mean giving away content to prospective customers in exchange for permission to talk to them. In a sense, you are saying to somebody, "If you give me permission to talk to you, I will send you my monthly newsletter."

Or a retailer might say, "Every week I will send you $10 worth of coupons for shopping at my store." Then, he can go to vendors and say, "These people shop at my store and they want your ad as content."

Broadcast media are having a particularly difficult time dealing with the new technologies. TiVo and Replay TV make commercials on television an option. Satellite Radio allows listeners to pick and choose exactly the content they want to hear, with no commercial interruptions. Ever!

The bottom line: Viewers and listeners may never have to hear a commercial again unless they want to. Broadcast may become a totally "opt-in" media.

How can TV make the transition? Here's one way: Let's say you're ready to buy a car. With nearly an infinite number of cable channel options, you simply tune into the General Motors Channel and watch infomercials about their array of automobile alternatives. Or switch over to the Used Car channel to find an array of used vehicles of all makes and models.

Need to go clothes shopping? Tune into the clothing channel. Perfume? Try the fragrance channel. You only watch what you want to watch. Opt in or opt out. Your choice.

The Internet may prove the most interactive marketing tool. If word-of-mouth is the best form of advertising, the Internet digitally enhances it.

First, everybody has more acquaintances today than ever before. There are all sorts of people you can touch today using email that you never would have picked up the phone to call previously.

So now, when you have a bad experience

## TIVO OR NOT TIVO

*Broadcast media are having a particularly difficult time dealing with new technologies.*

*Remote controls have made it easier to zip from channel to channel. And VCR users frequently zap commercials when recording their favorite shows.*

*Now, with new technologies like TiVo and Replay TV, zappers will only make it harder for advertisers to reach them.*

with a car rental firm, you might tell your whole email list. Or if you have a terrific meal at a new restaurant, you might tell fifty people, whereas before, you might have told two. And this word-of-mouth doesn't lose something in the translation. It's digital; it can simply be forwarded.

Second, people are way more receptive to new technologies. It took radio forty years to reach ten million listeners. Napster had fifty-seven million users

## Case Study **PROCTOR & GAMBLE**

### THE PROBLEM

Proctor & Gamble, the consumer products company, recognizes the need for products sensitive to the needs of niche markets.

When P&G introduced Cheer Free, a laundry detergent without perfumes created especially for consumers allergic to them, the company needed a way to remain respectful of customers' privacy while avoiding the waste of mass media advertising.

## A NEW IDEA IN WEB PUBLISHING

*Opt-in advertising is a system that allows content publishers to pick who their sponsors will be. Advertisers simply release their ads to the Web. Each ad is tagged with information about its target audience, how much the advertiser will pay for each click through, what type of website is acceptable (e.g., no porn sites), and any number of other characteristics.*

*Content publishers simply copy and paste the ads onto their websites. The ads, which are really tiny pieces of software, report back to the advertiser which websites have opted in and how many clicks they have received. The software also pays the content publisher automatically based upon the number of clicks.*

*Web logs (or blogs, for short) are the ideal users. Many of these microp-ublishers have assembled loyal online communities, they know their demographics and readers' tastes, and can pick and choose the advertisers they want to use.*

after just one year. So, new ideas and new products have a much better chance of reaching more people sooner.

Lastly, personalization is king. If it doesn't appeal to your particular peculiarities, your specific needs, it's not really marketing to *you*.

The future of marketing is in Permission Promotion. Consumers want what they want, when they want it. Those hunting new business will bag their game if they can come up with a deal for their prospect that says, "Watch this because there's something in it for you."

## LEADING ECONOMIC INDICATORS

One of the most critical elements in business planning is predicting the economy. So much is riding on whether it's going to go up or go down.

When you begin hunting new business, you naturally hope that the economy will smile favorably and allow prospects the flexibility to try a new supplier: *you*. But how do you know, before you launch your aggressive hunting expedition, where the economy is headed?

Someone once said that economics is the merging of finance and fortune-telling. Predicting the U.S. economy has become big business, with Wall Street gurus and Wharton business geeks madly analyzing everything from warehouse inventories to skirt length.

They push pencils and erasers with equal abandon, run complicated computer scenarios, and hang on every word of the Federal Reserve chairman. Then they wager fortunes on the whims of a fickle public.

Leading indicators are used to forecast the overall health of the economy or to predict the financial markets. Examples include annual inflation, prime interest rates, unemployment figures, and inventory levels. They are, at best, a reasonable guess when the economy is headed for trouble, or ready to rebound.

Truth is, despite all our best analysis and better intentions, those leading indicators don't work nearly as well as economists might have you believe. If they did, there would be far less volatility in the markets, and businesses could predict their future sales with far better accuracy.

There is a better forecasting tool, one proven amazingly accurate over the years, one that consistently predicts the rise and fall of our economy in advance by about two to three months. It's the advertising industry.

Advertising is typically one of the first budget cuts a company makes when it senses a softness in the marketplace. Magazine and newspaper ad pages decline. Radio and TV stations can't sell their inventory.

While a magazine or newspaper can simply limit the number of pages it prints, TV and radio stations sell time. If you begin to see more public service announcements, beware! That station has not been able to sell out its commercial time.

## CUSTOMIZED MARKETING

*Several leading food companies now allow you to customize your food and beverage choices.*

*Go to General Mills's www.mycereal.com and create your own cereal blend from ingredients that meet your specific tastes or health needs.*

*Proctor & Gamble's www.personalblends.com lets you customize your personal coffee blend. Answer a few questions about your ideal cup of java and your taste in certain foods, and receive a personal "tasteprint" for your perfect cup of coffee. A pound is ten bucks, plus shipping.*

*Ever had a hankerin' to try Asparagus-Anisette Ice Cream? Now's your chance. Ciao Bella Gelato (ciaobellagelato.com) will make you whatever flavor tickles your fancy (five-gallon minimum).*

Just as advertising declines as a recession is imminent, likewise, when the economy is about to pick up, industry suppliers begin to hear the phone ring.

As soon as TV and radio station inventory gets tight, as soon as I hear that freelance artists, photographers, voice talent, and modeling agency telephones are beginning to ring, I know that advertisers are returning to the marketplace.

**Case Study** > **PROCTOR & GAMBLE**

**THE SOLUTION**

P&G used a marketing method called self-selection to introduce Cheer Free laundry detergent for allergy sensitive consumers.

Without knowing who these allergy-sensitive people might be, Cheer ran mass media advertising offering free samples to anyone allergic to perfumed detergent.

In this way, Cheer Free collected the names of a unique target segment based upon self-selection. Those who responded to the offer identified themselves (or someone they knew) as being in need of such a product. Then, Cheer Free switched to less-expensive direct mail and online ordering.

www.pg.com

The economy is about to rebound.

You don't need to be a fortune-teller to know the economy is heating up. The advertising industry may just be the best leading economic indicator there is.

Just as hunters need to understand the environment in which they will be stalking their prey, so too do small businesses need to understand the changing marketplace in which they will be hunting new business.

Your company must hunt new business to survive. Choose new hunting grounds using demographic criteria, create awareness using powerful technology and word-of-mouth tools, and be prepared to adapt to changing markets and customer needs.

It sounds simple in the abstract, but is undeniably one of the more difficult strategies to execute effectively. Nevertheless, every customer eventually leaves. So, every business must hunt.

# TESTIMONIALS

One more word about hunting. Entering new markets takes credibility. And nothing creates credibility better than word of mouth. If I can get Tom to tell Sue what a great product I have, Sue is more likely to buy than if she simply sees an advertisement for my product. But how do I get Tom to tell Sue? In a word, testimonial.

If I can get Tom to tell me, I can take Tom's testimonial and pass it along to Sue. When Sue sees Tom's endorsement, she might say to herself, "If it's good enough for this Tom fellow, maybe I should try it, too."

Testimonials are one of the cornerstones of good advertising. The largest and most successful advertisers in the world use them. Why? Because they work. The endorsement of a fellow consumer is far more credible than the witty bromide of an anonymous copywriter.

How do you get customers to talk up your product? Simple. Ask them. Satisfied customers who believe in your product may be willing (even flattered) to endorse it. The most credible testimonials come from your customers. It's one more way to solidify your relationship with your customers, creating deeper brand loyalty.

Ultimately, farming is the easiest and cheapest way to increase your revenues. Developing brand loyalty among your existing customers and encouraging them to buy more from you creates additional revenue at the least possible cost.

# CHAPTER 7

## Kick-Ass Strategy #3: Farm

Purpose: *The purpose of chapter 7 is to identify various methods of harvesting more sales from your current field of customers.*

———◦———

**You may always need to hunt. Eventually, even your best customers may decide to leave you for a less-expensive competitor. Or they may leave you to do business with a friend or brother-in-law. Others simply die or move away. So new business will always be a necessary part of your marketing strategy.**

While you will always need to hunt, **farming** is the easier, cheaper, and more effective way to increase sales and profitability.

To change people's habits and customs is more expensive than to reinforce existing ones. So it costs much more to introduce your product to a new market than it does to build sales from your existing customer base.

## SELL ACCESSORIES

*I once operated a company that sold uniforms to schools of nursing. It was a tough business, with cheap offshore competitors and tiny profit margins.*

*Our highest profit items were sweaters, stethoscopes, sphygmomanometers (blood pressure kits), and watches with glow-in-the-dark numerals and sweep-second hands.*

*We paid the bills with uniforms, but we made our profit from accessories.*

To farm is to win more sales from your existing customers. Much easier. Much cheaper. Statistics show that the cost of selling to new customers is twelve times more expensive than selling to current customers.

Your current customers know you already. You don't need to create awareness and credibility with them. They already appreciate you and trust you. This provides you a distinct advantage. Cultivate them. Sell them more of your products or services.

There are lots of different ways to farm. Here are five:

1. **Suggestive Selling**
2. **Trade Up**
3. **Sell Complete Systems**
4. **Incentives**
5. **Rotation Farming**

# SUGGESTIVE SELLING

This is perhaps the easiest way to farm. I call it the You-Want-Fries-With-That-Order? strategy. Your customers are already in a buying mood. Their wallets are open. You're simply suggesting they spend a little extra to enhance the quality of their purchase.

If you sell a desk, suggest a matching chair or floor lamp. If she wants a new sweater, why not suggest a matching scarf? If a customer buys a new machine, suggest he purchase the special machine lubricant to make it run smoother. Or the conveyor belt that is compatible with the new machine.

While this seems like a simple concept, it is amazing how often it is overlooked. Sometimes, people feel as if they're being too pushy. But think of it as if you are simply trying to enhance the benefits of the purchase your customer just made.

If she buys life insurance from you, suggest financial planning options as well. You both win! She's happy having financial freedom, and you get an additional sale.

# TRADE UP

Last year, he bought the standard model from you. This year, sell him the deluxe model. And sell him an extended service warranty, too.

Even if he doesn't need a new model, sell him the new bells and whistles (and any other accessories) that enhance his purchase.

Trading up works on the concept of brand loyalty. If your customer is happy with the starter model, he is more likely to remain brand loyal. It makes it easier for him to buy again from you rather than starting over with a competitor's model.

General Motors had made this theory work for them for decades. Chevrolet is their starter car, ideal for young families and lower-income buyers. Pontiac is the stylish performance vehicle for the more affluent. Buick appeals to still more affluent buyers, a more luxurious car with all the modern conveniences. Cadillac is the status car, the one that says, "You've made it." If they kept you happy in a GM car through every stage in your life, you remained loyal to GM cars and no others.

Even if you don't bring out a new model every year, your industry changes, innovations occur, equipment becomes outdated. Keep your current customer informed of these marvelous new innovations that he shouldn't be without. Then, trade him up next year.

# SELL COMPLETE SYSTEMS

This is the age of convenience. People want an easy turnkey operation because of its convenience.

If a couple wants to plan a wedding, they can rent a hall, hire the caterer, order the flowers, audition the musicians, and so on. Or they can call your wedding planning service, because you offer all those services in one package.

If your customer wants to build a new plant, he can make all the separate decisions himself, hire architects, engineers, contractors, legal staff, and so on. Or he can call you because you offer all these services in one complete package.

GE Medical Systems sells not just a piece of Magnetic Resonance Imaging (MRI) hardware, but a whole set of accompanying services, including customized software programs, instructional services, financing, delivery arrangements, and maintenance and repair programs. And, naturally, a service warranty.

## SELL COMPLETE SYSTEMS

*I once asked a sales rep why she sold so few of a particular product line.*

*Stung by my implied criticism, she countered that it took too long to sell those penny-ante little products. By the time customers decided what to buy, she had spent ten minutes selling a five-dollar item.*

*She went on to criticize the company for not prepacking an assortment of the bestselling products. Then she could sell $50 worth in half the time.*

*It was, of course, a brilliant idea and we all wondered why nobody had thought of it before. The company did just as she suggested and everybody was happy, including the customers, but especially the saleswoman.*

*Are there any products you sell that could be ganged together and sold as a package?*

# INCENTIVES

Using incentives is not just a hunting strategy. It works for farming, too. Free gifts, premiums, and discounts are all effective ways to hunt new customers, but they can also be used to build more sales from your existing customer base.

Try offering an incentive for multiple purchases. For instance, buy one hamburger and get the second one for half price. "Try this new collection of cosmetics and get a free tote bag." Many businesses use this tactic with a simple offer like: Buy two cases, get the third case free.

Or motivate a buyer to purchase a complete set or bundle of items, rather than just one. For instance, "Buy a dozen Krispy Kreme Doughnuts and get a thirteenth FREE!"

Incentives work for hunting new business or for encouraging multiple purchases from your existing customers. A free gift with any purchase is an excellent way to attract customers.

Premiums can improve your image, gain goodwill, attract new customers, produce an immediate increase in sales (albeit short-term), and reward your current customers.

The trick is to find a premium attractive to your target market. Fast-food restaurants never fail to attract buyers for distinctive Coca-Cola glasses. Paying an extra buck (cost to restaurant, about thirty cents) for a collectible glass that customers can take home seems a real bargain.

When choosing a premium, consider:
- Does it appeal to your target audience?
- Does it have a perceived value?
- Is it in keeping with the image of your product?

- Is it a consumable or collectable, so that consumers will want one even if they already have one?

Particularly when selling commodity products or services, a premium offers a means to augment the products and a way to differentiate yours from the pack of competitors. Think about how your business could package its product with a sure winner to increase your sales.

## ROTATION FARMING

This is a simple way to instill brand loyalty. Some products or services lend themselves to periodic purchase, often at regular intervals, the frequent visit, or the regularly scheduled appointment.

Gas stations need to replenish their supplies of wiper blades, belts, and hoses every month or so, not to mention refilling their underground tanks with fuel. Smart suppliers contact the service station managers periodically to take their order for more fuel and accessories.

In similar fashion, that same service station manager might send a reminder every three months or so to his steady customers telling them it's time for an oil change. They appreciate the reminder, and his business benefits. If he encloses a coupon for a discount, his chances of snagging that customer for an oil change increase dramatically.

My barber (he calls himself a "hair designer") had some customers who stopped in only at their convenience. Unfortunately, too many of them often found his shop busy and then went elsewhere. He lost their business, for at least another four or five weeks. Other times, his shop had no customers and he sat idly reading the sports pages.

I suggested he simply ask all of his customers to schedule their next hair appointment as they left his shop. He did, and business increased over 20 percent. Fewer customers were turned away, and there was always someone in his barber

> ## PROMOTE THE PREMIUM
>
> *Incentives often work best when you promote the incentive rather than the product itself.*
>
> *For instance, when Godiva Chocolate sponsored a sweepstakes in which entrants could win diamond jewelry, the diamonds were featured in all advertising.*
>
> *An added benefit: the upscale prize, diamonds, enhanced the image of the product, fancy chocolate.*

## FARMERS FARM, TOO

*Discounts for multiple purchases are an effective method of farming.*

*I once saw a farmer selling eggs by the side of the road. Her sign said, "10 percent off any purchase of 13 or more."*

*After inquiring, I discovered she only sold her eggs by the dozen.*

*The promotion was a sham, but I bought two dozen anyway just because I liked her moxie, and her sense of humor.*

## ROTATION FARMING

*A florist contacts his good customers and requests their wedding anniversaries and spouses' birthdays.*

*He keeps the dates in his database and reviews them monthly.*

*Then, shortly before each date, he calls and suggests a floral arrangement appropriate for the occasion.*

*The customer is grateful to be reminded. The spouse is delighted with the thoughtful gift.*

chair (hair designer chair). He reads the sports pages on the weekends now.

Hunting for new customers may be necessary for the long-term health of your company. But selling more to your existing customer base is far easier. And far friendlier to your bottom line.

The whole point of farming is to generate more business from each of your current customers. Sell one customer at a time as much as possible.

# ONE-TO-ONE MARKETING

Wouldn't it be nice if all you needed were just one buyer buying all of your products? That's the principle behind one-to-one marketing. A one-to-one marketer does not sell products to as many people as possible. Rather, he sells a single customer as many products as possible over a lifetime.

He is the ultimate "farmer," constantly selling more stuff to the same people. Instead of gauging his success by the number of different sales, a one-to-one marketer achieves success by selling more to each customer. One-to-one marketers are after share of customer, not share of market.

Consider this: Would you rather promote to 100 percent of the area's consumers and get 10 percent of their business? Or sell to 10 percent of the consumers and get 100 percent of their business? Which method is more susceptible to competitive promotions? Which is has lower costs per sale?

To be a truly successful one-to-one marketer, you must determine the type of customer who is most likely to buy your products or services.

Start by using the old 80/20 rule (80 percent of your sales come from 20 percent of your customers). Once you have identified those top customers, identify others like them, customers with the same demographics, but who aren't spending as much with you.

Those are the ones you target. You want more of their dollars.

One-to-one marketing is about relationships with your customers. Customers, not consumers. The most successful marketers are those who build the deepest, most trusting relationships with individual customers.

One way to boost your farming production is to offer customization. More and more often, manufacturing is becoming "customer-ized," that is, made to each customer's specifications.

For instance, back in the early 1900s, Henry Ford made automobiles all black. (He was once quoted as saying, "Any color you like, so long as it's black.") Today, Ford Motor Company has no more than fifty in any one production run. Different colors, different accessories, different product packages. All customer-ized to dealer specifications or individual customer orders.

Technology has leveled the playing field, allowing even small businesses to customer-ize production. Technology allows you to direct market to specific customers (e.g., those who buy frequently, those who purchase larger sizes, or those who purchase unusual items). Technology makes contacting them easy and affordable. Your database can keep track of individual customers' special needs and wants. Sales Force Automation (SFA) systems allow your salespeople in the field instant access to information.

## MASS MARKETING VS. ONE-TO-ONE MARKETING

*Mass marketing requires product managers who sell one product at a time to as many customers as possible. One-to-one marketing requires customer managers who sell as many products as possible to one customer at a time.*

*A mass marketer tries to differentiate his products. A one-to-one marketer seeks to differentiate his customers.*

*A mass marketer seeks a constant stream of new customers. A one-to-one marketer seeks a constant stream of new business from current customers.*

Then, it's simply up to you to sell. One customer at a time.

# SELLING THIN AIR

Those who operate in the service sector can use farming techniques, too, though the methods may be different. Why? Because the selling of products or services you can't actually touch or feel in your hands presents some challenging problems. It's often called "selling thin air" because of its elusive and illusive nature.

Conceptual products include insurance, computer software, architecture, consulting services and the like, and if you are in the business of selling concepts, you understand some of the difficulties.

The idea of selling intangibles rather than hard goods is intimidating, puzzling, even humbling to many of the best salesmen and women. "How can I sell something I can't demonstrate? How do I point out my product's many features if I can't show them at work?"

Yet those who are good at it say they wouldn't sell anything else. What are their secrets?

Selling conceptual products and services is a four-part process:

## 1. Build Relationships

Some people are "revenue sellers." A revenue seller doesn't care about his customers. He only cares if they are qualified to buy and will they spend their hard-earned money *now*.

Telemarketers are revenue sellers. They call you on the telephone (usually at an inconvenient hour) and immediately ask if you are the person responsible for purchasing whatever product it is they are selling. They have no interest in building a long-term relationship; they're not interested in your family or that your dog had puppies last week. They want to know if you are qualified to buy, and then they deliver their pitch for your money.

There's nothing wrong with revenue selling. It is often the most efficient and expedient method of selling. It simply means there is no interest in repeat sales from that customer. And that's not what farming is all about.

Department store clerks are revenue sellers. Rarely do they attempt to build relationships with their customers. Do you want to buy that dress? It's definitely you! Will that be cash or credit card?

Revenue sellers are not looking to have repeat customers. Sure, the department store clerk wants you to come back to that store, but she likely won't be the sales clerk in that department again anyway. She doesn't have time to chit chat with every customer because others are waiting to check out.

A relationship seller wants that customer back again and again. He builds long-term relationships with his clients or customers. He knows that selling a good product and providing good service is expected of both him and his competitors. He knows he has to gain your trust so that you will prefer him to the competition.

Selling conceptual products and services takes trust. You're selling little more than

## SELLING THIN AIR

*Conceptual products and services are really nothing more than paper and promises. Credibility is critical.*

*Your customer must be completely confident that you will be able to perform as you have pledged.*

## BUILD RELATIONSHIPS

*Selling conceptual products and services takes trust. If he can't touch it, see it, smell it, or feel it, the only way your customer can have confidence in the results of your services is if he has confidence in you.*

*One successful financial planner I know seldom discusses money in his first meeting with a client. He creates a sense of friendship and camaraderie that builds to trust.*

*By the second or third meeting, his client has been sold on him as a person. After that, it's easy to sell financial planning solutions.*

paper and promises. Credibility is critical. Your customer must believe you can deliver on your promise. If he can't touch it, see it, smell it, or feel it, the only way he can have confidence in the results is if he has confidence in you.

## 2. Always Sell to Decision-Makers

You can sell "things" to the technicians, the implementers in a company. Folks with titles like office manager, shop foreman, data processing coordinator, or accounting supervisor.

Sell concepts to those with titles like CEO, COO, CFO, marketing director, and some vice presidents. These are the folks who establish departmental budgets, not the ones who must remain within one.

If you hear somebody say, "It's not in the budget," you're talking to the wrong somebody. You need to talk to the decision-maker who set the budget. Offer to help that somebody sell the idea to his boss, the one who set the budget. If your service is truly a benefit to the company, and his only objection is that it isn't in the budget, he'll appreciate your support in selling the idea up the chain of command.

## 3. Let Them Define the Problem

When selling concepts, we're really just selling solutions to problems. But first we need to figure out what the problem is.

The best way to do this is to ask questions and let the customer tell you. Keep asking questions until the decision-maker has defined the problem. Every company has them. It's simply a matter of asking the right questions and listening carefully until you hear a problem you think your firm may be able to remedy.

### ESTABLISH RAPPORT

*Selling concepts requires trust, and trust begins with rapport.*

*To help establish a connection at first meeting, try scanning the person's desk or office. A family photo or a sailboat on the wall may tip you as to the prospect's interests.*

## 4. Sell Solutions

When selling concepts to decision-makers, don't sell the "thing" itself. Whether it's computer software or building insurance, it's still just paper and promises.

Sell the ultimate benefit your product provides, the solution to the decision-maker's problem. Solutions should fall into one of three categories:

1. **Reduce Costs**
2. **Enhance a Company's Market Position**
3. **Improve Productivity**

Help the company run leaner by **reducing costs,** and you're a hero. If your software can reduce transaction expense, that's the ultimate benefit that your sales presentation must include. If your service can reduce your customer's costs while sales remains constant, the difference is *profit.*

> ## ASK QUESTIONS
> *Ask questions and listen carefully until you hear a problem you think your firm may be able to remedy.*
>
> *When probing for problems for which you may have a solution, have specific questions prepared in advance. My favorite—"Tell me about your competitors"—never fails to provoke discussion.*

**Enhancing a company's market position** allows the company to raise prices. Their customers recognize the greater value in the company's products. They pay more. Company sales and profits go up. If your service can improve your customer's market position and increase his sales while expenses remain constant, the difference is *profit.*

A service that **improves productivity** is often the easiest to sell. Better productivity can help reduce costs while sales remain constant, which increases profits. Productivity gains also can help improve quality or reduce delivery times thus enhancing the company's market position and increasing sales. If expenses remain constant, the difference is again profit. Your customer can use improvements in productivity to either reduce costs, increasing *profit,* or to increase sales, increasing *profit.* Ultimately, if your customer cannot translate your service into profit, it may be a difficult sale.

Selling intangibles may seem daunting at first glance. But follow these key tactics of successful concept sellers and you'll have shorter gaps between sales closings, and a healthier financial future.

## KEEPING THE CUSTOMER SATISFIED

Good service is the key to long-term relationships.

Think about the quality of service you tolerate as a (pick one) customer, client, passenger, patient, or patron. When it's good, it makes you feel good.

## PREVENT DEFECTION

*One company I know tells its customers that if they're not satisfied with their purchase, they can write the check out for any amount they believe is fair. (Remarkably few pay less than the invoice.)*

*This gives the customer a sense of control over the situation and helps identify customers near defection.*

You may even want to tell others about it. When it's bad, you feel demeaned, denigrated, and frustrated. You may even feel like throttling the clerk behind the counter.

To avoid having throttled clerks in your business, provide good service. Building a good service reputation for your business begins with you. As the owner or manager, you must set the tone. If you don't care, you cannot expect your employees to care. And if they don't care, don't expect customers. Period.

Start with training. Sam Walton, founder of Wal-Mart, said, "Communicate everything you can to your associates. The more they know, the more they care. Once they care, there is no stopping them."

Whether it's intimate product knowledge or a simple smile given to every customer, service is an attitude, a desire to do the little things extraordinarily well. An organization that delivers great service is one that recognizes the significance and dignity of every customer. Conversely, one that doesn't is saying, "We don't care about you. You don't matter to us."

Research shows that the number one reason companies lose customers is because of indifference. Not better prices, not better quality, not better selection. Customers leave because they think you don't care about them.

More important, one-third of your customers are in some phase of defection right now! And you probably don't even know which ones they are. Most companies have no formal process for spotting customers at risk.

Worse yet, nearly three-fourths of customers warn their vendors that they are thinking of leaving. They drop subtle hints, warning signals that, if you listen carefully, will tell you they soon may be former customers.

We all know that it is a lot cheaper to retain our existing customers than it is to hunt new ones. So retaining your existing customers can lower your costs and boost profits significantly.

Here are four ways to tell if your customers are about to bolt, and how to head them off at the pass.

**Case Study** ) **FORRER BUSINESS INTERIORS**

### THE PROBLEM

FORRER, the office furniture provider, had a problem with dissatisfied customers.

After a major installation that may include dozens of workstations and individual offices, invariably there were a few parts missing, incomplete deliveries, or mismatched furniture and accessories. Customers would call with a checklist of problems.

Soon, the company feared it could lose customers because of the time it took to resolve these complaints.

## 1. Listen to Your Purchasing Department

A long lapse between orders can be a tip-off that a customer is discontented. The longer the time between orders, the more likely you are to lose the customer.

Tracking your order frequency can throw up a red flag if there are problems. There are several nifty software programs that make this process relatively easy.

## 2. Make Your Invoices Work for You

Your customer makes the ultimate evaluation of your work when he is ready to pay the bill. If he's unhappy, it may be the last check he ever writes to you. And you may never know the reasons why.

Include a questionnaire with your invoice (see 3. Ask Your Customers). Ask the customer if there were any problems. This gives the customer an opportunity to sound off at the crucial moment: that point when he pays you.

## 3. Ask Your Customers

Sales clerks and service reps often have a good idea when a customer is unhappy. But it doesn't hurt for you to ask them, too.

### HOW AM I DOING? ........

*Ed Koch, the popular former mayor of New York City, made the question famous, "How am I doing?"*

*He didn't always hear widespread praise. But New Yorkers loved him because they felt he cared enough to ask their opinion.*

## Case Study

# FORRER BUSINESS INTERIORS

**THE SOLUTION**

FORRER decided the key was to develop an action plan, one that anticipated complaints and assured customers they would be resolved quickly.

After FORRER installs workstations and office furniture, the customer is given a checklist of potential issues to be resolved. The list includes such questions as, "Did the installation occur in a timely manner with a minimum of disruption?" and "Were the installers courteous and efficient?"

Any problems trigger a Call for Action (CFA) and are referred directly to the VP of Operations for immediate resolution. Result: Over 98 percent customer satisfaction rate.

www.forrersbi.com

Some customers may be reluctant to criticize you directly. Offer them an opportunity to sound off by distributing a questionnaire. A questionnaire serves several purposes. It offers anonymity to the person complaining. It identifies trends, pinpoints problem areas, and may well lead to a new product or service that hadn't occurred to you before.

Most important, it shows your customers you care about them, lets them know you value their opinion. Customers like that. It gives them a chance to let off steam, too. It's better they tell you what you're doing wrong rather than never calling you again for an order.

### 4. Beware the Milestones

A milestone event—end of the year, contract ending, renewal, etc.—can trigger a defection. These are situations that force customers to evaluate whether or not they want to continue doing business with you.

One company I know has a customer service representative call the account about a month before their annual renewal date. If the rep detects any unhappiness, the account is immediately referred to a "lifeguard," a specialist trained in save techniques, to rescue the customer. Result: they lose less than 1 percent of their renewal customers annually, a fraction of the industry average.

An early warning system that spots defecting customers will reap benefits for your sales team, and keep the customers satisfied.

# THE CARE QUOTIENT

It's part of the human condition. We all want to feel important. We all want to feel as if our business, no matter how meager, is important to our supplier. We truly want to feel as if we are valued customers.

No matter what your business, from hobby shops to hospitals, car parts to consulting, if you don't make your customers feel important, they will leave you for a competitor without a second thought. Don't let this happen to you.

Here's a little test to determine how valued your customers feel:

1. Are repeat customers becoming fewer and fewer?
2. Are they buying less frequently and spending less when they do?
3. Do you seem to be stocking the wrong items? Wrong sizes? Wrong accessories?
4. Are you losing customers to competitors?
5. Do your customers seem surly and uncooperative?
6. Have you received any unsolicited complaints from unhappy customers?
7. Has it been a year or more since you provided an opportunity for your customers to tell you how they feel they are treated?

If you answered yes to some of these questions, your "care quotient" is too low.

Research shows that two-thirds of customers leave their regular supplier for a competitor because they think that supplier doesn't care about them and doesn't respond to their needs—not because of better prices, better selection, or better quality. They leave simply because they don't feel important to that supplier.

Periodically, ask your customers, "How are we doing?" You'll be surprised at what you can

> ## HOW TO LOSE A CUSTOMER
>
> *Research shows that companies can lose customers just six ways:*
>
> **1 percent** *die*
>
> **3 percent** *move away*
>
> **5 percent** *are influenced by others to buy elsewhere*
>
> **9 percent** *are lured away by competitors*
>
> **14 percent** *don't like the product*
>
> **68 percent** *are displeased by the attitude of indifference on the part of a company employee*
>
> ***Incredible!*** *More than two-thirds of customers are lost because their supplier is saying, "We don't care about you."*

## A = GREAT QUALITY
## B = LOW PRICE
..............................

*A good way to find out what your customers want is by testing your advertising.*

*Send out a direct mail piece to half your customers using **headline A** touting the quality of your product, and half using **headline B** boasting your low price.*

*Then, count the results. Your customers will tell you which is more important to them.*

learn. Your customers will be delighted you asked.

The first thing you'll learn is your customers feel reassured that you took the time to ask them their opinion. Everyone likes to offer an opinion. The second thing you'll learn is that you should ask more often.

There are many ways of getting feedback from your customers. One way is by simply asking them while they're buying something from you. The information you learn is immediate and may help resolve a problem quickly before you lose a customer.

Restaurants use this technique effectively. Did you ever notice that within five minutes of being served, your waiter or waitress stops by your table (usually just after you took that huge bite of pizza) and asks, "How is everything here?"

It's standard practice in the restaurant industry because restaurants know that fickle customers won't return (and won't brag about the restaurant to their friends) unless they're made to feel important.

Here's another way of soliciting feedback, often used by retailers, but equally adaptable to many types of business: the questionnaire.

## Case Study    CPI

### THE PROBLEM

CPI is an audio, video, and film production studio that prides itself on having the latest and greatest digital production equipment, as well as creative personnel trained in its operation.

After a decade in business, owner Jim Kagan worried that the firm had grown stale. He needed to find out exactly what ad agencies and creative types around town thought of his studio.

Sometimes customers may be reluctant to tell you face-to-face if they have a problem. They may feel uncomfortable telling you your prices are too high, your merchandise is faulty, or you're not open at convenient hours.

Offer them an opportunity to sound off anonymously by distributing a questionnaire. A questionnaire serves several purposes. It offers anonymity to the person complaining. It identifies trends, pinpoints problem areas, and may even lead to a new product or service which hadn't occurred to you before.

Most important, it shows your customers you care about them, lets them know you value their opinion. It gives them a chance to let off steam, too. It's better they tell you what you're doing wrong rather than never calling you again for an order.

When distributing questionnaires, consider mailing them out to your database of customers

> ## RETAIL SERVICE
> *How do retailers say, "We don't care about you," to their customers? Most-often heard complaints include:*
>
> - *Clerks distracted, uninformed, or uninterested*
>
> - *Having to wait in line, on the phone, etc.*
>
> - *Help not around when you need it*
>
> - *Merchandise out of place or out of stock*
>
> - *Dirt, disorder, or safety hazards*
>
> - *Failure to stand behind the product*

rather than simply handing them out with every purchase. First, you reach the customers who haven't purchased from you in awhile, the very ones you most want to ask, "Why?"

Second, you're likely to receive more responses. Selling business-to-business, your chances of reaching a decision maker are better when you use direct mail. If you're a retailer, it's too easy for your customer to toss the questionnaire along with the bag and the receipt as soon as he gets home with his purchase. Most folks are more likely to answer their mail than a questionnaire casually tossed in among their purchases.

Questionnaires have many uses. Some companies use periodic questionnaires to determine the effectiveness of their advertising and the mood of their customers. McDonald's queries the public quarterly. "What's your favorite fast-food restaurant?" and "Who makes the best french fries?" are typical questions asked. Results are tracked and compared. If any category dips too low, they know they need to bolster their advertising in that area.

However you choose to query them, let your customers know you care. Periodically ask them, "How are we doing?" It's a great way to build your care quotient.

## THANK THE COMPLAINERS

Most people agree, word-of-mouth is the best advertising of all. The spontaneous testimony of a satisfied customer is trusted well beyond any fancy copy produced by some Madison Avenue whiz kid.

**Case Study** **CPI**

### THE SOLUTION

CPI distributed self-addressed questionnaires to all their customers over a period of three months.

Among other things, they learned that their customers wanted longer hours and lower prices.

Based on this input, the studio decided to offer evening hours at reduced rates. This change not only better utilized their capital equipment, it better served their customers' needs.

Revenues jumped 28 percent.

But what about negative word-of-mouth? What happens when a customer has a bad experience and tells someone else? It would be great if customers would tell only us about their unpleasant experiences, and tell their friends about their pleasant ones. But that's not reality.

Somewhere along the line, you will have a defective product or fail to provide acceptable service. And someone will complain.

Those are just the ones you will hear about. Only 4 percent of unhappy customers complain; the other 96 percent simply go away unhappy. That means every time a customer complains, you can figure there are twenty-four more with a similar problem.

If a customer complains to you, thank him. Profusely. He (or she) has done you a tremendous favor. He has alerted you to a problem experienced by (on average) twenty-four others. You better fix whatever he's complaining about—and fix it fast if you want those twenty-five people as customers again.

How you handle the complaint can make or break your business. Of those who complain, two-thirds will do business with you again if the complaint is resolved. That number goes up to *96 percent* if the complaint is resolved quickly.

The secret to positive word-of-mouth then is avoiding complaints, or by resolving them quickly when they occur. That's good service.

Beyond good service is what has come to be known as **extraordinary service**. The ability to exceed customer expectations.

Experiencing extraordinarily good service is a wonderful event for customers. It makes them feel good, sometimes only momentarily, but often on a deeper level, one that lingers beyond the event itself. It can affirm for customers that they are worthwhile people. Somebody cares about them.

It is also a positive experience for the service provider. When challenged to do whatever it takes to please a customer, employees are often amazed at how proficient they can become.

Good service is simply ordinary people doing ordinary things well. Extraordinary service is ordinary people doing ordinary things extraordinarily well, beyond expectations. Allow your people to give extraordinary service to your customers at all times. Give them the right to make decisions in the best

## PROCTOR & GAMBLE

### THE PROBLEM

When toll-free numbers first became available, Proctor & Gamble put their 800 number on boxes of Duncan Hines–brand baking mixes.

Calls began to come in from consumers who wanted to know why their cake or breads didn't look like the ones on the box. Or, was cooking with gas different than cooking with an electric oven? Or, what about cooking temperatures at different altitudes?

After a time, P&G wondered how many other people had the same questions or problems as those who actually called in.

interest of employees (within reason). You will find that the effect will extend beyond satisfied customers. You will have happier employees, too.

# THE GOAL: BRAND LOYALTY

The ultimate goal of any marketing campaign is to create brand loyalty. You want customers to remain loyal to you no matter what price your competitors offer them, no matter what product substitutes they offer, no matter what services they offer.

Brand loyalty is the elimination of two steps in the **buying process**. Once the prospect perceives a problem, a need is created. Without bothering to seek information about resolving that need, without evaluating alternative methods of resolving that need, the prospect simply buys from you.

Brand loyalty begins with the purchase. Until that first purchase, the customer simply had a need and perceived that you (or your product) could fill that need. With his purchase begins the opportunity for you to create brand loyalty. That step is called: **Post-Purchase Satisfaction.**

When you buy a lawnmower, you have made a substantial investment that you hope will solve your problem: your grass needs cutting. You hope that lawnmower will cut the grass, and you hope it will do it evenly and cleanly. You hope the lawnmower will not require a great deal of maintenance or repair, but if it does, you hope the dealer will do it quickly and inexpensively. In short, you have certain expectations about the lawnmower and its performance.

If the lawnmower performs up to your expectations, you are pleased. You have post-purchase satisfaction. But there are two parts to post-purchase satisfaction. Empirical evidence, how the product meets your expectations, is just one part.

The other part is how the product satisfies your need to be accepted and your approval by others. How does your neighbor feel about your purchase? "Wow! What a nice-looking new lawnmower, George. Pretty fancy. Wish I had one like that." It makes you feel good to have peer approval. It favors your self-esteem, bolsters your ego, and engenders a sense of pride in your ability to make good purchase decisions. If your

## BRAND LOYALTY
............................

*Create brand loyalty by eliminating two steps in the buying process:*

*1. Problem Recognition*

*2. Information Search*

*3. Evaluation of Alternatives*

*4. Purchase*

*5. Post-Purchase Satisfaction*

neighbor were to say, "Gee, George, that's an ugly-looking machine. I can't believe how much you paid for it. My brother-in-law could have gotten you a much better deal on a more dependable model," you might either smack your neighbor upside the head, or feel poorly about your purchase decision. Or perhaps both.

Typically, the larger the purchase price, the more important the need is for post-purchase reinforcement.

About one in ten new home buyers suffer buyer's remorse at some level. Many seek to get out of the deal within days after closing. Smart realtors provide corroboration in the form of gifts (e.g., a plant with "Best wishes in your new home") or simple verbal reinforcement (e.g., "This home is perfect for you. And with this location, it's bound to appreciate substantially.").

> ## POST-PURCHASE SATISFACTION
> ····················
> - *If product performance falls short of expectations, the customer is disappointed.*
>
> - *If product performance meets expectations, the customer is satisfied.*
>
> - *If product performance exceeds expectations, the customer is delighted.*
>
> - *These feelings make a difference whether or not the customer becomes brand loyal.*

Car companies know the importance of post-purchase satisfaction. Immediately after buying a new car, you will likely be inundated with calls from the dealer offering to answer any questions about the car's operation, or letters from the manufacturer congratulating you on your intelligent choice. All designed to guarantee post-purchase satisfaction.

The psychological factor is so important (many people judge others by the car he or she drives), car companies build it right into their advertising campaigns. ("Honda, the smart choice.") Good promotions support beliefs and attitudes that help the customer feel good about his or her brand choice.

Creating positive feelings after the purchase requires a good product that meets or exceeds customer expectations as well as positive psychological reinforcement for the purchase choice.

# THE THREE R'S

Try as we may, we know that sometimes a customer will be unhappy. What should you do if your customer has a problem with his purchase? Fix it. And fix it fast. How?

We know that statistically, 96 percent of customers whose problems are remedied quickly will likely buy again from you. So speed is important.

But it's more than that.

People want to feel reassured the problem will never happen again. And, ideally, they would like to have some compensation for the trouble and inconvenience the problem caused them.

---

**Case Study**   **PROCTOR & GAMBLE**

### THE SOLUTION

P&G conducted research to discover how many people had the same problems as those who called in, but never voiced a complaint. They were astounded to discover that, for every complaint they received, there were (on average) twenty-four others who had the same problem but never bothered to complain.

Similar results were found in other product categories—shampoo, potato chips, and restaurants. Only one in twenty-five people who had a problem ever complained.

When P&G began adding their website to packaging, they conducted the same research, assuming the percentage would increase because of the ease of email. But they discovered that the numbers held true. Only 4 percent of people who have a problem actually complain.

Think about that next time you have a bad meal at a restaurant or poor service at a department store. Are you one of the 4 percent who actually complain about a problem?

www.pg.com

---

Time to resort to the three R's: Recognition, Remedy, and Reinforcement.

Imagine for a moment you are in a restaurant. You're dining with your spouse. It's your anniversary. The waiter delivers your meals and, after a few bites, you realize your steak is fatty, tough, and overcooked. You complain.

If the restaurant has properly trained its wait staff, you will receive acknowledgment of the problem ("I'm terribly sorry."—**recognition**), an offer of a solution ("Can I get you something else instead?"—**remedy**), and satisfaction that the problem will not happen again, along with some form of reward for your trouble ("The cook assured me that your steak came from an inferior supplier we won't be using again. Here's a $20 gift certificate for your next visit here."—**reinforcement**).

Would you visit that restaurant again? You bet. Why? Research shows that consumers prefer the known to the unknown. Given the choice between that restaurant and some other restaurant where you don't know if they would solve your problem so satisfactorily, you would likely choose the restaurant where you know, if you have a problem, they will resolve it quickly.

So it is with customer service. Follow the three R's—recognition, remedy, and reinforcement—and you can create loyal customers.

Only 4 percent complain. You have an opportunity to create brand loyalty from that 4 percent. By encouraging others to complain (by asking them—personally or through a questionnaire), you increase your opportunities for brand loyalty.

# CHAPTER 8

# Kick-Ass Strategy #4: New Products

Purpose: *The purpose of chapter 8 is to explain the necessity of new products to your organization's long-term health, how to develop new products, and how to launch them successfully while avoiding the most-common pitfalls of new product introduction.*

————◄○►————

**E**very company needs new products.

New products replace all those old products nobody wants anymore, the ones that have reached the maturity stage of their product life cycle.

New products offer new opportunities for revenue. They present an image to the industry that your company is on the cutting edge. Best of all, they give your salespeople something to talk about at the trade show.

Where do new product ideas come from? Where is the next Post-It Note? The next iPod? And how can your company find it?

> *Nothing in this world*
> *is as powerful as an idea*
> *whose time has come.*
>
> —Victor Hugo

**New Product Development** is one part need, one part science, and one part magic. There are a host of creative techniques designed to foster new product ideas. The best are presented here. All have two things in common: creative discipline and an open mind. Creative discipline, because right-brain creative thinking requires some left-brain analysis. And an open mind, because there will always be someone who says it won't work.

New product development can be the costliest of the five strategies. It is by far the riskiest. Products come and go at whiplash pace. Fact: On average, fifty-eight new products are tested to make one successful new product. That one new product must pay for the cost of testing the other fifty-seven, plus make a profit.

Despite the risks, dozens of new products are introduced every day, and some of them make our lives a little better or a little easier. Where corner grocery stores once rested, mega-marts stand as monument to the ingenuity of consumer product research and development departments everywhere. Somebody somewhere must be doing something right.

You need to be one of those somebodies.

# THE PRODUCT LIFE CYCLE

Your company needs to develop new products and services for two reasons.

First, because your products are getting stale. To the people in your industry, they're as pungent as yesterday's fish. Tried and true is good, sure. But tried and true and improved is even better. Modify it and you could create a category to make your industry jealous. Or innovate, and start your own industry. But do not stand pat. The market is forever moving. Up, down, mostly forward. You stand pat and you are left behind.

And second, because customers prefer to work with suppliers who offer the latest and greatest. Push the envelope and they feel more assured, secure, and loyal.

New products eventually get old. Product categories, and more frequently, specific brands, have limited life expectancies. Eventually, progress makes everything obsolete. The **product life cycle** is a useful way to explain this phenomenon, how products go through four distinct stages from birth to death:

1. Introduction
2. Growth

## The Product Life Cycle

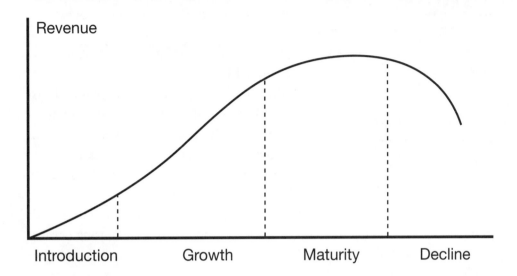

3. Maturity

4. Decline

During the **introduction** stage, you test the product, explore different distribution options, analyze target markets and marketing options, and investigate various price points (the Four Ps: product, place. promotion, and price).

As you gear up production, your product may not be available everywhere immediately. Rollout may need to come in stages. Profitability is modest or non-existent due to a lack of economies of scale and the cost of testing.

In the **growth** stage, the market begins to accept your product. Rollout is complete and some economies of scale are realized. Cash flow turns positive and you begin to realize some profit.

As the product reaches **maturity**, sales peak, cash flow peaks, and profits peak. Production is at full capacity and your costs are predictable. But the category has attracted competitors who begin to carve up market share.

Eventually, the market becomes saturated. There is only room for so many Starbucks coffee shops after all. Or perhaps some technological breakthrough, or maybe just a modest product enhancement, makes your product obsolete. You have entered the **decline** stage of the PLC. Cost containment becomes critical.

## JUST SAY "NO" TO THE PLC
················································

*Edwin Artzt, former president and CEO of Proctor & Gamble, once said that P&G didn't believe in the product life cycle.*

*P&G continually improves its products, then relaunches them as "New and Improved."*

Competitors vie for market share. Niche players begin nibbling around the edges and margins grow thinner. Profits are precarious.

# HOW TO AVOID THE DECLINE

A Boston Consulting Group study found that twenty-seven of thirty brands that were number one in 1930 were still number one in their category fifty years later, including Gold Medal flour, Campbell's Soup, Kellogg's Corn Flakes, and Ivory Soap.

The ability to cycle and recycle products helps keep number one brands number one. Modifying the product—adding improvements and using cheaper or sturdier material—can extend the PLC, perhaps indefinitely in some categories. This process is called "scalloping."

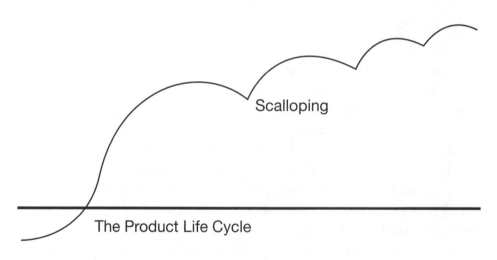

Scalloping

The Product Life Cycle

Ivory Soap, a brand first introduced in 1878, has undergone a multitude of product improvements over the decades. Yet it is still 99 and 44/100 percent pure. It still floats. And it's still number one.

Other products and categories come and go quickly. Remember the Nash Rambler? Evening in Paris perfume? The pet rock?

Fads and fashion aside, products and categories can be extended. Only a "category killer," that is, some major advance in technology, can make a product category obsolete. Computer word processing has virtually eliminated the need for a conventional typewriter. Email is quickly eroding the need for a fax machine.

Extending the life of a product through improvement may not always be the best use of your budget. Better is to find new uses in other markets (see "Hunt," chapter 6). When good locations for new fast-food restaurants

> ## MARKETING MADONNA
> ....................................
> *Madonna began as a punk rocker, then relaunched her career as a lacy virgin, Marilyn Monroe clone, aerobic queen, and mom.*
>
> *In 2004, her face appeared on the covers of* Rolling Stone *and* Good Housekeeping *in the same month.*

became harder and harder for McDonald's to find domestically, they redoubled their efforts to build new stores in other countries. When the market for disposable diapers matured, P&G's Pampers found a new use for the product (Depends).

# RISKY BUSINESS

The failure rate for new products is high. How high no one knows for sure. So many new products and services are introduced every day, falter, and fade so quickly, they may not even be noticed.

Of those that are tracked, we know that over 30,000 new consumer products are introduced annually. The number of B2B products is even higher. Most fail in the first year, 80 percent within three years.

The most common reason for new product failure is the **illogical champion**. Some high-level executive has made this his or her pet project—he or she feels it's going to be a winner—and he pushes it through despite a lack of supporting evidence. "Gut feel" is great, but it can be expensive, too.

**Market ignorance** is the next most common reason for new product failure. If you fail to plan properly, plan to fail properly. Poor market research, poor forecasting, or poor positioning can sink a new product quickly.

**Poor design** and execution come next on the list of reasons for new product failure. Sometimes, the product is at the wrong price point to interest customers. Occasionally, it's just plain ugly (remember the Edsel?).

The **wrong product** will fail to entice customers to change what they are presently using. It lacks distinction, a discernable difference, or it has no perceived benefit. Nobody knows what it does or what it's good for.

The last and least frequent reason a new product fails is because of **high cost**. Usually your research has identified costs well enough that you anticipate them accurately. But supply problems or a strong competitive response or misreading the time necessary to generate cash flow could throw your projections out of whack.

Despite the myriad obstacles, don't give up. You need new products. The right idea could generate millions for you and your organization.

## HOW TO GET GOOD IDEAS

New products come from within and from without. Within are those you or your company develops yourself. Without are those suggested by customers, the trade, or through scientific exploration. Start within.

The best advice I ever heard for creating a new product was to "think like a kid."

Remember what it was like to be six years old? Hide and seek, cops and robbers, skateboarding after dark, games and mischief, and make-believe.

Kids are playful and unencumbered by life's natural boundaries. Responsibilities are few. Time is unmeasured and limitless.

Kids recognize they don't know everything. "Why?" seems to be they're favorite phrase. New ideas are absorbed as if by osmosis.

Kids are fearless and naïve. Consequences mean nothing to them. "Let's try this. Let's try that." Ever watch a six-year-old snow ski? Straight down the hill fast as the slope allows. No fear of failure. This positive attitude about play, about life, about everything, lends itself to creativity. Anything is possible if it can be imagined.

Imagination is unlimited—yours included. Using it just takes a little practice. Channeling your creative DNA through the Imagination Machine is a discipline that can be learned. I refer to this discipline as **The Four I's**.

### The Four I's
...................................

• *Information*

• *Incubation*

• *Inspiration*

• *Implementation*

You don't need to be a creative genius to come up with compelling ideas. But it does take hard work, just like any other task worth doing well.

Good creative ideas begin with good analysis. Immerse yourself in **information**. All kinds.

Trade journals, competitive reports, articles on business trends and your company's weekly inventory levels. Analyze it. Connect bits of information and write down a few key ideas.

Then, put it away and don't think about it for a while. Allow the information to percolate, to **incubate**. Let your brain rest. Think about something else entirely. Take a shower. Go to a movie. Or putz in your garden.

Your brain chews on the information you feed it, analyzes the problem while you're doing other things. When it is ready, it will provide your conscious mind with an inspiring idea.

Then suddenly—K-Pow!—the muse strikes: **inspiration**. It may come while you're driving to work. Sometimes it happens in the middle of the night. Your best ideas frequently come without warning, when you least expect them. Write it down so you don't forget it. Even if it's just a kernel of an idea, save it. You may come up with the rest later. But get your idea down on paper, no matter how crazy it may seem. You can fix it later.

### WHERE TO GET NEW PRODUCT IDEAS

*1. Your Customers*
- *Sales reps*
- *Dealers*
- *Surveys*
- *Focus groups*

*2. The Trade*
- *Suppliers*
- *Trade associations*
- *Magazine reps*

*3. Scientists*
- *R&D labs*
- *Universities*
- *Think tanks*

The last step then is **implementation**. An idea is no good without it. Many are the brilliant new product ideas that lie dormant and useless simply because they were never implemented.

Writing down your inspiration is a first step to implementation. Then, break the idea into bite-sized chunks. Finally, execute each step. Or delegate.

New product ideas also come from outside your company. Who better to offer new product ideas than your customers? Here's another opportunity to get feedback. But don't say, "Tell me a new product you'd like to see." Rather, "What sorts of problems do you have?" If necessity is the mother of invention, fill the need. Your customers will tell you what they need if you ask them.

At your next sales meeting, include a discussion of new product ideas. You may be surprised at what your sales staff tells you. It could be next year's big winner.

Suppliers have a vested interest in your new product's success. You are finding other uses for their materials, so they sell more, too. But suppliers may only offer an imitation of a competing product or a minor improvement over last year's model. For breakthrough ideas, talk with your sales representative at your industry trade magazine. Sales reps—good ones—have vast knowledge of industry innovations. Pick their brains for the price of lunch. Then, combine two or more technologies to get new product ideas.

Some companies exist for the sole purpose of inventing new products. They may license them or simply sell marketing and distribution rights. Many are affiliated with universities or foundations. Maintaining contact with leading educational institutions in your trade keeps you in front of innovation in your industry.

## IMPROVEMENT, MODIFICATION, OR INNOVATION

New products typically fall into one of three categories, depending upon the level of customer re-education.

Product **improvement** requires no radical change in a customer's behavior. Air-conditioning improved automobile driving comfort, but required little change in product usage. Product extensions (Honey Nut Cheerios, Ivory Shampoo, ergonomically-designed computer keyboards) are **improvements.**

Automatic transmission represented a **modification** to the way people drove. Long-play records (LPs) of crooner Bing Crosby gave way to eight-track tapes, then cassettes of his, "B-b-b-boom." Later generations heard him on CDs or downloaded mp3 files. Convergence of technologies can lead to radical **modification**. Futurists predict that we'll be watching TV and conducting ecommerce on our combination Internet/TV/radio/telephone/credit card technology system.

The automobile itself was an **innovation** that changed the way we live. The fax machine, birth control pills, homogenized milk, panty hose, and the Apple Macintosh were all **innovations** that radically disrupted our known worlds.

## BRAINSTORMING

Probably the most familiar method of creating new products is through **brainstorming**. Gather a group of people together who know your company's products and customers and toss around some ideas. The crazier the better. Add technologies together to create hybrids and mutations. Invent artificial needs that customers might desire. Spin outside the box. No limitations, no evaluation, no criticism. Just ideas.

Avoid evaluation of ideas at your brainstorming session, no one saying, "We've tried that before" or "That will cost too much." That way, good ideas won't die before they're fully developed. And participants will be more inclined to suggest something completely wacky without fear of being criticized.

*Brainstorming Corollary:* Ask a nonparticipant to record ideas as they occur. Use big sheets of paper posted on the walls so everyone can see them. Later, have the scribe type them up and distribute them to participants within twenty-four hours. Participants then should

## BRAINSTORMING

- *Group size: six to ten people*
- *Address ONLY one problem*
- *AM better than PM*
- *No evaluation, just ideas*
- *Use a nonparticipant scribe*

*Follow Four Rules:*

*1. No criticism*

*2. Ideas, ideas, ideas (the crazier, the better)*

*3. Go for quantity*

*4. Link ideas for improvement*

**Case Study** | **UNION CARBIDE**

### THE PROBLEM

Back in the early 1980s, Union Carbide, the makers of Glad bags, had an excess of polyurethane plastic. The brand manager approached Leo Burnett Company and asked us to develop new ideas for plastic garbage bags.

We began by applying sensory modification. First, we thought about something that looked different. That netted colored bags—pale green for the bathroom, yellow for the kitchen, and pink in the nursery. They bombed in test. Research showed consumers did not think of their trash containers as decorative items.

Next, we addressed the sense of smell—pine scent in the bathroom, lemon for the kitchen, and baby powder in the nursery. They bombed in test, too. If consumers wouldn't use their wastebaskets as decoration, they sure wouldn't expect them to freshen a room.

combine and modify at least three ideas for further consideration. Reconvene and choose the best for development.

Following are three brainstorming techniques you can use in your sessions.

**1. Sensory Modification**

**2. Attribute Modification**

**3. Morphological Analysis**

The first two techniques are most useful for product **improvement**.

**Sensory modification** tests a product against the five senses: touch, taste, smell, sight, and sound. Take your product and imagine it feeling different (longer, shorter, heavier, lighter, slipperier, leather instead of cotton, aluminum instead of steel), tasting different (sweeter, saltier, chocolate-coated), smelling different (spicy, floral, scent-free), looking different (colors, packaging, stealth), and sounding different (imagine a quiet Harley).

**Attribute modification** is ideal for improving an existing product. This method addresses its specific features and benefits.

When applying attribute modification, think about your product and how you could:

- Magnify
- Micro-fy
- Combine
- Reverse
- Substitute
- Rearrange

Start by listing the attributes, e.g., a screwdriver with round steel shank and wooden handle. Apply modifications to the attributes, e.g., hexagon shank allowing users to apply more torque, a rubber handle to insulate, a motor for more power.

Focus group research can be helpful in generating ideas for attribute modification. Customers tend to focus on benefits. They are more likely to point out problems based upon product attributes, attributes that you can then modify to relieve the problem.

At Burnett, we used focus groups to learn how consumers felt about Glad garbage and trash bags. We heard users complain about the method of closure, those annoying twisty ties. So we suggested modifying this attribute, that is, adding handles. Test markets loved the new bags. Handle-Tie bags were an instant hit and carved out a whole new market.

To create significant product modification, try **morphological analysis**. This technique is probably the most fun and can generate the most interesting new product ideas.

First, pick your product category's most important issue. For example, moving stuff from here to there. Next, describe the process. In a container (cart, box, sling, chair, bag) through some medium (air, water, rail, rollers) using some power source (cable, magnetic field, internal combustion engine).

**Case Study** ⬤ **UNION CARBIDE**

**THE SOLUTION**

After colored Glad bags and scented Glad bags both bombed in test markets, we finally gave up on sensory modification and opted instead for attribute modification.

Our research said that consumers found twisty ties to be inconvenient as they were hard to find and they often came off, spilling garbage everywhere.

A modest manufacturing modification put handles on the bags, and a whole new product category was born.

www.unioncarbide.com

You begin to see the possibilities. By mixing, matching, and **morphing**, you might come up with a box on rollers pulled by a cable. Or a chair on rails powered by an internal combustion engine. Or even a cart on air powered by a magnetic field.

Successful new product ideas can come from anyone. You, your staff, your customers, dealers, distributors, or suppliers—all may have ideas worth exploring. Just remember: there are no bad ideas (except maybe those scented garbage bags).

# FROM CONCEPT TO CONSUMPTION

Once you have decided upon your new product, it must pass six stages of testing.

New Product Launch Sequence:

**1. Concept Stage**

**2. Investigation Stage**

**3. Design Stage**

**4. Prototype Stage**

**5. Introduction Stage**

**6. Product Transition**

At the **concept stage**, ask yourself, "Is this product feasible? Does it follow the company's mission? Does the customer want it? And will it make money?"

If you can answer yes to these questions, you can move to the **investigation stage**. Here, you conduct focus group research, test it in-house, and show it to a few trusted colleagues for their opinions. You also begin to estimate what it might cost to make it, and what it might cost to launch it. Are these funds available? Could you borrow the money?

At the **design stage**, you begin testing the new manufacturing process for volume runs. Take a look at timing. Will this product fit your production schedules? Will it require new capacity? Skilled labor? Better rethink your costs. Recalculate your ROI.

The **prototype stage** lets you touch it and feel it. Examine it closely. Does it perform to expectations? Can you build it? Install it? Service it? And still make money?

You're finally ready to foist your new product on an unsuspecting public. At the **introduction stage**, users will have their first opportunity to experience the product, apply it, operate it, scrutinize it, and tear it to pieces. Listen to their feedback. Learn from them. Make any changes necessary quickly before too many people experience problems. Are you able to produce the product in volume? Ship it on time? Have you found the right price point? And, as always, can you still make money?

> ## FAST FACT
> *Your product is new for a limited time. After six months, you can no longer legally advertise it as new.*

The **transition stage** features market acceptance. You've made it. The new product is a success. It's contributing to your company's continued growth. The industry acknowledges your innovative leadership. Sales and profits are up.

It's time to start brainstorming new ideas.

# INTRODUCING!

The **introduction stage** may be the trickiest part of new product introduction. Promoting a new product is one of the most difficult and highly studied areas in marketing.

The fact is, you only have one chance to make a first impression, so don't blow it. Customer impressions, once formed, are difficult to change. It's important to be sure your product is the best it can be.

Nothing will destroy a bad product faster than good marketing. No matter how skillful your promotion plan, if you have a bad product, your target market will find out that much faster.

The primary marketing objective at the introductory stage is to induce trial. You must get those **early adopters** to try your new product. Early promotion is aimed at informing your target market about the product, how it works, and its promised benefits.

> ## CONSUMER PROMOTIONS
> *Promotion options that can help* **pull** *your new product through channels and into the hands of users:*
>
> • *Discounts*
>
> • *Samples*
>
> • *Coupons*
>
> • *Publicity*
>
> • *Advertising*
>
> • *Sweepstakes/Contests*
>
> • *Bonus Packs*
>
> • *Premiums*
>
> • *Ad Specialties*

Awareness comes first. Before anyone will purchase your new product, they must first know about it. Start with publicity. If you start with any other promotion, you lose the opportunity for publicity because the press will not print a story that isn't news. Then, advertise heavily, far more than the industry average percent of sales.

Next comes credibility. They must believe your new product fills a need or solves a problem. And it must solve it better than anything they are currently using. Your promotion therefore must be persuasive and foster trust.

Lastly, tell them where to get it. A new product likely will not be available everywhere immediately. You will need time to load the channels of distribution, push the

## TRADE PROMOTIONS

*Promotion options that can help **push** your new product through the supply chain:*

- *Quantity Discounts*
- *Credit Terms*
- *Trade Allowances*
- *Samples*
- *Sweepstakes/Contests*
- *Trade Shows*
- *Point-of-Purchase Displays*
- *Incentives*
- *Ad Specialties*
- *Publicity*
- *Co-Op Advertising*

product through the supply chain. "Available in limited areas" can be used to alert the market they may have to look to find your product. Using words like "Quantities are limited" or "Available to select customers only" may also spur demand.

Heavy advertising, coupons, sampling, and publicity pull in customers. But a number of trade promotions may be necessary to ensure adequate distribution.

Choosing a price point may depend upon several factors:

- Competitive Alternatives
- Cost to Manufacture
- Demand

Price your new product either high, to recover R&D costs (called "skimming"), or low, to maximize trial.

When Panasonic first introduced the digital camcorder, it was priced nearly twice as high as its non-digital competition. Targeted to people who were willing to pay for the latest and greatest technology, the high price helped Panasonic recoup much of its R&D expenses.

Low-end pricing helps overcome skepticism. If your new product is priced lower than alternative products, the prospective customer will be more likely to decide to give your product a try.

## THE MIDDLE MAJORITY

Now that your new product has been introduced, naturally, you would prefer your entire target market to adopt it immediately. But that's not how it works. Customers differ in how quickly they are willing to try something new.

Typically, users fall into one of three categories: **early adopters**, **middle majority**, and **late adopters**.

Innovators are adventurous and willing to take risks. You probably knew someone in high school or college who had to have the latest and greatest techno gadget—computer peripheral, stereo equipment, cell phone—and was willing to pay dearly to be the first among his peers. He was an **early adopter**, willing to take a risk on a new product simply because it was new.

**Early adopters** are typically well educated, well traveled, younger, and have above-average income. They often know all about new technologies before others are even aware they exist. Others look to them for their opinions and advice on various topics making them key to a new product's success.

Smart marketers use early adapters to provide feedback. Testimonials can be especially useful when introducing a new product. Those first users of your product, those **early adopters**, will have opinions. Use their testimonials (assuming they are favorable) to show others that people are already benefiting from your new product. This can help sustain the momentum from your introduction.

> ## SKIMMING
> ........................
> *If you are the first in a new market with a highly innovative product much in demand, as Texas Instruments was with the first calculator, you can use a "skimming" strategy to price your product.*
>
> *TI's first calculators sold to banks and large accounting firms for hundreds of dollars. The accuracy and time savings was worth the premium price.*
>
> *This allowed the firm to recover its R&D expenses before competitors came into the market with cheaper models.*

While the first to buy are important, the **middle majority** is key to your product's long-term viability. If they buy, you can rest assured your product has been accepted by the marketplace. They are willing to buy a new product, but usually don't want to be first. They need to be persuaded that your new product isn't simply new, but better than what

**New Product Adoption**

| 10% | 80% | 10% |
| Early Adopters | Middle Majority | Late Adopters |

## BETA TEST

*Some companies give key customers their new product free or at a reduced price in exchange for feedback.*

*A software developer may offer their next generation program to a few key customers at a greatly reduced price. These customers try the new software and point out glitches, inconveniences, or tendencies to crash.*

*The developer then addresses these concerns before launching the product to the general market.*

## CREATE HAPPY CUSTOMERS

*Make your best customers **early adapters** and build credibility among the rest of the market.*

*Send a free sample of your product to a prospective customer in exchange for permission to use his comments in your advertising and promotion materials.*

*Your customer is happy to receive something for free (or at a reduced price, if necessary). And you're happy to have the testimonial.*

they are currently using. A majority of your promotion efforts must be directed squarely at this **middle majority**.

**Late adopters** are laggards. They will try your new product only when there is little or no risk involved, when the purchase becomes an economic necessity, or when social pressure is applied. These people are typically lower in social class and bound by traditions. Often, by the time they adopt a product, it may already be superseded by new technology.

Ignore the **late adopters**. Their numbers are small. Unless your market is a mature one and they are the only non-users remaining, they are not worth a concerted effort. Better to devote your energies to developing your next innovation.

New products offer a multitude of opportunities for increasing your company's sales. Their high risk of failure is far outweighed by the benefits to your company's prestige within the industry, and to your bottom line.

Some companies devote a huge percentage of their annual sales to research and development of new products. They understand that innovation is key to unbridled growth in virtually any industry. They recognize creative imagining can lead to new product magic.

Not every new product is a megahit right away. Look at your cell phone—bulky as a shoe box when first introduced. It was costly and undependable, too. Today, it is lights, buttons, and information, carrier of messages around the world, and a storage unit for music and photographs—an alien concept just two decades ago and pure heresy two centuries ago. Two thousand years ago, it would have been worshiped as a god.

All innovation begins with the sharing of information. Information is the one commodity you can give away and still have. It is completely recombinant. Rip it apart, categorize it, unbundle it, reconfigure it, and recombine it in an infinite variety of ways to come up with practical (or impractical) products for tomorrow.

Dare to dream the impossible; create the improbable. Take a little technology, a hardy dose of discipline, and a dash of magic. Mix thoroughly. Then dazzle your customers and your industry.

# CHAPTER 9

# Kick-Ass Strategy #5: Merge or Acquire

Purpose: *The purpose of chapter 9 is to outline the benefits of merging or acquiring another company, examine typical acquisition search methods, and determine the target company's worth to your business.*

———◦———

**The last and fastest way to build your business is to merge or acquire.**

When interest rates are low, money is cheap. Big companies all over the planet get hungry. They know that expansion may best be served cold, like a fresh new market for their products, a crisper operation with combined talents and technologies. They merge or acquire new companies. With interest rates low, it may be the least expensive method of acquiring new customers, new markets, new products, or that magic they call "synergy."

Why not your company?

## 4 OUT OF 5 = M&A

*Buy Market Share*

*+ Hunt*

*+ Farm*

*+ New Products*

---

*Merge & Acquire*

A partnership with a competitor (**horizontal integration**), or with a supplier or customer (**vertical integration**), could build your sales dramatically.

Gain access to new markets that others have mastered, with new products and new people who could bring in more new customers. The melded company would offer a multitude of cost savings as you combine overhead expenses (like accounting or human resources). The benefits that come from merging or acquiring another company often lead to greater profitability.

Mergers and acquisitions are being used more frequently as a route to dramatic growth because of a relaxed regulatory environment and lower interest rates. About a third of Proctor & Gamble's sales come from acquisitions made since 1980. Often, the larger a company gets, the more clout it has in the supply chain, the more acumen it has in diverse markets, and the more money it makes.

But before your eyes fill with dollar signs and you start bidding on companies, recognize there are key factors that must exist:

• Your business must be healthy.
• Your debt to equity ratio must be low (lower than your industry average).
• There must be a strategic benefit to the partnership.
• Your partner must be willing.

Four of the 5 Kick-Ass Strategies are inherent in the **merge or acquire** strategy.

By merging with or acquiring a competitor, you **buy market share**. You sell more of the same stuff to a whole lot more people—your customers plus the new company's customers. Your piece of the pie just got bigger.

By merging or acquiring a supplier or customer, you **hunt** new customers. You sell different stuff to the same people. Invariably, the new company has product lines that suit the needs of your customer base. Supply chain costs are minimized, making your price points more attractive to a wider target base.

By merging or acquiring a competitor, you **farm** both your customers and your partner's customers. Cross-selling each other's product or service offers the best of both. You sell more stuff to the same people, i.e., your combined lists of customers.

By merging or acquiring a customer, supplier, or competitor, **new products** emerge. Research and development departments are combined. Shared testing results along with shared technologies, new ideas, and new stuff being sold to new people.

# FINDING THE RIGHT FIT

A good partnership is like a marriage. Fit is critical. That's why the screening process must be rigorous and thorough.

There are three basic approaches to locating a strategic partner:

1. Passive
2. Aggressive
3. Outsource

The **passive approach** simply means you wait for someone to come to you. You may encourage the process by notifying your attorney, accountant, or banker that you are interested in making an acquisition. They become your eyes and ears in the marketplace. This approach is the least expensive as it requires little added time or investment. It's also the least effective.

Taking a more **aggressive approach**, you look at contacts and relationships among customers, suppliers, competitors, or firms that sell related products. You gather information at trade shows about firms like yours, selling similar products in different territories. You research various companies using SIC codes, visit their websites, begin screening potential candidates, as well as comparing products lines, target markets, and supply chains for compatibility. This assumes you have the time and energy to devote to the process.

If not, consider an **outsourced** consultant, attorney, or investment banker versed in mergers and acquisitions. He or she can begin the screening process anonymously so as not to tip your hand. Eventually, you will need to make direct contact with the other company decision makers to investigate their level of

> ## HOW TO APPROACH A POTENTIAL M&A CANDIDATE
> ·············································
> *Directly: CEO to CEO (or other senior officer).*
>
> *Third Party: Investment Banker, Commercial Banker, Business Broker, Accountant, Attorney, Consultant, etc.*
>
> *It's often best to use the third party approach for the initial contact/stages of the solicitation, but not to negotiate the deal.*
>
> *Principals must get involved early to avoid misunderstanding and develop a comfort level between key decision-makers.*

interest. This is the most expensive method. Professionals, however, have greater experience and expertise, and will drive the process to a successful conclusion.

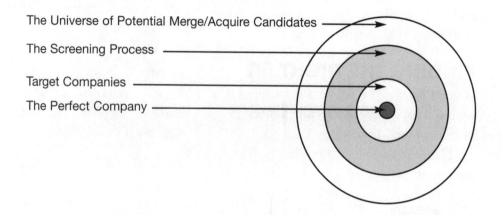

The Universe of Potential Merge/Acquire Candidates

The Screening Process

Target Companies

The Perfect Company

# THE SCREENING PROCESS

Out there are thousands of companies, a vast panoply of manufacturers, distributors, and retail companies eager for your call. How do you cull the bad from the good, the inappropriate from the perfect fit?

Most successful mergers or acquisitions among small- to medium-size companies are within the same (or a related) industry.

Typically, the ideal M&A candidate will be through either **horizontal integration** or **vertical integration.**

**Horizontal integration** is when one organization partners with another at the same level of the supply chain. You may partner with a competitor—another company selling many of the same things you sell, maybe even in the same territories—or a company selling related products in the same industry.

A distributor of outdoor electrical construction equipment might partner with a distributor of indoor electrical construction equipment, or a distributor of outdoor gas-powered construction equipment, and so on. But always another distributor.

**Vertical integration** is when you partner with an organization at a different level of the supply chain, either a supplier or a customer. You might merge or acquire a manufacturer of outdoor electrical construction equipment. Or you might buy up one of your customers, a construction firm, for instance—but almost always a direct supplier or direct customer. (In rare instances, it might make sense to partner with an indirect supplier—e.g., a manufacturer of indoor electrical construction equipment—but almost never does it make sense to partner with a non-customer at a different level of the supply chain.)

Your search should include both direct and indirect competitors, as well as other players in your supply channel. Begin by establishing ideal acquisition characteristics—sales, number of employees, industries (by SIC code).

Then ask yourself a few questions. What resources or expertise are you seeking that you do not currently have? What new customer groups would you like to serve that you are not serving now? What new geographic territories make the most sense?

> ### FINDING THE PERFECT COMPANY
> ....................................
> *The ideal candidate will possess most or all of the following:*
>
> - *Offers new product or process capabilities.*
>
> - *Provides access to new markets (industrial and/or geographic).*
>
> - *Introduces you to new operations technologies.*
>
> - *Has a strong management team in place.*
>
> - *Is financially sound.*

Once you have established your search criteria, use it to identify possible candidates. Industry trade associations, your local library, and the Internet all offer a host of research options.

## TARGET COMPANIES

The next step is to make contact with some of your candidates. Don't send out a mass mailing; you won't have time to follow up all of them. Prioritize your list. Establish a "Top Ten," those you most want to investigate further. They are probably the ones you already know the most about, the ones you see at your industry trade show, or the ones whose CEOs you met at a golf outing.

The next step is to initiate contact with target candidates to determine their level of interest in opening discussions. Send a letter directly to the presidents or CEO introducing yourself and your company. Tell him or her that you are exploring acquisition possibilities and found his/her company a possible candidate. Be frank. Explain your reasoning, the benefits to your combined operations. Close by asking if there would be any interest.

## THE DUE DILIGENCE PROCESS

. . . . . . . . . . . . . . . . . . . . . . . . . . . . .

*A CEO will be reluctant to reveal much about his or her company to a stranger.*

*Begin the process by offering to exchange summary information. For instance, gross revenue for the past three years, any extraordinary expenses (e.g., building rent paid to CEO owner is high for area), owner compensation range, general company strengths and weaknesses.*

*If it still looks like a good fit, consult your attorney and arrange to sign confidentiality agreements.*

Invariably, the CEO will reply, "Sure, I'm interested. Make me an offer." The "Everything is for sale" attitude needs to be filtered before you can find a seller willing to negotiate a fair price.

If you find a motivated seller, one who is considering retirement with no logical heir, or one whose circumstances suggest genuine interest, set up a meeting. No accountants. No lawyers. Not yet. Just two people getting to know one another.

How do you know if the candidate is truly motivated to sell, or just blowing smoke? Gauge seller's motivation upon:

- How much information is the candidate willing to share?
- Age of owner—is he/she nearing retirement?
- Are there family members in management?
- Is there another logical buyer, a major supplier or customer?

As part of your examination process, perform a SWOT analysis on the target firm. What are its strengths, weaknesses, opportunities, and threats in the marketplace? How does that fit with your own strengths, weaknesses, and market opportunities? Ideally, the new company's strengths will be your weaknesses, and vice versa.

Look hard at the Q, S, & P factors, too. How does it fit with your image? If they are known for great service and inexpensive products (big S, big P), how does that jell with your great service and high-quality products (big S, big Q)?

Once you have found a truly "motivated" seller, dig deeper into the company. Are the managers effective? Is the company's financial condition sound? You don't need a turn-around situation. Lastly, what is the company's reputation in the industry? Look for quality reputation and ethics here. How much "goodwill" will you be buying?

Do **due diligence**. Get permission to review the books. This is when a professional—investment banker, accountant, attorney, etc.—is invaluable. You have neither the time nor expertise to examine accounts, interview customers and suppliers, inspect the property, plant, and equipment, and the myriad other duties necessary to determine value.

What you need to know is the four methods of valuation:

**1. Asset Evaluation**

**2. Discounted Cash Flow**

**3. Comparable Market Analysis**

**4. Make or Buy**

Perhaps the simplest evaluation is to simply look at all the company's assets, subtract the liabilities, and arrive at a number. These assets may be both tangible and intangible.

Tangible assets are the property, plant, and equipment. Be careful. Some property or equipment may no longer be useful. When I purchased an apparel company, we discounted the value of much of the inventory as obsolete, then sold it at auction. Many of the rolls of cloth were perfectly good, but they had not been used in years because there no longer were any customers for it. We paid pennies on the dollar, and even that was too much.

Intangibles are patents, copyrights, territory exclusivity agreements, and goodwill. Very difficult to assess value. At the apparel firm, the prior owner had stiffed some suppliers. So we actually had "badwill" as a part of our equation.

## Case Study : EXEC PC

### THE PROBLEM

Greg Ryan, president of ExecPC, the largest internet service provider (ISP) in Wisconsin, faced a dilemma. He wanted to expand into the Chicago market, but knew he faced enormous obstacles.

Advertising costs in Chicago were expensive. Did it make more sense to buy a Chicago-area ISP or advertise and begin signing up subscribers?

# DISCOUNTED CASH FLOW (DCF)

This method assumes those assets have no value unless they can actually churn out cash, now and into the future. If the assets cannot be used to generate income, they have no benefit.

DCF approach focuses on the present value of projected earnings to reach a value. (For more on present value, see chapter 10.) Forecast five years of earnings before interest and taxes (EBIT) and add in depreciation and amortization (if the candidate company's owner is not part of the merged company, add in his or her salary as well). DCF is particularly useful for determining the present value of intangibles.

By combining DCF with asset evaluation, you can use simple return on investment (ROI). (See chapter 10.) If you purchase the assets for $1 million, and they churn out $80,000 in earnings before interest and taxes each year, that's an 8 percent ROI. Or, looked at another way, if the company is expected to churn out $80,000 annually, offer a $1 million for the assets to get an 8 percent ROI.

# COMPARABLE MARKET ANALYSIS (CMA)

CMA is the most sophisticated method of analysis. It uses the standard real estate practice of looking at other companies in similar industries and determining a multiple, or P/E, ratio. The problem is that most smaller companies are bought and sold without price disclosures. Investment bankers and some consultants and attorneys specializing in mergers and acquisitions may have access to the information. Otherwise, simply look at public companies within similar SIC codes. Get their annual reports or 10 K reports. Look for earnings per share (EPS) and compare it to sales price.

# MAKE OR BUY

This evaluation is as it suggests: "What would it cost to make this company from scratch?"

If you are a widget maker in Walla Walla, Washington, and want to buy a widget company in Spokane, do a **make or buy** analysis. How much would it cost you to lease space in Spokane, hire employees, and create enough awareness and credibility in the marketplace to attract new customers? It may turn out it's cheaper to start from scratch in Spokane than to buy the other company.

The best way to valuate the candidate company is to use all four methods. Start with assets and discounted cash flow. Investigate comparable acquisitions in your industry and their earnings as a percent of sales. And finally, imagine what it might cost to start a similar operation from scratch.

Then, strike a balance, and make an offer.

Mergers and acquisitions are the fastest ways to grow a business. Used most effectively when interest rates are low, they can vault your business to industry leadership, help you enter new markets, allow you to offer more products and services to your current customers, and build an arsenal of creative new product ideas.

And you might get to meet some nice people in the process.

## Case Study ) EXEC PC

### THE SOLUTION

ExecPC (since acquired by CoreComm) began advertising in Aurora, an isolated suburban Chicago market.

We spent a lot of money and quickly determined that, to enter the Chicago market, it would cost more per subscriber in promotion expense than it would to buy up a small, established ISP in Chicago.

That made Ryan's decision an easy one: merge or acquire rather than start from scratch. It also gave him an idea of the value of the candidate company.

www.execpc.com

# CHAPTER 10

## Managing Your Growth

Purpose: *The purpose of chapter 10 is to provide guidelines for making changes in your workplace (both factory and office) to maximize efficiencies and set the stage for expansion.*

———◦———

**T**o grow exponentially, the entrepreneur needs to maximize his business systems. That means optimizing three things:
- **Operations**
- **Finances**
- **Human Assets**

*Operations*

This is your property, plant, and equipment. Are your property and your plant (building, floor layout, etc.) capable of handling the additional business? If not, will more space be required? Or can you outsource some tasks less expensively? Your equipment is the tools you use to build stuff. Tools transform raw materials into output. They can be physical (drill press, computer, delivery van) or conceptual (creative ideas, a manufacturing process, intellectual property).

*Finances*

Does your company have the financial strength to grow? Increasing sales requires cash. You pay for raw materials on day one, take ten days to build your widgets, take ten more to sell them, and wait forty-five to sixty days to collect the money. That's a long lag time. Diligent cash management and the strength of your financial statement together create the environment for exponential growth.

*Human Assets*

Hiring and training new people, or developing from within, will also be necessary to accommodate your growth. Your management team must be in place, trained, and motivated.

The five strategies will build your business. As it grows, you will need to grow the supporting infrastructure—more space, more equipment, more tools to meet the needs of your growing business.

If your company develops the wrong structure, you may misdirect resources and waste energy on unimportant matters. This chapter will help you design your organization to operate in perpetuity. It explains the structure of operations, how to coordinate multiple functions and maintain your company's balance, setting up your office for maximum efficiency, why a service organization has unique growing pains, and how to break a bottleneck no matter where it happens.

# THE TRANSFORMATION PROCESS

| Input | Auto Manufacturer | Output |
|---|---|---|
| Materials, Parts | Labor, Plant, Equipment | Automobile |
| | **Hospital** | |
| Sick Patients | Doctors, Nurses, Technology | Well Patients (or Corpses) |
| | **Retail Store** | |
| Prospects | Clerks, Selection, Ambience | Customers |

Whether you're in manufacturing, distribution, or retail products and services, all companies have a transformation process, where input is transformed into output. The rate at which this transformation occurs is called **productivity.**

An automobile manufacturer, hospital, and retail store all have several factors in common. They all forecast sales and expenses; they all have inventory; they all adhere to strict policies and schedules; they keep track of earnings and expenses; and all are subject to quality control. Most important, they all transform input into output. How well they do this is a measure of their productivity.

Productivity—the amount of output per unit of input—is a basic yardstick of a company's health. Your labor productivity is measured by the amount of output divided by the number of man-hours of labor (some service businesses use earnings before interest and taxes divided by number of employees). That output can be measured in tons of iron ore for a mining operation, an airline's revenue passenger miles, or a barber's number of haircuts.

## PRODUCTIVITY LEADER

*U.S. productivity growth averaged about 2 percent a year from 1900 to 2000. That means U.S. living standards have doubled, on average, about every thirty-five years.*

*That the U.S. enjoys one of the world's highest standards of living is a reflection of its productivity. It wasn't always so.*

*From the thirteenth to the sixteenth centuries, Italy led in productivity, the Dutch republic in the seventeenth and early eighteenth, Britain in the late eighteenth and most of the nineteenth, and the United States throughout much of the twentieth century.*

*Who will lead the world in productivity in the twenty-first century?*

There are two primary ways to boost productivity—either by investing in technology, the tools you use to create products and services, or by investing in human capital, smart people who will find new ways to increase efficiency, and find faster, better ways to do the work.

Technology plays a key role. Imagine the supermarket clerk who has an automatic scanner instead of an old-fashioned cash register.

Specialization, too, is crucial. Henry Ford's auto plants turned out many more cars per man-hour than competitors because of the assembly line and each worker's responsibility for just his one job on the line.

# START WITH THE LITTLE THINGS

Periodically, you will need to consider whether your production capacity is sufficient for the growth plans outlined in your marketing objectives. Can you actually make/provide all the products/services your plan calls for?

If not, there are short-term solutions and there are long-term solutions, depending upon your need. Short-term solutions may resolve the immediate capacity problems, but eventually, if your company is to grow exponentially, you will need to add property, plant, and equipment.

Short-term solutions include overtime, second or third shifts, or outsourcing. All will help increase your production output. You may also gain efficiencies and free up capacity by applying any of the following measures:

1. **Level Your Production Rate**
2. **Alter the Production Schedule**
3. **Rebalance Your Flow Process**
4. **Decentralize**
5. **Make Modest Improvements First**

## Level Your Production Rate

If you level your production rate, you can build up a backlog of finished goods and sell them during peak demand periods. At the apparel firm, we sold uniforms to schools of nursing, and most students needed their uniforms in the fall. So we spent the spring and summer building up inventory in various sizes. The larger lot runs made for economies of scale, increased the efficiency of our sewers so they sewed uniforms faster, and lowered overall costs. When orders began to flood in, we simply picked uniforms out of the storage bins, quickly pressed them, and shipped them to the students in time for class.

## Alter the Production Schedule

By altering the production schedule, you can reduce capital equipment downtimes. Setup of each new job means an idle machine. Coax more production out of each machine by altering the product mix or planning longer run times.

## Rebalance Your Flow Process

Adding or changing the labor makeup on a piece of equipment can increase productivity and increase capacity.

## Decentralize

Improve information movement by decentralizing. Computers on the factory floor rather than at the supervisor's desk allow decision-making at the point where the work is performed.

## Make Modest Improvements First

Even a modest investment in technology, a simple process modification, or tiny product redesign can decrease manufacturing cycle times and free up capacity.

Short-term measures to increase capacity can be planned quickly, require limited investment, and can be implemented informally. And while they may have dramatic impact on your company's output, most of them are simply substitutes for acquiring additional space and production equipment. They're a good starting point, but they are only a start.

# LONG-TERM CAPACITY CONSIDERATIONS

At the same time you are implementing these measures, you should be looking at one of three long-term solutions:

1. **Expand Your Existing Facility**
2. **Open a Branch Office**
3. **Relocate to New Quarters**

Any expansion of capacity must be judged against alternatives. You have choices. Build, lease, subcontract, or add a third shift. Using sophisticated net present value techniques and internal rate of return analysis, you can determine which will have the most immediate impact and add the most to your retained earnings.

Your accountant or financial advisor may be able to apply these financial tools to the options available. As an entrepreneur (and the decision-maker), you need to understand what they're advising you to do (more on financial calculations in chapter 10).

## RELOCATION FREQUENCY

- *Only about a third of relocations contemplated are ever carried through.*

- *Three percent of all manufacturing facilities relocate annually.*

- *Six percent of all manufacturing companies add branch plants annually.*

- *Annually, less than 1 percent of U.S. manufacturing facilities (with one hundred or more employees) relocate.*

Source: Milwaukee Metropolitan Association of Commerce report

## WHEN CONSIDERING ADDITIONAL SPACE:

• *What is the impact on existing operations?*

*Transition can be disruptive and time-consuming. Processes and systems may be altered, materials handling changed, new learning required. Engineering and management may be so tied up in the move that everyday work is ignored.*

• *How flexible is your new capacity?*

*In fluid, evolving industries (e.g., electronics or pharmaceuticals), where new markets, new products, and new distribution methods are the norm, production must remain flexible. A new space may even hinder the company's ability to keep abreast of changes in your industry.*

• *Are you overthinking the project?*

*Plant managers are often required to jump through hoops just to get capital equipment that may be fairly inexpensive when compared to just one individual worker's capitalized stream of earnings.*

## Expand Your Existing Facility

Expansion at your existing facility is by far the most practical option. Businesses frequently seek ways to build on to their current plant, such as an addition, a new room, added floor, or renovated basement. Its low cost—no new land acquisition—short lag time, and the fact that it is a known quantity make it appealing.

But there are pitfalls in on-site expansion. As more production space is added, the layout of your plant may become less optimal. Materials handling and storage may become disjointed; chances for delayed deliveries increase. Staying at the same site may delay technology advances, too. You use the same old machines, same old methods. With more production at the same plant, management runs the risk of complicating supervision, inventory control, and cost accounting.

## Open a Branch Office

A branch office has its advantages, too. You can avoid overloading one plant with either too many products or too many workers. You can specialize at each branch and keep cost accounting simpler and more controllable. New technologies can be tested, new processes explored. A branch office could open new markets (see chapter 6).

## Relocate to New Quarters

Relocation is best when the problems are less related to size and more related to processes, technology, or control. Close down old technology, old process methods, and old policies in exchange for new. Plant relocation can exploit the latest production technology and the most sensible plant design.

Most relocations are less than twenty miles distant. This helps retain a skilled labor force so they don't have to drive too far. It also ensures continuity of customer and supplier relationships.

Most manufacturing firms follow a **product plant strategy**, where different products or product lines are made at separate plants. Plants specialize and gain economies of scale through repetition. This strategy corresponds with a decentralized management structure, with decision making at the plant level.

A **market area plant strategy** allows plants to service specific market areas. Each plant manufactures most or all of a company's product line. This works best when freight costs are a major part of the overall cost (e.g., the brewing industry, magazine printing, food processing and canning) or when quick response is necessary. This strategy requires centralized management, calling the shots for multiple plant production and distribution.

Some companies use an assembly-line approach. The **process plant strategy** uses separate plants to make goods to be shipped to another plant for final assembly. A rare occurrence, fewer than 10 percent of all manufacturing companies utilize this strategy. Centralized control is a must to coordinate materials and product between plants. Most process plants are in easy driving distance of one another to reduce transport costs.

Some people introduce elaborate rating schemes that quantify every variable for each location. There are really only six major factors that need to be considered, and, generally, one or two of these are so important that they make your decision for you.

1. Cost and availability of skilled labor.
2. Cost of taxes and other governmental payments.
3. Proximity to customers.
4. Proximity to suppliers or raw materials.
5. Proximity to another company facility.
6. Quality of life (defined in any number of ways).

Other factors to consider may include the cost of utilities; workforce attitude toward unionization; cost to build access roads and parking; access to freeways, airports, or railroads; aesthetic and cultural options; location of direct competitors.

Over the past several decades, another factor has been thrown into the mix. Local and state governments may offer incentives to woo companies that will employ local workers and generate tax revenue for their communities. Nevada has mounted a campaign specifically to attract California companies, offering lower corporate tax rates, lower worker compensation rates, and cash incentives.

While no site may rate high on all factors, it should rate high on those that truly make a difference in your company's ability to compete effectively.

## Case Study  JONCO INDUSTRIES

### THE PROBLEM

JONCO Industries' president, Tom Ryan, was in a quandary. His packaging and fulfillment company had a contract to fill over 100,000 one-quart bottles annually with specialty oil. But the customer had begun ordering smaller quantities, just 2,000 or 3,000 at a time.

His equipment was set up for larger runs and the smaller quantities did not allow for economies of scale. Production costs began to eat up his profit margins. In addition, his cost of raw materials began to increase, and his contract with his customer had a long-term fixed price.

What to do?

## Licensing and Outsourcing

Other options for increasing capacity include **licensing** and **outsourcing** production.

**Licensing** allows another firm to produce and market your goods for a specific purpose for a specified period of time. **Outsourcing** production is the process of obtaining outside vendors to provide goods and services that might otherwise be obtained in-house.

A licensing agreement means you sell the right to use your name or logo or the product itself to another company for a specific purpose and for a limited period of time. It can provide a company instant recognition and consumer interest.

For instance, Jack Daniels licensed its name to T. Marzetti to produce bourbon-flavored mustard. Movies license products to manufacturers for everything from T-shirts to tattoos and key chains to candy.

You have spent years and thousands of dollars creating awareness and credibility for your brand. You may decide to license your name or product to another company to both increase credibility for that company as well as awareness for your name brand. For instance, the Intel Corporation's reliability is so well known, manufacturers tout Intel chips in their computers. The "Intel Inside" campaign creates added credibility for any company using the Intel chip in the manufacture of computers or component parts.

You may also choose to increase your sales by paying a license fee to use a famous brand name. If you produce clothing, could your firm benefit by an exclusive agreement to manufacture and distribute sports team clothing? If you make key fobs, how about a license to make fobs with car logos? Or NFL team logos?

There may come a time when your firm has an opportunity to make more profit by seeking an outside vendor than by producing an item in-house. Outsourcing can be either a short-term solution or a long-term production strategy.

Let's say your facility is set up to make a million widgets annually. Your factory is really humming; you have three shifts going; the equipment is running at peak performance. As your growth accelerates, you suddenly anticipate a need for ten million widgets a year. But your cost structure is not set up for such a large quantity.

You could begin planning a new factory, which could take years. Or you

 **Case Study**

## JONCO INDUSTRIES

### THE SOLUTION

Ryan contracted with a smaller outside supplier who was set up for short runs. He specified the production constraints and monitored the process carefully in the early stages to ensure quality.

The outsourced supplier was set up for shorter runs. His costs were lower than JONCO's, with the new supplier's more sophisticated equipment.

Both the outsourced supplier and JONCO make a tidy profit packaging the specialty oil.

www.joncoind.com

could expand your existing facility, which could take almost as long. Or you could find a vendor, perhaps in another state or another country that is better set up for larger quantities. His costs are so low, he can sell you the item, produced to your unique specifications, at a price low enough that you can turn around and sell it to your customers and still manage a significant profit.

Some companies exist solely as marketing firms, subcontracting or outsourcing *all* production. Samuel Adams beer is manufactured by big beer companies and independent brewing facilities throughout the U.S. Shipping beer, which is mostly water, over long distances is costly. It makes sense for the small brewery to tap into other brewers' excess capacity rather than build manufacturing plants all over the country.

## CAPACITY IN A SERVICE BUSINESS

Service businesses have different problems than manufacturing companies. Capacity decisions in service businesses are more complex. Before making any capacity decision, you need to take into consideration things like competitive reactions, amenities, and demand modifications.

Because service capacity is often created at the time of the sale, the relationship between marketing and operations is closely tied. Services cannot be stockpiled in inventory to help smooth out peak demand periods (e.g., your hairdresser can serve only one customer at a time). Services have dated obsolescence, that is, when the service time has passed, it cannot be retrieved (e.g., when the airplane takes off with empty seats, they cannot be sold later).

Under such circumstances, capacity planning becomes critical. Because the capacity itself is often the product, it is important to understand buying motivations. Why does a person use this service? Will she be more likely to use it if it were near her place of work? Or her home? Would the additional revenue from extended hours offset the added costs? Would service amenities, either free or for a fee, create more revenue?

Because service businesses often have low entry barriers, competition can easily throw off your earning potential. If customers decide to try a new hairdresser opening down the street, your carefully scheduled calendar (and profit projections) suddenly goes awry.

## Case Study ) YMCA

### THE PROBLEM

The parking lot at the local YMCA is full during peak periods (early morning and 5 p.m. to 7 p.m. on weekdays).

New members complain about lack of convenient parking. Some long-time members even quit their memberships in frustration.

The YMCA needed an inexpensive way to increase parking capacity despite a lack of additional space.

When your service business is expanding, a conservative approach to capacity expansion may be more realistic. Short-term measures for increasing capacity in service industries include:

1. **Hire Part-Time Workers**
2. **Encourage Self-Service**
3. **Share Capacity with Other Businesses**
4. **Make Modest Improvements First**

## Hire Part-Time Workers

Using part-time help during peak times may keep the customers satisfied. But part-timers may not offer the same level of service you would prefer.

## Encourage Self-Service

Asking your customers to assume responsibility for providing some of the service themselves has proven satisfactory in many service industries. Salad bars in restaurants have been particularly popular, allowing customization of the service provided.

## Share Capacity with Other Businesses

There may be opportunities to offset some capacity problems by sharing with non-competing businesses. For instance, a dry cleaner with too many deliveries might offer discount coupons to a printing firm to borrow a delivery truck for an afternoon.

## Make Modest Improvements First

Cross-training or job specialization may increase efficiencies. If your manicurist doubles as a hair stylist, she can fill in during peak demand periods.

Demand can be manipulated through pricing policies. If most everyone wants to use the tennis courts after 4 p.m., discounting play before 4 p.m. could alter demand. Price elasticity analysis can tell you whether raising your prices or lowering your prices will result in an increase in revenue.

Demand can also be manipulated through service policies. A reservation system for peak periods can regulate demand. Services—availability of a teaching pro at a golf course or tennis club, for instance—private lockers, nursery care, and other extras may mollify capacity problems somewhat. Make some of these added services free during off-peak periods to level demand.

Often, amenities are just as important in service businesses as capacity.

For instance, a popular tennis club with ten indoor courts is busy from dawn to closing. The manager decides to convert the locker rooms into an additional tennis court to increase revenues. But members who prefer to shower after a match stop coming. Capacity is increased by one court, but revenue drops. Instead of eliminating the locker room, he might decide to eliminate one court and convert the space to a juice bar and grill. Despite the loss of a court, revenue might actually increase as patrons stop for a fresh drink and a sandwich after their match.

Sometimes, the addition of service amenities can both manipulate demand and create more revenue. Adding free lessons from a golf pro at the local golf course on Tuesdays can create demand during a traditionally slow time period. Adding a bar to the clubhouse creates opportunities for additional revenue and makes the golf course a more attractive destination.

# PROFESSIONAL SERVICE FIRMS

Manufacturing companies have different problems than professional service firms, e.g., accounting firms, law firms, and consulting organizations.

Manufacturing companies take raw materials and add labor to produce tangible products, things you can see and touch and feel. Service professionals use judgment to apply abstract thinking to a client's problems. Their talent is unique, rare, difficult to develop and nurture, and harder still to duplicate.

**Case Study** ) **YMCA**

**THE SOLUTION**

Facing frustrated members due to a lack of parking space during peak periods, the local YMCA struck a barter agreement with the church next door.

The YMCA offered reduced membership fees for church members in exchange for the use of the church parking lot on weekdays.

It turned out to be a win-win for both groups, and the YMCA members now have ample parking.

www.ymca.com

Economies of scale rarely exist in service firms. Having a big office with many professionals seldom yields cost advantages. Typically, costs go up under such circumstances. Entry barriers therefore are lower in professional service firms. Any new firm would probably not require a whole lot of investment capital. A consultant starting up a new practice, for instance, would not need a lot of money the way a new manufacturing concern might.

The objective at any service firm is to deliver high-quality service at an economical price. While price is easily measured, quality of service is not. Over time, quality might be measured in terms of increased trust, or long-term satisfied clients. But even these are intangible and difficult to assess.

In reality, success is measured by the sum total of actions taken by the professionals working in the firm. The best strategy: Hire good people, focus on a clear set of values, and be totally responsive to client needs. Success is the outcome of the collective professionals' efforts.

In general, service firms follow a **practice spectrum**.

With **commodity services**, common and simple problems are solved with specific procedures. McDonald's delivers fast food simply and efficiently. It's served the same way in Bangor, Bangkok, or Bangladesh.

## Service Firm Practice Spectrum

|  | Commodity Service | Procedure Service | Experience Service | Expertise Service |
|---|---|---|---|---|
| Client Problem | Common and simple problems | Choosing among several complex alternatives or implementing a complex process | Deciding a major issue for which the client has little experience | A unique and difficult problem with major consequences |
| Sales Pitch | Efficiency in delivery | Systematic and comprehensive approach | Past experience with similar problems | Analytical ability to solve problems |
| Example | Hairdresser | Dentist | Civil Engineer | Consultant |

Source: Adapted from David Maister, *Managing the Professional Service Firm*, Free Press: NY, 1993.

A more complex **procedure** requires deeper thought and perhaps customization of the service provided. Life insurance is sold using a systematic and comprehensive approach, yet is fitted to individual needs. Agents follow pre-rehearsed procedures to secure a client's business.

## LEVERAGING YOUR EXPERTISE
• • • • • • • • • • • • • • • •

*If you are an expert in your field, you may find that, to grow your professional services firm, you will have to rely more on the work of subordinates with less expertise.*

*They will need to be directed more toward experience or procedure services.*

*While their labor rates may be less than yours as an expert, the greater volume of work results in greater overall revenue.*

Sometimes, "gray hair" **experience** is what is needed. An accounting firm may be asked by a client to solve a major issue—an IRS audit, for example—for which the client has little past experience. The accounting firm, however, has encountered similar problems with other clients over the years and can draw upon its experience to assist the client.

When facing a difficult problem that may have long-term repercussions, specific **expertise** may be required. This is when a consultant, an expert in that particular discipline is required.

The further you move toward expertise on the **practice spectrum**, the more you can charge for your services. Labor utilization must be high (and wages low) for **commodity**-based service firms in order to compete on commodity services. Higher wages are paid to **procedure**-based firms as customization becomes more important. For **experience**-based firms, listening skills are paramount. Personnel must be knowledgeable, creative, and attentive to client needs. For those with **expertise**, so much time is spent in research to remain on the frontier of knowledge that labor rates can zoom off the charts.

Growing your professional services firm requires a balance between nurturing the growth of your subordinates and maintaining the expertise that attracts new business. Marketing strategies affecting a manufacturing operation or retail establishment may seem to have little bearing for a service firm, but many similarities exist. For one, all organizations have an office.

# OFFICE SPACE

Smart business leaders recognize the importance of space in optimizing performance. Too often, your workspace, relative to people, processes, and technology, may be overlooked as a factor in determining your bottom line.

Whether in the factory or in the office, space matters. In the factory, time-and-motion studies may help create faster workflow. Materials-handling studies do the same in warehouse settings. Job shops have their unique utilization rates. Efficient solutions can be assessed for each unique factory, warehouse, or job shop.

But every growing company has an office. How you use that office space will assist or hinder your growth.

Retailers judge their performance on revenue per square foot; factories measure their success in output per square foot. Yet most companies fail to measure the productivity of their office. To most, it's simply overhead, fitting the most people in the least amount of space regardless of the tasks performed by each.

## SPACE—THE FINAL FRONTIER

*Space is no longer simply a cost to be managed.*

*Rather, workspace is an asset that can be leveraged to help a company grow exponentially.*

## TYPICAL OFFICE ENVIRONMENT

- *Offices on outside walls*
- *Cubicles in the "bullpen"*
- *Little informal interaction*
- *Infrequent interdepartmental meetings*
- *Stuffy conference rooms*

If your office is like most, space is allocated and equipped based upon status, not the type of work performed. The guy with the corner office and the big windows must be the boss. Informal interaction among employees is limited to the water cooler. Otherwise, folks sit at their desks all day and rarely leave their departments. Formal meetings are held in someone's private office or a stuffy conference room. It's tiresome, unproductive, and inefficient.

Office workplace design is gaining favor among operations gurus as a means for creating efficiencies and maximizing output. As you grow, your workplace needs to grow with you. How your employees interact, the way they work, and the tasks they perform—highly collaborative work or individual efforts requiring strict concentration—play an important role in the design of your workplace.

The following diagram shows the different levels of collaboration and various configurations best suited to maximize your workplace performance.

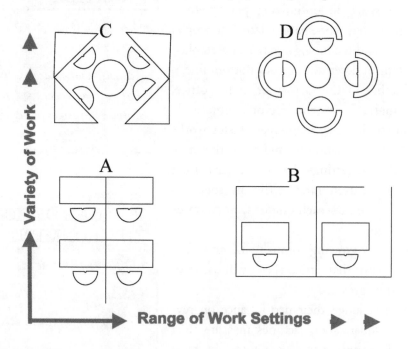

Your office personnel perform a wide variety of tasks. Some people do the same thing all day. Some work individually at times but may also collaborate with others in small groups. Some may meet with a variety of people throughout the day. The point is, one size does not fit all.

**Case Study**

# FORRER BUSINESS INTERIORS

## THE PROBLEM

FORRER Business Interiors was determined to use its new offices as a show-place for workplace design.

In addition to utilizing the most efficient workspace design techniques, FORRER wanted to express their company's personality as soon as guests stepped through the doors.

If the variety of work performed is minimal and the range of work settings is low—for instance claims processing or bookkeeping—work setting A would be most appropriate. These people work with computers and do repetitive tasks. Give them ergonomic support to minimize health and safety risks.

Consultants, architects, and the creative people in advertising agencies or design services firms perform a variety of tasks. They conduct research, share ideas, and talk on the telephone. Configuration B works well for creative types. They need privacy, personal computer support, and access to small meeting rooms.

Collaborative tasks, like sharing ideas, maintaining constant feedback, and heavy telephone and computer usage, are best suited to work setting C. Customer service representatives, telemarketers, and in-house salespeople should use this configuration. Give them handy storage space for reference materials and documentation.

## DECORATE TO INSPIRE

*A few decorative pieces in keeping with the nature of your business can help inspire teamwork, or serve as a reminder of why you're in business.*

*An acquaintance whose firm manufactures avionics has the propeller from the vintage P-40 in which he was shot down over Holland during World War II. (It was discovered by Dutch excavation workers several decades after the war and returned to him.)*

*It hangs in the reception area of his plant and serves as both an inspiration and a conversation piece.*

## USE THE FIVE SENSES AT YOUR WORKPLACE

### Sight

*Does your office look like good clean fun? Adequate lighting is a minimum. Small, dark rooms inhibit performance and feel claustrophobic. Clean up. Remove the clutter. It makes you look disorganized and may make your people disorganized, too.*

### Sound

*Music playing in the workplace can be soothing and help employees perform better. It can also mask conversations, so workers in open offices or cubicles maintain a level of privacy.*

### Touch

*Displays, counters, and plants all play a role in creating a comfortable, "touchable" workplace.*

### Smell

*Aroma is receiving increasing attention among interior designers. Your real estate agent recommends you bake bread before showing your house. This same principle works in your office, too. Even the smell of fresh-brewed coffee can create a sense of warmth and hospitality.*

### Taste

*A good cup of coffee can brighten an early-morning meeting.*

Teams and task-force leaders, like project managers and research and development groups, function best in configuration D. This allows team members to interact frequently, but they can also switch easily to individual tasks requiring concentration, or work separately using portable computers. Give them marker boards and easels for impromptu presentations.

Your office layout is an area typically overlooked when you begin to experience dramatic growth. Yet it is key to using technology effectively, implementing new business initiatives, and contributing to employee satisfaction. In short, space matters. Your workplace can either impede or contribute to your growth. Your workspace must facilitate the work performed there.

The goal is simple: Make sure your office space is adequate to absorb the growth your marketing plan will feed it.

## THE HOLISTIC WORKPLACE

Ever think about your company as an environment? Part of a holistic world in which your employees spend a third of their lives?

Imagine your employees as a component of the environment in which they work. How they interact with their workspace, and how it interacts with them, can play a big part in increasing efficiency, effectiveness, and employee morale.

Workers are happier if they like their workspace. An attractive work environment makes it easier to attract good people. Once hired, they perform better, they treat their coworkers better, and they like their jobs better.

It isn't feng shui, but it is a growing trend in commercial interior design—"sensory" or "holistic" layout. It takes stock of the five senses—sight, hearing, touch, taste, and smell—and making sure they all work together to create a comfortable workspace.

## Case Study   FORRER BUSINESS INTERIORS

### THE SOLUTION

FORRER decided to use the entire office area as an interactive brochure. At the front door, Jane Devine, director of design, used seven different carpets in the company's new reception area.

The design immediately offers traffic-flow options, and the varying textures create a sense of warmth and welcome for new arrivals.

Traffic is led through the various work areas, from design to sales and accounting, ending at the president's office in the center of the building (no isolated window office here).

www.forrersbi.com

Lighting, color, and music of a certain tempo can create an atmosphere that encourages employees to linger, or to leave. Fast-food restaurants, for instance, want customers to buy, eat, and leave quickly to make room for more customers. But a bookstore or clothing store may want customers to relax and explore at a more leisurely pace.

### Sight

Colors should be bright and cheery, but not too busy. Try using colors in a color scheme. Browns and olive greens, for example, with an accent of dark red for contrast, can create a sense of excitement. Blues and deep greens create a sense of calm and tranquility.

### Sound

Whether yours is a retail establishment, manufacturing facility, or office space, sound, or the lack of it, can greatly affect the mood, pace, concentration, and overall perception of your workplace.

Annoying sounds—stark echoes, noise from the service department, a radio blaring from someone's office, or two coworkers trading recipes—can be an irritant. Some folks may mentally block out the noise, but it can still slow their productivity and add to stress.

Workspace that is deadly quiet can also be unsettling. Every little noise then becomes conspicuous, magnified, even disturbing.

Music playing quietly in the background is the easiest, and often the best solution. Background music should be just that, music that remains in the background. Stay away from unusual music styles. No rap or hard rock n' roll. Smooth jazz or classical music often work best.

### Touch

Tactile images give a sense of warmth and security to your work environment. Plants, sculpture, or tapestries used smartly can be combined with other design elements to create a mood, delineate work areas, or separate workstations. Many retailers use tactile surfaces and décor effectively. A local shoe store emphasizing outdoor boots and hiking equipment used a working waterfall, the sound of crickets chirping, and pine scent in the air to create an ambience consistent with the sale items.

### Smell

Olfactory senses can create a mood, a sense of "home" in your workplace. Vanilla creates a sense of calm among the chaos of a busy office. Fresh-brewed coffee is always a welcome odor.

### Taste

You might think the sense of taste would be difficult to apply in the workplace, unless you operate a restaurant or bakery. But it can be featured even in environments that do not serve food. For instance, every training session at SBC Communications features some form of food, candy, gum, and beverage. Leo Burnett Company has a bowl of apples on every reception desk in every one of their offices throughout the world. Breaking bread together creates a bond between coworkers. It's why so many deals are done over breakfast or lunch.

Using this holistic approach in your workplace can make your employees more productive, too. It can improve their sense of camaraderie. Happy employees are more likely to stick with you longer, and they are more likely to make your customers happy, too.

In any rapidly growing organization, quality must remain the primary focus. Too often, management is so intent upon growth it neglects its core competencies, the qualities that made it successful in the first place.

> *Top-level managers are responsible for 85 percent of quality problems and workers for 15 percent.*
>
> —W. Edwards Deming, leading guru of quality management

## QUALITY COUNTS

Everybody wants high quality. The executive who seeks low quality has yet to be found.

But quality means different things to different people. Is it how the product looks? How well it performs? Whether it performs a variety of functions? Or how long it lasts? All are subjective issues.

Quality, like beauty, is in the eye of the beholder—or rather, the customer. Mercedes and Rolls Royce are not the only quality-built automobiles. The lowly Ford Escort is a quality product if it meets Ford Motor Company specifications, one of which may be "low price."

Quality then might be defined simply as whether or not the product or service conforms to specifications. But not every product is "quality" if it conforms to specifications. Not if the specifications are lousy to begin with. Quality, then, can be defined as delivering products and services according to specifications that conform to customer needs and wants.

Making quality happen in your organization means making products or delivering services according to specifications, and making those specifications conform to the wants and needs of the customer. This removes subjectivity and provides a quantifiable means of measuring quality.

### THE THREE COSTS OF QUALITY

1. **Failure Costs:** *the cost of product failure, unhappy or lost customers.*

2. **Detection Costs:** *the cost of inspection, to detect failure before delivery.*

3. **Prevention Costs:** *the cost of preventing failure in the first place.*

It also means you can apply a cost to it.

The cost of quality is really the cost of doing things wrong. It is the cost of not conforming to specifications and therefore disappointing your customer. This cost can be broken down into three parts.

**Failure Costs** include external failure costs (after the product is delivered) like customer complaints and returns, field service and repair, product liability (insurance and settlements), guarantee, and warranty costs. And internal failure costs (before the product is delivered) like downtime due to defects, engineer and purchase change orders, redesign, retest, rework, or reject.

**Detection costs** are your efforts to stop defects before they lead to failure. They include capability tests, prototype inspection, supplier surveillance, receiving inspection, work-in-process testing, and finished goods inspection.

**Prevention costs** are the costs of stopping defects before they start. They include design reviews, engineering drawing checks, specification reviews, preventive maintenance, quality audits, supplier evaluations and rewards, tool and machine controls, and worker training.

Add them all up and you find "quality" costs a bundle, perhaps as much as 20 percent of the cost of sales. To avoid most of these costs, you must produce the product or deliver the service right the first time, and every time.

W. Edwards Deming, a leading quality-control expert, insisted that quality should be built in from the worker level up. Working in Japan after World War II—

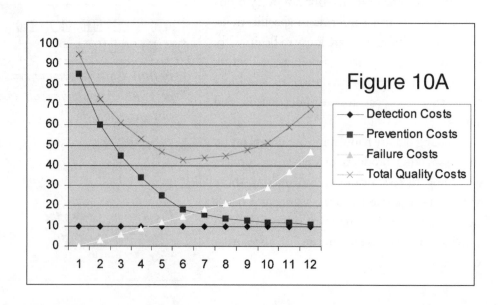

Figure 10A

Detection Costs
Prevention Costs
Failure Costs
Total Quality Costs

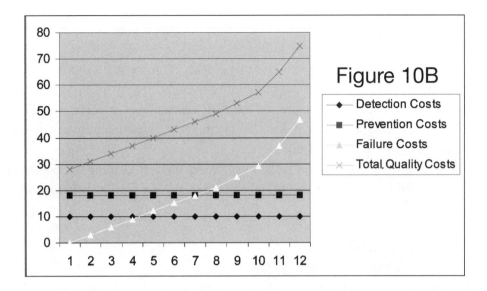

Figure 10B

- ◆ Detection Costs
- ■ Prevention Costs
- ▲ Failure Costs
- ✕ Total Quality Costs

many claim the Japanese auto industry quality improvements in the 1960s and 1970s are directly attributable to Deming—Deming proved that quality should be implemented at each worker's station, rather than something dictated by management. Everyone in the organization must be convinced that things have to be done right the first time, every time.

The biggest step towards better quality comes when everyone agrees that perfection is not just the goal. It must be the standard.

A zero-defect standard says that everyone is expected to produce with zero defects. Either that, or you should change the procedure until zero defects is the result. Ultimately, this leads to a shift in quality costs. Typically, **failure costs** shrink while **prevention costs** rise. But overall costs decline.

Workers are no longer simply executing the designs of engineers. Rather, engineering must be a resource for solving any quality problems, problems that are, for the most part, first known by the workers. To truly create a no-defects environment, engineering (and management) must serve the worker, not the other way around.

When determining the cost or acceptable level of quality, the debate rages in academic circles. Some theorize that **prevention costs** increase dramatically as an organization gets closer and closer to zero defects. They reason that those last few defects are harder to find and harder still to correct. A sense of diminishing returns sets in as more and more errors are found and corrected.

Therefore, some optimum level of defective products is seen as acceptable (see Figure 10A).

Another school of thought states that it takes no more money to detect and remove the last error than it does to remove the first. It may take more time to determine what these last errors are, but their correction is no more complicated or costly than any other defect. Under this scenario, the optimum level of defects is zero. (see Figure 10B).

Whoever is correct in this debate, one thing is clear: Deming has taught us that the optimal level of defect is far lower than anyone previously imagined.

## SIX SIGMA

Today's competitive environment leaves little room for error. One effective way to limit errors is through the use of a quality control system known as Six Sigma.

Quality has become a commodity. It is expected. It's a given. Your quality must meet your customers' expectations or even exceed their expectations. That is why Six Sigma Quality has become a part of our business culture.

Six Sigma (driving towards six standard deviations between the mean and the nearest specification limit) is a highly disciplined process that helps focus on eliminating defects in any process—from manufacturing to retail, whether a product or a service.

The central idea behind Six Sigma is that if you can measure how many "defects" you have in a process, you can systematically figure out how to eliminate them and get close to zero defects (defined in Six Sigma as 3.4 defects per million).

Motorola first began Six Sigma Quality training in the 1980s. Since that time, the company claims the defect-reduction process has saved more than $16 billion (that's billion) over a fifteen-year period. General Electric, one of the most successful companies implementing Six Sigma, has estimated benefits on the order of $10 billion during its first five years.

### Why "Sigma"?

$$\sum \text{ or } \sigma$$

The word is a statistical term that measures how far a given process deviates from perfection.

There are two Six Sigma sub-methodologies:

1. DMAIC (define, measure, analyze, improve, control)
2. DMADV(define, measure, analyze, design, verify)

Use DMAIC to improve *existing* products or processes. The latter, DMADV, helps you to develop *new* products or processes at Six Sigma quality levels.

Six Sigma consultants, known in the trade as Green Belts, Black Belts, and Master Black Belts, can help you execute the Six Sigma process. Even if you're not a Motorola or a GE, your savings could be significant. According to the Six Sigma Academy, Black Belts save companies approximately $230,000 per project and can complete four to six projects per year.

Six Sigma is not just for large companies, either. Small companies can streamline their processes and obtain substantial savings with Six Sigma initiatives. Key to success for small companies, according to the Six Sigma website (www.isixsigma.com), is:

• Commitment from management
• Employee training
• Time commitment from those employees to be trained
• Link to compensation

Smaller companies usually have an easier time gaining managers' commitment, but may find training more expensive per person. Also, participating employees may be asked to spend up to 100 percent of their time on Six Sigma

## Case Study    WILSON PRINTING

### THE PROBLEM

Printing quality brochures, annual reports, and promotional pieces is a complicated process.

Inevitably, some equipment will break down, often slowing schedules and delaying delivery of customers' projects.

Sam Fecundis, print shop manager, is a veteran of printing press malfunctions. Despite his title, he found himself spending more and more time fixing bottlenecks and repairing equipment rather than managing the shop.

efforts. Keep in mind, however, that any time spent on process improvement will be recouped in process productivity as you grow.

For more on Six Sigma, or to find out how your organization can benefit, there are any number of training organizations that advertise on the World Wide Web.

# BREAKING BOTTLENECKS

Every company's got 'em. They can strangle your growth, wring the enthusiasm from your employees, and cause you stress, anxiety, and fear.

Stationary bottlenecks are easiest to cope with. Something has broken the process of production—a machine is down, a key employee is absent, parts are missing, or demand has outstripped the capacity to produce. Work-in-process inventory backs up against the bottleneck. Stationary bottlenecks often occur in service operations, causing customer wait times.

> ## TWO TYPES OF BOTTLENECKS
> ......................................
> *Episodic bottlenecks are the fires you have to put out.*
>
> *Chronic bottlenecks require long-term planning or design modification.*

More difficult to deal with are those sneaky, shifting bottlenecks that have no clear cause. Frustrating because inventories build up for no apparent reason in different places and at different times. Maybe a new worker can't keep pace with the production line. Or a part is missing, or defective.

These more subtle bottlenecks are episodic rather than chronic, that is, they are intermittent, always different, cropping up when you least expect. And usually at the most inopportune time.

If they recur frequently, episodic bottlenecks can become chronic problems. They then require serious consideration, a design change, or long-term planning to correct.

**Episodic bottlenecks** fall into three categories:

1. Machine Breakdown
2. Material Shortage
3. Labor Shortage

A machine breaks down and you have lots of frantic people scurrying about to fix it, or reroute the work it was doing. One solution is a good program of preventative maintenance. But planned downtime, while easier to cope with, may exceed the breakdown time of the machine. Assigning the factory's best maintenance tradespeople—a fix-it guy to firefight such problems—is gaining favor among many companies.

A broken machine may be the biggest fire you fight, but material shortages are the most common. Sometimes it is a vendor problem; other times it is another department in your company. Just-In-Time (JIT) procedures or EOQ formulas (for Economic Ordering Quantity) can take into account demand, ordering costs, carrying costs, etc. to minimize shortages and costs. EOQ models vary by industry, company, and individual circumstances too numerous for detailed discussion here. But a qualified consultant can be of value in adapting JIT or EOQ to your situation.

Unexpected absences, vacations, under-trained workers, and other labor shortages can cause bottlenecks in production. These can quickly evolve into a

**Process Flow Diagram for an Apparel Company**

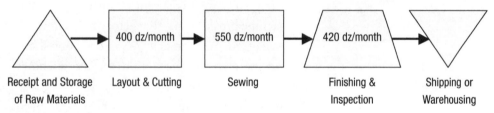

| Receipt and Storage of Raw Materials | Layout & Cutting 400 dz/month | Sewing 550 dz/month | Finishing & Inspection 420 dz/month | Shipping or Warehousing |

## Case Study   WILSON PRINTING

### THE SOLUTION

Service is paramount at Wilson Printing. Delays in the production schedule caused by machine breakdowns began to hurt the company's reputation for on-time deliveries. Owner, Dale Wilson, needed to make a change.

After careful consideration, Sam Fecundis, formerly the shop manager, was reassigned the position of Mr. Fix-It.

While many employees still rely upon Sam for his expertise in matters of printing and binding, a majority of his time is spent fighting machine breakdowns and maintaining equipment.

www.wilprint.com

## WAITING LINES

*At Disney resorts, waiting lines are long, but they don't seem long. Diversions and speed are the key.*

*While lines may snake over a hundred yards or more, people keep moving rather quickly.*

*Wait times are posted at intermittent locations ("15 minutes to the Magic Mountain") and diversions dot the path (e.g., a graveyard with humorous grave markers entertain those waiting to see the Haunted House).*

chronic problem in any growing company. To solve it, keep a constant flow of new hires coming in the door, train them well, and promise them promotion opportunities as your company grows.

The bottleneck at this apparel factory is the Layout & Cutting operation. Cutters are skilled laborers and are difficult to hire and train. It is a chronic bottleneck that can be solved in the long term with an apprentice cutter program. The secondary bottleneck, Finishing & Inspection, uses unskilled labor and can be resolved quickly.

Other bottlenecks occur when a specialized sewing machine breaks down or a skilled worker (e.g., a cutter) is absent or on vacation. For machine breakdowns, the factory may employ a specialized maintenance man to troubleshoot stubborn machines, or a preventative maintenance program to service machines when they are not in use. Skilled workers' vacations are scheduled during off-peak times. Absences due to illness or other reasons are the greatest unresolved bottleneck in this factory.

**Chronic bottlenecks** typically are either materials problems or process problems.

Materials problems, like not enough or the wrong stuff, suggests a problem in purchasing. It could be the vendor, but it could also be poor forecasting, incorrect purchase orders, or a host of other problems. Using an EOQ formula or JIT techniques, you may solve this problem quickly.

A product mix that changes constantly can also cause material shortages. Even if your vendors and your purchasing department are in perfect sync, the rapidly changing mix can place irregular demands on individual departments. Your factory has the capacity, but specific departments are overworked. The bottleneck may be a single department that needs upgrading.

Process problems include insufficient capacity, quality problems, or poor plant layout. Capacity is discussed earlier in this chapter, as is quality. Poor layout, convoluted routing, or overcrowding can drain a plant's productivity. Plant layout is a highly specialized process unique to the character of each individual situation. A plant layout specialist in your industry may be the solution.

# SERVICE BOTTLENECKS

Process flow diagrams can be particularly useful in a service organization setting. Analyzing the time required at each service point can identify bottlenecks and alleviate waiting times.

For service firms, typically a capacity "range" may be necessary. Who knows whether a customer requires twenty minutes or twenty-four minutes for a haircut? The bald guy may take only five. Nevertheless, process flow diagrams can be invaluable tools in delivering services in a timely manner. Seemingly minor adjustments can often yield significant improvement.

Waiting lines are one of the most studied problems in operations management, and one of the most hated problems of consumers. How often have you kicked yourself for getting in the wrong line at the ticket counter or supermarket?

Waiting line problems are dependent upon a variety of factors, from arrival process (singly or in groups), to queue discipline (first come, first served or random), and serving process (constant or variable, multiple lines, etc.). The possibilities are numerous and complicated.

The goal: simplify the problem so that it can be grasped easily and bottlenecks remedied quickly. If the problem is still too complex to tackle, computer simulation models are available. They rely upon mathematical distribution theory, the probability that some event (e.g., phone calls, people entering a line) occurs in a given time period.

Waiting time is a function of your ability to match capacity with need. Excess capacity means you have employees sitting around with no one to serve. A shortage of capacity means long waiting lines and customer frustration (perhaps even lost sales).

Not only is having some spare capacity crucial to avoiding lengthy waiting lines, but when possible, equipment, supplies, or products should be prepared in advance. Also, your capacity must be available when needed. No sense having extra workers at noon when five o'clock is your busy time. Labor must be scheduled to match peaks in demand.

For customers, the length of time waiting in line is crucial to overall satisfaction. But in many service industries, waiting lines are inevitable. What to do?

Make the line *seem* shorter.

Use diversions—entertainment, reading material, background music, anything to keep the customer's mind occupied during long wait times. Lines can be made to appear shorter by creating multiple channels, even though they may all land at the same place. Careful supervision of line length—knowing when to open another checkout station for instance—can go a long way toward keeping the customers satisfied.

Bottlenecks can occur due to supplier problems, too. Understanding purchasing habits and streamlining buying procedures can eliminate many bottlenecks in your production process.

# PURCHASING

Purchasing has a direct and powerful effect on your company's bottom line.

Your role in this strategic function is a complex one. You have to orchestrate a dynamic chain of events from bid solicitation to final delivery and set-up, and satisfy the needs of your company without breaking the bank.

Your natural tendency is to ask for the lowest price.

Don't.

Price is only the most obvious solution, the first of three elements of cost. The principle of **total cost ownership (TCO)** takes into account all three elements of cost: quality, service, and price (Q, S, &P).

Inferior quality can generate production problems and customer complaints. Poor service results in slow response time, missed orders, and inadequate support.

When buying from your suppliers, make them prove (and periodically reevaluate) how their wares consistently yield the lowest TCO, especially in the cost elements most important to you.

Once you have identified your high TCO suppliers, either abandon them or work with them to reduce the TCO. Purging high-TCO suppliers saves you money.

## TOTAL COST OF OWNERSHIP
••••••••••••••••••••••••••••

*Machine A costs $1,000. It has a life expectancy of two years.*

*Machine B costs $1,600, but has a life expectancy of four years.*

*Machine B is 60 percent more expensive, but in terms of TCO, Machine B is the better value. It costs $400 per year, while machine A costs $500 per year.*

Reward your low-TCO suppliers by increasing your spending with them. Doing so increases their profitability because their fixed costs are spread over a larger base, and their marketing and sales expenses are reduced. This allows you to ask for more preferential treatment, a better price, for example, which leads to even lower total costs.

> ## USE TCO TO SELL TO YOUR CUSTOMERS
> ...........................
> *Identify which element is most important and focus on the **total cost of ownership**.*
>
> *For medical supplies, it's quality. For software, it's service. For manufacturing customers, it's on-time delivery.*

# Total Cost of Ownership

| | | | Supplier A | | B | | C |
|---|---|---|---|---|---|---|---|
| 3 | **Quality** | Rejection Rate | 2% | 1 | 7% | 2 | 12% |
| 3 | **Service** | On-Time Delivery | 90% | 1 | 80% | 2 | 75% |
| 1 | **Price** | Price | $24.00 | 3 | $22.00 | 2 | $19.50 |
| 7 | **Total Cost Rank** | | | 5 | | 6 | |

This is a simplified chart illustrating how to use TCO. Suppliers are ranked against one another using 1 for lowest, 3 for highest. All Q, S, & P elements are assumed to have equal weighting.

Good suppliers work with customers to reduce high-cost elements and shrink TCO, not argue over price.

# NEGOTIATING

Ever feel like you paid too much, got a raw deal, or were roped into a bargain that didn't turn out to be a bargain? Ever put off negotiating a new contract simply because you feared the give and take, the compromising and debating necessary to strike a fair deal?

Negotiating need not be intimidating or avoided. Follow these few simple steps and the process becomes more gratifying, less stressful, and win-win for both parties.

**Do your homework.** Good negotiating is very much like good marketing. First, do a little research. Understand the other party's needs and wants, what he or she might be willing to give up, and when he will dig in his heels.

> ### NEGOTIATING TIP #1
> ....................................
> *Everything costs something in a negotiation.*
>
> *Don't give up something without getting something in return.*

Compare this list with your needs and wants. What are you willing to give up, and when do you need to dig in?

You may have a particular need the other party is unwilling to relinquish. Be creative. There may be ways to accomplish the same goal by negotiating a different point. Concede in other areas in little steps and divide your goal into small steps the other party is willing to concede. Which brings me to the next step:

**Be willing to compromise.** Start by getting to know the other party. Exchange small talk and listen to the other party's, or parties' personal information. It may help to understand motivations later in the negotiating process. Also, it will be much easier to receive a concession if the other party likes you.

Expect to adapt to change during your meeting. Recognize that in compromise, no one receives everything he or she wants. Instead of dwelling on each concession you make, appreciate your gains. Assess their economic and legal impact, and applaud your accomplishments.

> ### NEGOTIATING TIP #2
> ....................................
> *Don't sweat the small stuff.*
>
> *Too frequently, negotiations get mired in minutia. Don't lose sight of the big goals in order to gain some small point.*

Likewise, it is best not to make any firm commitments until the final agreement is reached. That is, recognize that *everything* remains "on the table" until *nothing* remains "on the table." When the negotiation is complete, you put it in writing and both parties sign. Until then, the other party may balk, may want to make changes, or may back out of negotiations completely, which leads to the next step:

**Be patient.** Negotiating is a process. If you have a deadline, it will work against you. The other party may make an effort to delay the process, knowing you will concede an issue simply to reach a conclusion. For instance, they could delay giving you a draft of the agreement (and throw in a few "minor" changes) simply as a negotiating ploy. The one who is more willing to wait it out, often has the advantage.

A few more negotiating tips:

- Avoid meeting in the other party's office where a telephone or intercom may be turned on without your knowledge. This allows a third party to eavesdrop, which could be to your detriment.
- Watch out for the good guy/bad guy strategy, where the bad guy rants and raves and fusses over some crucial point, finally stalking from the room. Then, the good guy turns to you and offers you the same deal in a less threatening tone.
- Don't bluff unless you can't get caught. If you're called on it early in the negotiations, your credibility is damaged for the remainder of the process.
- Call the other party's bluff. If they threaten to go to a competitor, it may be best to let them.

If planning is the "eyes" of your organization, operations is the "feet," the execution of the vision proscribed by your plan. To grow exponentially, you must manage capacity, avoid bottlenecks, and maintain the smooth flow of supplies to your organization.

> ## NEGOTIATING TIP #3
> ..............................
> *Know when the negotiation is over.*
>
> *When your goals are met, stop the negotiation before the other party decides to argue for any more details.*

> ## DECOY STRATEGY
> ..............................
> *Sometimes, the other party will inflate the importance of a minor issue to mask the importance of a larger issue or a hidden agenda.*
>
> *If the other side is willing to concede what they would have you believe is a major issue, but what is actually just a minor one, they will then expect you to concede on one of your truly important issues.*
>
> *Do your homework. Know their "hot" issues and which are less important. Understand the industry value of various issues to recognize "decoys."*

# CHAPTER 11

# Cash Is King

Purpose: *The purpose of chapter 11 is to help you make financial decisions for your rapidly growing company. Included is a comparison of different business entities, basic principles of debt and equity financing, and proven techniques for cash management.*

————◇————

**A**sk any accountant, bookkeeper, or banker. They will all tell you that money is the lifeblood of industry. Cash flows through the system and the more that flows through your company, the healthier your business.

Operations people may argue the point as will marketing people (see chapter 1). But cash management is critical to any small business, especially as that small business grows into a bigger business.

To run a small business successfully, you must run it like successful businesses are run. You must do the things that successful businesses do.

They keep track of inventory costs, accounts receivable, and accounts payable. From order to cash, and from purchase to pay. The money coming in and the money going out. The whole ball of wax.

The first step is to keep accurate records using the three basic financial reporting formats:

1. Balance Sheet
2. Income Statement
3. Statement of Cash Flow

These three form the financial picture of your company. They are necessary to borrow capital, get credit, pay taxes, and to know whether or not you made a profit. Just as a picture is worth a thousand words, these three tell you how you're doing.

## DYNAMIC GROWTH

You have embarked upon a strategy of growth that will require cash to implement. By executing the 5 Kick-Ass Strategies, your business may likely grow faster than your financial condition can support.

You may need new facilities, new personnel, employee training, more inventory, more accounts receivable, advertising costs, and myriad other expenses. All these require cash.

> *"If you would know the value of money, go and try to borrow some."*
>
> —Benjamin Franklin

Take a look at the "Fast 50" growth companies in your state (usually sponsored by one of the big accounting firms and published by one of your region's major business publications). All embarked on rapid growth plans. Their sales are up, visibility up, stock price up, everything up, up, up. Yet few are profitable. Why? Because they are cash starved.

Fear not.

The need for cash can be resolved by relinquishing some equity. In a sense, you trade some control of your company for increased wealth. Just as it takes money to make money, selling off equity allows you to expand and increase your wealth exponentially.

How?

You already have a proven cash machine, your business. You have made it successful over the years. Now, you simply want to expand on the skills, experience, and ideas that got you this far. You just need cash to do it.

You can raise that money one of two ways. You can borrow it (**debt financing**) or you can give up some ownership and take on a partner or partners (**equity financing**). Simply put, debt has to be paid back from the profits of the company. Equity doesn't.

# EQUITY FINANCING

Equity is an ownership interest in a company. If you own stock in Microsoft, either common stock or preferred stock, you have an equity interest. You own a piece of Microsoft. Granted, it's a small piece. You're one of thousands of partners who own an **equity interest** in Microsoft.

If you aren't already, get incorporated. A corporation can sell stock for cash. No repayment schedule is required. No interest, either.

If the entire amount is lost, your stockholders are out everything. Naturally, your investors hope to build their investment through a rise in the stock price. As you grow, you should even pay a dividend. But by sharing your equity, you share your risk.

Raise money in stages. A start-up company has to give away a substantial portion of equity for seemingly very little money because of the higher risk involved. But as you expand, you can ask a higher price for equity. The success of your company justifies a higher share price. You end up selling off less equity if you sell it in stages than if you sell it all at once.

When you sell equity in your company, the buyer pays money or barters goods in exchange for ownership, usually in the form of stock. To divide the ownership of your company, you need to form some sort of ownership structure.

There are various methods of structuring the sale of equity. Here is a brief description of each, but you should consult with an attorney to structure your business.

## DYNAMIC GROWTH AT AMAZON.COM

*It took Amazon.com almost ten years before it had its first full year of profit.*

*The Internet retailer launched its website in 1995 and went public in 1997, despite never having shown a profit.*

*Today early stockholders, having weathered the dot-com boom and bust, Borders and Barnes & Noble competition, and several stock splits, are worth millions.*

## C Corporation

Think General Motors. All profits are taxed annually, at a rate of as much as 48 percent. There are no long-term capital gains tax benefits. That is, if your company realizes a long-term capital gain, it is taxed the same as income. Stockholders may receive wages, taxed as personal income, or dividends, taxed at a maximum rate of 15 percent. Legally, all stockholders are protected personally against civil suits to the company. Board members may be subject to suit from stockholders.

## S Corporation

The S corporation pays no income tax. Rather, the annual income is passed through the corporation directly to stockholders. Profit distributions are taxed as wages or as dividends, but the first distribution is usually taxed to the individual as wages. As with the C corporation, stockholders are protected personally against civil suit.

## WHEN YOU SHOULD NOT GIVE UP 51 PERCENT

• *You retain ultimate control over key strategic decisions of the company.*

• *You can take a longer-term perspective on key corporate decisions.*

• *A majority of the benefits accrue to you.*

*(Despite having the voting control of the company, majority shareholders still have significant fiduciary obligations to minority shareholders)*

## Limited Liability Corporation (LLC)

As in the S corporation, the LLC must file a tax return but pays no income tax. The net income or loss passes through to the equity holders. Most LLCs have a managing partner. The LLC can convert to a corporation through a Section 351 tax-free exchange should the needs of the entity warrant. There is no maximum number of shares, though most LLCs define a maximum number of membership units when seeking funding. LLCs enjoy similar protection to that of the S corporation.

## Limited Liability Partnership (LLP) or Limited Partnership (LP)

Partners are typically passive investors dependent upon the efforts of the general partner. The LLP and LP are perfect when you are looking for a handful of well-heeled investors for a limited-term project, like a real estate development project for example. Net income or loss is split between partners equally, with a disproportionate share to the general partner.

## Service Corporation (SC)

A group of licensed professionals (lawyers, accountants, architects) who band together and issue stock similar to either the S corporation (income pass-through) or C corporation (income taxed).

The best advice when deciding to give up some equity in your company is to seek the counsel of your attorney and your accountant. They will best be able to advise you on the benefits, and drawbacks, of each entity.

# RAISE MONEY IN STAGES

Most equity is raised in stages. The younger your organization, the greater the risk involved and the more equity you are liable to have to relinquish. The more stages, the more equity you can retain, because, as your company grows, its value grows, and the value of its stock grows, too.

Investment stages include:

**1. Angel Investment**

(Highest risk—usually seed money for start-ups, new products, or inventions)

**2. Venture Capital**

(High risk—usually for companies with limited track record of success, sometimes called second-round investment)

**3. Mezzanine Financing**

(Limited risk—usually bridge financing to fix a problem or divest an unprofitable unit before taking the company public)

**4. Hybrid Funding**

(Limited risk—a combination of debt and

### WHEN YOU SHOULD GIVE UP 51 PERCENT

- *You need additional capital for growth.*

- *You cannot generate sufficient capital internally or obtain it from other sources.*

- *You want to diversify your risk.*

- *You need to finance a redemption or buyout of a significant block of ownership without over leveraging the company.*

- *You know your equity partner well and have compatible strategic and investment interests.*

- *To attract management talent or a successor who requires stock ownership.*

## STAGES OF EQUITY CAPITAL

*Stages of investment are associated with the level of risk:*

**Seed Money** *(for start-ups, highest risk)*

**Second Round** *(for growing companies with track record of success)*

**Mezzanine Level** *(short-term funding in preparation for an initial public offering)*

**Hybrid Funding** *(debt funding with an equity "kicker")*

**Initial Public Offering** *(least risk but riskier than conventional lending)*

## WHERE TO FIND ANGEL INVESTORS

*Indiana Angel Net, Ohio Tech Angel Fund, and Central New York Angels are typical groups. Most have websites. A few have full-time staffs.*

equity funding usually provided by investment bankers who are willing to lend but want a "kicker" if your company really takes off)

## Angel Investment

Unpredictable, often undisciplined, and just plain hard to find, angel investors are well-heeled individuals (or groups) who like to take a gamble on emerging companies. They tend to invest locally, in industries they understand, and usually conduct limited due diligence on your company.

A trade group of about 200 angel groups, Angel Capital Association (www.angelcapital association.org), helps raise awareness of angel investing.

Typically, they are wealthy folks who use their own money to help fund start-up companies at a very early stage—after you have already hit up all your friends and family members, but before you move on to a venture capitalist. A typical angel investment might be a few hundred thousand dollars, or a tenth of the amount that might be put in later by VCs, who have money from pension funds and the like to work with.

Angel investors frequently form clubs that meet in various cities, either monthly or quarterly, to hear a half-hour pitch from entrepreneurs, inventors, and others who need seed capital to create their business dream. If any of the angels are interested, they meet later, separately, with you to discuss your idea or review your business plan.

Many angel investors pool their funds and decide upon investments as a group. This reduces their risk considerably. If ten angels pool funds and invest in ten companies, only one or two have to be winners for the group to earn a healthy return.

## Venture Capital

If yours is an unusual, potentially high-risk opportunity, and conventional financial institutions are unwilling or unable to bear that risk, you may wish to consider **venture capital** as a source of financing for your business.

Many firms or individuals call themselves venture capitalists but may in fact be brokers looking to present deals to investors or companies that invest. A true **venture capital** fund is managed by an individual who looks to invest in particular types of businesses.

In order to strike a deal, you and your partners will be put through a rigorous due diligence process. If you pass muster, you will be offered an agreement that requires you to sign away your life and that of your unborn children, or so it will seem. This agreement may be negotiable up to a point, but don't expect them to be too flexible.

Venture capital money is difficult to find and very expensive, meaning you should expect to relinquish a substantial portion, perhaps more than 50 percent, of your company. A venture fund will invest in many companies, most of which do not do nearly as well as the original owners expect. The few winners must pay for the rest. So if one hits, they want a big payoff, typically five to ten times their investment.

## TYPES OF ANGEL INVESTORS

### Classic Investor
*A successful entrepreneur who wants to invest in other entrepreneurial ventures. The largest and most active group of angel investors.*

### Retirement Investor
*A senior manager at a large company who may be looking to maintain a foothold in his or her former industry. Often uses pension or retirement fund to invest.*

### Professional
*Doctors, lawyers, and accountants who often invest in their particular field, or a related field. A group of doctors, for instance, may decide to back a new film documentary on the AIDS epidemic, or cleft palate problems in third-world countries.*

### Manager Investor
*Let go in a corporate downsizing, a manager buys back his old job in the hope of contributing professionally. If your company is short on industry know-how, this could be a good fit.*

### Company Investor
*Some companies seek out entrepreneurs to provide ancillary products and services for their equipment. For example, Apple may be willing to provide you with seed money if you are designing application software for use on their computers.*

---

## WHERE TO FIND VENTURE CAPITAL

· · · · · · · · · · · · · · · · · · · · · · · · · · ·

*Pratt's Guide to Venture Capital Sources* by Edwards and Angell

*Dictionary of Venture Capital* by Lister and Harnish

*Venture Capital Resource Directory*, a service of vFinance, Inc. www.vfinance.com/ent/ent_3. asp?ToolPage=vencaentire.asp

*National Venture Capital Association (NVCA)*

*Note: Know what kind of companies a fund invests in before submitting your business plan.*

---

Here are the top four factors both Angel Investors and Venture Capital firms seek:

1. **Good management**—the most important factor. Your experience and industry connections are critical

2. **Commitment**—one that demonstrates your sharing of the risks, one that indicates a strong motivation and an intense focus on the business.

3. **Exit strategy**—one that leaves both you and the investors with a substantial return, usually in the form of an IPO or sale of the company within five to ten years.

4. **A good product**—one that the market clearly needs, with sound marketing strategies and production capabilities

One advantage of venture capital funding is that, once your company is funded, more funds from the VC may be available for subsequent growth stages. The venture fund may also offer (or require) management help, either in a consulting role or, more often, a board position. Their talent can also help you ramp up for substantial growth, or even a public offering if the market warrants.

## Mezzanine Financing

This is used as bridge financing to take a company to restructure debt or take a company public. Usually, it is available from a venture capital firm—typically, one that has already made an investment in your company. The VC will invest additional funds in your company to fix a problem, divest a division or branch office, or acquire another company that is necessary to round out a product line or category.

## Hybrid Financing

There are some firms that will offer a combination of debt and equity funding. The debt gives the investor some liquidity while the equity offers possible upside growth. One method is to use unsecured promissory notes that are convertible to stock in the company, usually at some discounted price.

### Debt vs. Equity

| Debt | Equity |
|---|---|
| ▪ Time required to secure debt is shorter than equity | ▪ Payback schedule is usually longer |
| ▪ Cost of debt is easily measurable | ▪ Better-looking balance sheet |
| ▪ Documentation costs are less than equity | ▪ Does not constrain cash flow as debt will |
| ▪ You don't have to give up ownership | ▪ No personal guarantee required |
| | ▪ Less record keeping required |

You may wish to offer a debt instrument coupled with equity or some level of participation by the lender as an inducement to invest. (The LLC format works well for this type of investment because of partnership taxation rules.) See your attorney or accountant for the best advice.

Whichever method of equity funding you choose, you will find myriad advantages. Equity on the balance sheet looks better than debt. You need not pay interest so it helps your profitability. And no personal guarantee is required, so you don't have to worry about losing all your worldly belongings.

But equity funding may not always be available. To finance your growth, you may choose to borrow the money.

## PERSONAL GUARANTEE
..............................

*A bank may require you and any partners' personal credit history. Most do.*

*They may even demand a personal guarantee from you and your spouse.*

*If so, ask if the bank will remove your personal guarantee after some reasonable period of time. (They may not, but it won't hurt you to ask.)*

# DEBT FINANCING

Most every small business needs to borrow money at some time or another. To finance your rapid growth, you will need at least a line of credit. There are a variety of sources for borrowing money:

- Bank Loans
- Small Business Administration (SBA)
- Credit Cards
- Home Equity Line of Credit
- Retirement Fund
- Life Insurance
- Financial Brokers
- Factoring
- Friends and Family

## Bank Loans

Probably the most common method of borrowing. The bank will require a personal financial statement and (usually) a proposal or business plan (see chapter 1).

Banks like to lend money. That's what they do best. They will gladly loan you the money if they believe they can make a profit doing so. Banks like to feel secure when lending money. Their security is reflected in how they evaluate your proposal. Typically, they look at **Five Cs**: credit, collateral, capital, conditions, and character.

You need to show them you are creditworthy. Your company has a history of making money. You have a well-conceived plan for growth. You will pay back the loan as scheduled. You will pay the interest as scheduled. You will make them happy.

Interest is the profit to the bank on your loan. All banks charge it one form or another. One word of caution: the lower your interest rate, the more carefully they watch the performance of your business.

## Small Business Administration

The SBA offers a variety of loan programs for small businesses. Typically, they guarantee a large portion of loans delivered by your bank. The maximum loan is $2 million (under the SBA's basic 7(a) loan program). The SBA also offers micro-loans for as little as $25,000.

There are specialized programs targeted to women, minorities, veterans, and Native Americans. Other programs focus on exporting. Still others offer long-term fixed-rate financing to acquire land and buildings. For more information, go to the SBA website at www.sba.gov.

The SBA is often viewed as lender of last resort, but that is a fallacy. The SBA finances healthy ventures that have immediate needs for bridge financing to grow or acquire new facilities.

## Credit Cards

Some entrepreneurs use their credit cards to finance operations. It is one of the most expensive means to finance your company. Credit card companies typically charge 18 percent interest or more. It is best to use credit card debt for *short-term* financing. If you can't pay it off in thirty days, try to find some other way. Any other way. Avoid the interest and penalties that can bury you. Pay it off. Fast.

If you have to use your credit card, a good strategy is to use it only for purchases of hard goods (computers, machinery, etc.) or inventory to fill an order. Something that will generate cash quickly.

## Home Equity Line of Credit

Your home can be a source of funding. Offering your personal residence as collateral represents a strong commitment and shows confidence you intend to make your plan work.

---

### THE FIVE CS LENDERS USE TO LEND MONEY

**1. Credit**

*Your personal and the company's credit rating.*

**2. Collateral**

*Tangible physical property or equipment you have to offer to the bank in event of default on the loan, usually the company's property or equipment, but may include personal property— house, car, stock, artwork, jewelry, anything easily converted to cash.*

**3. Capital**

*The capital strength of your company, usually expressed as a debt-to-equity ratio.*

**4. Conditions**

*What are the economic conditions? Or does the lender have too many companies in your industry already in its portfolio?*

**5. Character**

*Your character—how well they know you and their judgment about your likelihood of paying back the loan.*

## HOW TO PRESENT TO YOUR BANKER

*Meet with your bankers before-hand to determine exactly what they require in your proposal.*

*Present believable projections. Better still, present both "most likely case" and "worst case" scenarios.*

*Plan a meeting on your home turf. Not only are you more comfortable, your key employees can present portions of your proposal. Bankers prefer to see your management team, the people who will be using their money.*

While you may already have a mortgage on your house, you may be able to generate cash by establishing a second mortgage. Your first mortgage may be paid down sufficiently, or your home may have appreciated sufficiently, to allow you to borrow against its additional equity.

This is a flexible loan that allows you to borrow only as much as you need at a time. You only pay the interest on the balance. Note: You may be required to pay down the line to zero at some point each year in order to retain this type of loan indefinitely.

## Retirement Fund

If you have a self-directed IRA or even some types of pension funds, you can invest in a private company (not your own, unless you hold a minority interest.) In some circumstances, investors can use 401(k) money to invest in private companies.

You should talk to your attorney or accountant before casting your retirement money into the pool, however, as tax laws change frequently, and retirement fund money has an array of rules and regulations attached to its use that can make the average layperson dizzy.

## Life Insurance

Your life insurance policy is a source of capital. If you have a whole life plan, ask your agent how you might free up some of the cash value in your policy. You may be surprised at the low interest rate available on the money. The loan remains in place as long as you pay the annual premiums. If you die before the loan is repaid, your benefits are simply reduced by the outstanding balance.

## Financial Brokers

These guys are scary. They are not regulated like accountants or bankers and there is seldom any public information available on their lending practices.

Their job is to shop your loan around until a lender is found. They may charge you an up-front fee or other expenses. They'll want a piece of the loan, usually 10 percent or more. They may even want a piece of your company. Or all of the above.

The broker may bring you a financing arrangement that you don't like, but then demand a fee anyway. Be sure you don't sign any agreement that pays the broker even if no financing is forthcoming.

Some will try to convince you that your business plan needs upgrading, and charge you several thousand dollars to upgrade it. If you have a good business plan, with accountant-approved pro forma statements, avoid that particular financial broker.

## Factoring

Also known as receivables financing, factoring converts your accounts receivable into immediate cash. You assign your receivables to the factoring company, who will then be responsible for collecting the money.

Factoring provides immediate cash flow to your business without the obligation of long-term debt. But it can be expensive. The factoring company may take as much as 20 percent. For example, if you assign the factoring company $10,000 in current receivables (nothing over ninety days—they don't want any bad debts either), you may receive $8,000. Look for factors in your industry at www.edwardsresearch.com, or visit your local public library.

## Friends and Family

When first starting out, many entrepreneurs look at home first. After all, your friends and family know you best. Who better to go to when you need money?

---

### WHEN TO DECLINE THE MONEY

*Some investors are just not right for your company.*

*While an investor is investigating your company, you should investigate them as well. What other companies have they funded? What have been the outcomes? How active a role did they play in management? If they refuse to provide references, don't take the money.*

*If it's a family member who loves you, someone who is making do on a fixed income, willing to give you his or her last nickel because of a belief in you, be grateful for the faith, but don't take the money.*

Unfortunately, it's a great way to end a friendship or a family relationship if things don't work out as planned.

If you do find yourself with hat in hand knocking on the door of friends or family, do it in as professional manner as possible. Present a written proposal (business plan) with the amount required, its use, and a payback schedule, just as you would a lending institution. Include a reasonable interest rate. And get any agreement in writing.

## INTEREST RATES (A PRIMER)

When borrowing money, it is helpful to have a rudimentary understanding of interest-rate theory.

When the economy is expanding, companies need money to expand with it. This pressure to borrow pushes interest rates up. Also, inflation pressure is stronger during boom times. The Federal Reserve will try to counteract this pressure by tightening the money supply, forcing rates even higher.

During a recession, the Federal Reserve increases the money supply, making the cost of money cheaper. Slack business reduces the demand for credit, and interest rates fall. When negotiating the interest rate on your loan, keep these factors in mind.

(These tendencies do not always hold up, of course. During the recession of 1974–1975, the price of oil increased dramatically, touching off one of the highest inflationary periods in history. But, over time, these maxims generally hold true.)

A loan's interest rate is usually tied to some floating governmental-controlled rate, like the prime rate. Some banks will lend to their best customers at prime or a quarter over prime. But they watch these customers like hawks, ready to pounce if one financial ratio gets out of whack, or one payment is a day late. It may be better to pay the extra quarter point than have a banker require a stack of paperwork from your staff.

Once acquired, either through equity, through borrowing, or from profits, managing your money efficiently is critical to rapid growth. Following are several essential money management techniques vital to the health of your business.

## COLLECTIONS

If cash is the lifeblood of a business, collection is the lifeguard. Bad debt is a scourge that can rob you of cash and bury your successful business. Your sales staff makes a big sale. They're happy. Your shipping department ships it on time. They're happy. Your new customer loves your products. They're happy. But they don't pay the bill. You're miserable.

*If your profit margin is 10 percent, a $100 bad debt requires $1,000 of additional sales just to break even.*

For many people, especially those in a small business, the psychology and process of collecting debts is a complete mystery. You ask for the money, and you receive an excuse. The excuse seems reasonable. But you still don't have your money. You don't want to stop shipping products for fear of losing the customer. And the bad debt mounts.

How do you avoid bad debt? Any time you make a sale for something other than cash—check, credit card, or a purchase order number, you are extending credit, which entails risk. Your first line of defense is to protect yourself before you sell anything. Do this by establishing a **credit policy**. A credit policy, established in advance, while not foolproof, can help protect you and reduce your risk.

Credit policies differ widely because all situations—customers, products, economic conditions, locations—differ so widely. Selling to individuals often entails more risk because they may not be easy to trace once the sale is made on credit. Credit cards have reduced much of the risk for merchants, but consumer fraud still takes its toll on small businesses every day.

# EXPAND SALES OR REDUCE RISK?

*Some argue that your sales will increase if your credit policy is more relaxed. "Make it as easy as possible for people to buy." "Take advantage of the impulse sale."*

*This is true. There's no question your credit policy is a delicate balancing act between credit leniency and cash only.*

*You must constantly ask yourself the question: "Would the increased profit from greater sales balance out the risk of losses due to giving more credit?"*

Protecting yourself includes getting proper identification so you can find the debtor or any assets later. It also means writing up a strongly worded agreement or contract so you have the law on your side when it comes time to collect. Ideally, you can even pass along any costs incurred in collecting from the debtor.

When dealing with a corporation, a contract or purchase order, a form of contract, can moderate much of the risk. It is not

## NEW CUSTOMER QUESTIONNAIRE

*Whether an individual or a corporation, it is often well advised to ask new customers to fill out a New Customer Questionnaire ("Credit Application" sounds intimidating).*

*Include questions about the customer's needs, how he/she heard about you (always helpful), and the customer's bank name and location.*

*For individuals, a social security number can be useful in obtaining credit information. For a business customer, request the Employer Identification Number.*

uncommon to call a new customer's bank and request a credit rating. You may even decide that, given the high level of risk involved, it is best to request a letter of credit (LOC). The LOC is a deposit from the customer in favor of the seller that cannot be touched by the seller unless the buyer defaults on a payment.

Obtaining a credit history on your new customer is an ongoing process, one that may proceed in stages as the customer grows and places larger orders, thus becoming a greater risk.

Begin with credit rating services, like TRW, Trans Union, Equifax (CBI), or Dun & Bradstreet. They provide credit ratings of individuals and companies for a modest fee. You can also get credit ratings through rating agencies associated with particular industries. For instance, there are special agencies in the furniture, apparel, and jewelry industries that offer credit analysis. Check your industry for credit rating information.

If the customer places a larger order, request financial information. A preprinted questionnaire may be sufficient, but be sure it includes the following:

- How long the company has been in business (a sign of stability).
- Where the company is incorporated (necessary if it ever comes to suit).
- What bank the customer uses (so you can check credit references).
- Who its present suppliers are (call to see if there are any credit problems).
- How much the company expects to buy from. you each year (so you can weigh risk and reward).
- What other trade names are used by the company (so you can check on these, too).

Your banker may be a source of information. You may not want to ask too frequently, but if the account is a large one, ask your banker to check for you. Bankers have vast resources for obtaining credit information. They also have a vested interest, as they don't want to see you incur any bad debt either.

As your business expands, you may have to extend more and more credit. You become, in effect, an investor in the success of your customer. You don't own stock; you have no say in the management of that customer. But you are an investor all the same.

You increase your company's sales by extending credit. But profit may elude you if you fail to get paid.

# PRESENT VALUE AND FUTURE VALUE

Should you buy or lease? If a supplier offers "thirty days, net ten," should you take it? What sort of credit terms can you offer your customers and still earn a profit?

These questions require a rudimentary understanding of the time value of money. Following are two simple formulas to help you determine the present value of a dollar received at some future date, and the future value of a dollar received today.

We all know a dollar received today is worth more than a dollar received next week. Inflation and opportunity cost dilute the value of money over time. Inflation takes a bite out of every nickel you own. Steadily, inevitably. Plus, if you had that dollar now, you could invest it for the week and earn interest.

Conversely, the dollar spent today is more costly than a dollar spent in the future. Put simply, the dollar has a value that varies with time. How much it varies is dependent upon your company's cost of funds, that is, how much interest you have to pay to your banker to borrow money.

The following formula is used to figure out the **future value** of a lump sum at a particular interest rate:

$F_n = P(1 + k)^n$

$F_n$ = The future value of a lump sum of money after n time periods

$P$ = The present value of a lump sum of money invested at the beginning of a period

$k$ = The interest rate or cost of funds, expressed as a percent

$n$ = Number of periods over which your money (P) is invested, plus any accrued interest

Let's say you put $1,000 in a financial vehicle that guarantees 6 percent interest rate compounded annually. At the end of the first year, you will have $1,060.

$$F_1 = \$1,000(1 + .06)^1$$
$$F_1 = \$1,000(1.06)^1$$
$$F_1 = \$1,060$$

What if you left the money in for five years?

$$F_5 = \$1,000(1 + .06)^5$$
$$F_5 = \$1,000(1.06)^* (1.06)^* (1.06)^* (1.06)^* (1.06)$$
$$F_5 = \$1,000(1.33822)$$
$$F_5 = \$1,338.22$$

At the end of five years, you would have accumulated $1,338.22. The six percent interest is earned both on the principle and the interest earned during each period.

What if you have decided to attract more customers by offering generous credit terms? You put together an aggressive advertising campaign and buy newspaper space to tout this stupendous deal for your customers: "Buy Now! Just $999.99! No Payments for Twelve Months!"

How much does this cost your company if your cost of borrowing money is 8 percent? Simply put, what is the value today of $999.99 (call it $1,000) received a year from now?

To determine the **present value** of money received in the future, use a variant of the same formula:

$$F_n = P(1 + k)^n \qquad P = \frac{F_n}{(1 + k)^n}$$

$P$ = the **present value** of some money received at some point in the future.

So, how much does your promotion cost you (not including the advertising costs)?

$$P = \frac{F^n}{(1 + k)^n}$$

$$P = \frac{\$1,000^1}{(1 + .08)^1}$$

$$P = \frac{\$1,000}{1.08}$$

$$P = \$925.93$$

Your No-Payments-for-a-Year promotion cost your company about $74 for each unit sold. Was it worth it? Could be. You may have induced new customers to purchase your product rather than a competitor's. Even though you did not receive the money right away, it still showed up on the books as an asset (accounts receivable).

**Present value** and **future value** arithmetic can be useful in a variety of situations, including leasing decisions, figuring the value of annuities, credit terms, and payment methods.

# RETURN ON INVESTMENT (ROI)

The fundamental measuring stick of the free market system is ROI, the return you receive for your investment. If you put $100 in a savings account and close the account at the end of a year with a balance of $105, you earned a 5 percent ROI. Simple.

The same principle applies to your business. ROI refers to the annual profit of your business divided by the total cash you have in it, which includes all the money you've invested in property, equipment, inventory, and supplies that you have not yet taken out or sold.

**Annual Profit $ 10,000 = 10 percent ROI**
**Total Cash Invested $ 100,000**

Could you do as well in other markets? Could you invest your money in the stock market, for example, and get a 10 percent ROI? Sure, you could. You could also lose it all. Or you could fly to Vegas and bet it all at the blackjack tables.

Point is, your money, invested in your company, is something over which *you* have control.

You could invest your money in the stock of some other company and allow the management of that company to use your money to get some ROI that they

## Case Study    JONCO INDUSTRIES

### THE PROBLEM

Rather than buy new, expensive equipment, owner Tom Ryan, frequently purchases used machinery and equipment at auction for his packaging and product fulfillment company.

He may buy ten machines for $50,000, though he only has use for one or two of the machines.

The others machines sit idle taking up warehouse space until he can find a use for them.

then pass along to you in the form of a dividend, or in the increased value of your stock. But you have little if any control over how they manage your money. (In some cases, you might be better off in Las Vegas. At least then you control whether or not to hold on seventeen.)

Use ROI to calculate purchases of equipment. For instance, you are about to add a new machine at a cost of $10,000. This new machine will produce $80,000 in annual sales at a profit margin of 4 percent, or $3,200.

$$\frac{\text{Annual Profit} \ \$ \, 3{,}200}{\text{Total Cash Invested} \quad \$ \, 10{,}000} = 32 \text{ percent ROI}$$

Buy the machine. Thirty-two percent is an outstanding ROI.

But wait. Now add in the cost of setting up the machine ($2,000) and the added cost of training your personnel in its operation ($4,000). The cost of the machine is now $16,000.

$$\frac{\text{Annual Profit} \ \$ \, 3{,}200}{\text{Total Cash Invested} \quad \$ \, 16{,}000} = 20 \text{ percent ROI}$$

It's still a good investment. Where else can you get a twenty percent ROI?

For more information and applications using ROI, see the Value-Based Management website (www.valuebasedmanagement.net/methods_roi.html).

Should you rent it, or buy it? New or used? These are questions faced every day by rapidly growing companies. Following are some hints for when to do which.

# NEW VS. USED

An uncontrollable urge to invest in long-term commitments is one of the top causes of business failure. The auction houses are filled with fancy furniture and equipment from those entrepreneurs whose grandiose plans went up in smoke.

Those long-term commitments impact your business in three ways:

1. Big down payment
2. Debt service reduces future profit
3. Principal repayments further reduce profit

Buy used equipment instead. Excellent used equipment can often be obtained for less than half the cost of new.

Your company can only support a certain level of investment. Anything larger and your ROI begins to drop, making alternative investments more attractive. Always make the least possible cash commitment as a hedge against lean years.

Don't let the glitter of "new," and the image you hope it will project, outweigh the value of conserving cash. Should it turn out your business can afford to go with "new," by all means, take the plunge. Just remember that while "new" may be less troublesome, it is seldom less costly.

## JONCO INDUSTRIES

**THE SOLUTION**

Ryan assigns all the value to the machines he puts into production, and depreciates them over time.

The remaining unused machinery does not appear on his books. No sense paying personal property taxes on it if it sits idle.

Later, he bundles idle machinery for sale at auction. In this way, he frees up cash and realizes the full amount in profit.

www.joncoind.com

## RENT VS. BUY

Simply put, buying is usually better than renting. If cash flow permits. A big "if."

The primary advantage to renting is that the commitment is limited to the term of the lease, and cash flow is impacted only in small monthly chunks.

Buying a building, for instance, requires a down payment (cash), closing costs (more cash), interest payments (some more cash), property tax payments (still more cash), and the monthly principle and interest and insurance payments (cash, cash, cash). Plus you're stuck with the building if your needs change—you outgrow it, or you need to be closer to transportation, or you don't like your neighbors.

But buying a building also has many advantages. This asset will likely appreciate in value. You can do what you want with the build-out, customizing the property to exactly suit your requirements (within zoning restrictions), including adding on when more space is needed. And when renting, many leases require a significant portion of your profit to be passed to the landlord, especially in retail.

But furniture, equipment, or cars almost never appreciate in value. Buy used (see above) and you're way ahead in the long run.

The only time it may make sense to rent is in a fast-changing industry. Your computer system, for example, was probably obsolete the day you bought it. That industry changes so fast, purchase (or a long-term leasing arrangement) almost never pays out. Better to sign a short-term lease.

In summary, rent when you must, but buy (used) when you can.

Using just these few fundamental principles of cash management and investment strategy, you can accumulate the capital you need to grow your business exponentially.

# CHAPTER 12

## Managing Your Human Assets

Purpose: *The purpose of chapter 12 is to help you manage your most valuable asset, your people. How to hire (and fire), lead, motivate, delegate, and prosper through the minds and efforts of your workforce.*

———◦———

**I**f you are the owner of a small company, your organizational chart probably looks like this:

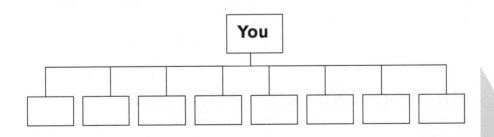

But as your business grows, you will need to add people.

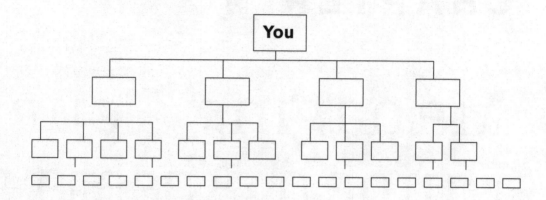

> *"People are disturbed not by things, but by their perception of things."*
>
> —Epictetus

This chapter offers methods for hiring, training, and motivating the most valuable assets your company has: people. You must gain the commitment, the "hearts and minds," of your employees through involvement, communication, and trust to grow your company exponentially.

This is the "heart" of human resources management.

Here are five steps to help you maximize the value of the human assets in your organization:

1. Hire and train skilled employees in the right jobs at the right time.
2. Develop the capabilities of employees to their fullest potential through training and advancement.
3. Foster a culture of trust and loyalty between management and the workers.
4. Provide for the needs of a diverse workforce, with all their differences in needs, work styles, and aspirations.
5. Assure that equal opportunities are available to all.

# THE PERSONNEL DEPARTMENT

If you're going to grow, you need a department (it could be just one person to start) to handle the screening and hiring of employees, along with all the record keeping that goes with them. Your personnel department is responsible for implementing policies and procedures to ensure your company obtains and retains the people it needs to accomplish your company goals.

The personnel department serves several functions:

- **Audit**
- **Stabilization**
- **Training**
- **Service**

## Audit

It is always easier to print a policy manual than it is to uphold the principles it contains. Auditing procedures help to assure that policies are followed. A company may pride itself on promoting by merit alone, but an audit may reveal that a vast majority of promotions go to senior white males. Management is often too engrossed in day-to-day problems to recognize the gradual erosion of hiring and promotion standards.

Sometimes, personnel programs are not cost effective and need to be changed. For instance, an audit of company-sponsored tuition reimbursement programs might reveal employees using this education opportunity, and then leaving the company for a better job. It is the personnel department's responsibility to alert management when such policies should be changed.

## PERSONNEL AUDIT TECHNIQUES

### Attitude Surveys

*Both standardized questionnaires and customized surveys are used to monitor employee receptiveness to company policies, organizational changes, and staffing issues.*

### Absenteeism Ratio

*A sign of employees' dissatisfaction usually expressed as a ratio:*

$$\frac{\text{\# employee days lost/month}}{\text{Avg. \# employees} \times \text{\# workdays}} \times 100$$

### Turnover Ratio

*Compare to industry averages*

$$\frac{\text{\# employee separations/month}}{\text{Avg. \# employees}} \times 100$$

## Stabilization

The personnel department assures the uniform implementation of policies. Line managers can't go ahead and hire someone before clearing it with personnel. This could include pay increases, union grievances, or disciplinary action. This

## THE EMPLOYEE MANUAL

*Most companies have an employee manual that specifies policies, procedures, and benefits. But they can be legal booby traps. A few pointers now that can save you a lawsuit later:*

- *Carefully review and update your employee manual at least once a year.*

- *Record usage dates that will enable you to determine and produce a copy of the exact version of the manual in effect at any given time.*

- *Distribute the manual to all employees and get a signed acknowledgment from each stating the employee understands that the policies, procedures, and benefits contained in the employee manual are subject to change, and that the manual is neither intended to be, nor does it constitute, an employment contract.*

helps insure larger company objectives are met. A seemingly trivial decision regarding one person's work schedule could disrupt production, safety, quality, or any number of other costly issues.

Many line managers resent these restrictions, and begin to wonder who the boss really is. Other times, the supervisor may simply use personnel to pass the buck. "Sorry, I'd like to give you that raise, but personnel won't let me." Personnel, however, can also serve as the benevolent boss, someone an employee can turn to if the supervisor is being unfair.

### Training

As your company grows, you will need more employees. Many will not be trained in the skills your company requires. New sales representatives need product information training. New laborers need machinery instruction. New technicians need software instruction.

The capacities and skill sets of your current employees will be tested by your company's expanding needs. Personnel should coordinate continuing education, both within the company as well as the use of outside institutions.

Here's the opportunity to promote good employees from within. Send Joan to a skills-training seminar, Jason to a software convention, and Anthony through a series of management courses. Your employees feel valued, they move into roles of greater responsibility, and their newly acquired skills add value to your company.

## Service

Somebody has to show you around on your first day of work. Somebody has to explain the company health insurance plan. Somebody has to write the job descriptions, undertake recruiting, screening, and testing. These are just a few of the services provided by a good personnel department.

Other services simply fall to the department because they don't fit anywhere else—e.g., management of safety programs, manning the reception desk, writing the company newsletter, serving as liaison with community or government groups, running the company vending services or cafeteria—the list goes on.

Ideally, the personnel department should lobby for the humanity of the company. Just as finance emphasizes cash flow and marketing stresses the customer first, personnel's focus is on your people—their skills, their training, their "fit" within the culture of your organization.

Human beings are psychological animals, less predictable than facts and figures, materials, or formulas. Your people are a unique blend of skills, experience, personalities, styles, capabilities, and quirks. They do not always easily fit into organizational box charts in neat rows or columns. It is the personnel department's responsibility to manage and control this diverse asset to the overall benefit of the company.

# STAFF ORGANIZATION

Up until now, you have probably run your organization on a loosely defined set of rules and policies suited to your personality and those of your employees. And it's worked. You know each of your employees' first and last names; you probably spend time with some of their families, even socialize frequently outside the office.

As your company grows, you may have less opportunity to interact with your workforce on a regular basis. It is therefore imperative that you organize your staff in the manner best suited to achieve your corporate objectives. This means matching resources to your needs, improving performance, and achieving competitive advantage.

How? There are myriad designs for successful organizations. All stem from two basic premises:

**1. Vertical Coordination**

**2. Horizontal (or Lateral) Coordination**

All organizations differentiate work into specific functions, units, and roles in a variety of different specialties and disciplines. People going in different directions with different tasks, different motivations. Then they tie all these disparate parts together using vertical and horizontal coordination.

## Vertical Coordination

Use this method to control the work of subordinates through authority, rules and policies, and planning and control systems.

Authority figures—boss, supervisor, foreman—form a chain of command that allows orders to disseminate throughout the organization. Simple. Obey the rules. What the boss says goes. The military is a typical example.

Rules and policies limit discretion and ensure uniformity. Standard processes are established and enforced. Two employees with the same problem should be treated identically, regardless if one is a vice president and the other a clerk.

Plans and control systems offer reliable measures of how everybody's doing, both the effectiveness of individual and company performance. Any methods you can specify in advance will help guide your employee's behavior. At McDonald's, the policy says to greet every customer with a smile. The objective is satisfied customers, but it's easier to monitor an employee's behavior than how the customer feels about it.

> ### STANDARD OPERATING PROCEDURE (SOP)
> .............................................
>
> *In the commercial airline industry, flight crews rotate frequently. Pilots never know with whom they may fly.*
>
> *SOPs govern all significant aspects of their work in order to assure safety. Crews are trained to follow a checklist before every takeoff and landing.*
>
> *So long as they all follow the SOPs, the crew members mesh. If not, disaster could follow.*

People are unpredictable. Rules and policies remove some of that randomness. Theory is, if you always do it the same way, you should always get the same result. Surgeons work with a different anesthesiologist, different nurses, a different group almost every operation. If each member of the group follows procedures, the crew works as a team. If not, a malpractice suit may result.

## Horizontal Coordination

Vertical coordination works well within a department or work group, but sometimes vertical levels need to talk to each other. Use horizontal coordination when your vertical parts need to get together—**meetings, task forces, networks,** and **matrix structures**.

**Meetings**—love 'em or hate 'em—hold your company together. Boards confer to make policy. Managers gather to develop strategies. Review committees convene to assure quality and performance standards are met. Every company has meetings.

As your company grows, it becomes more complex. More people. More technology. More problems. A **task force** draws people together from different departments and different experience levels to break a bottleneck or review a new procedure. Project teams or tasks forces coordinate development of new products or services, too.

The Internet has created a wealth of **networking** opportunities. Beyond the local service clubs and chambers of commerce, whole industries communicate through chat rooms, web logs ("blogs" for short), and news groups. A knowledge-based industry like nanotechnology is so complex and widely dispersed that no organization can operate unconnected. Projects are developed by teams of scientists at a host of companies, universities, research centers, and government laboratories.

If you're forming franchises or multiple-location operations, you may want to think about a **matrix structure**. Each location develops its own vertical and

## CORPORATE CULTURE

......................................

### Power Culture

*One central figure, probably you, that has control. Few rules. Everybody does what you tell him or her to do.*

### Role Culture

*Procedures and rules ensure that the role, or job description, is more important than the person who fills it.*

### Task Culture

*Put the right people on the project and let them alone. Expertise creates influence. Teamwork is critical.*

### Person Culture

*Your company exists only to serve certain star performers. The insurance company that exists to serve its agents, or the brokerage house that exists to service its account executives.*

horizontal coordination, a boss telling subordinates what to do, meetings, some networking, maybe a task force or two.

Yet your multiple locations need to be coordinated by product group or SBU as well. Enter the matrix. It's a complex structure of reporting that takes place through supervisors from business or product lines on one axis, and countries or locations on another.

If your organization operates in a stable and defined industry, you should use a less complex, more centralized structure. Create rules and responsibilities for each employee. Policies and procedures coordinate the work and assure quality through uniformity. Lean toward vertical coordination.

A turbulent, complicated, or overlapping industry requires more flexibility. Otherwise, when information pours into top management faster than it can be processed, decisions get backed up at the office door. Nothing gets done. Lean more toward horizontal coordination.

Your goal is to maximize performance while minimizing costs. Applying structure can enhance your company's performance and increase your efficiency through specialization and a clear division of labor.

Standardized policies and procedures allow you to view your staff as interchangeable parts. Management decides roles and relationships. Moving good employees throughout your organization with training, promotion, or rotation. This allows for both company goals and individual differences.

## HIRING

Finding kick-ass people to grow your company is critical to your success. It ain't easy. They have to have the right skills, the right experience, the right "fit" with your company culture.

A study of highly successful organizations suggests that effective hiring policies follow a four-step process:

1. **Job Description**, specified in your advertising.
2. **Résumé** screening and automated search methods.
3. **Interview**, in which a candidate describes specific examples of his or her skills and how they fit the job requirements.
4. **Investigate** the candidate's past experience and references.

## Job Description

Good hiring practices begin with a job description, a clear definition of the job to be filled. This process is coordinated by the personnel department and the manager of the department where the candidate is to work. Together, they describe the function in simple terms, including any required experience.

Many candidates come to your company through word-of-mouth. Most high-level positions are filled through referrals or professional recruiters rather than published advertisements. Even so, a clear job description is essential in the screening process.

## Résumé

All candidates have a résumé. Depending upon the job and the pool of qualified candidates, you may be inundated with résumés. To the point you have stacks of dozens, even hundreds.

You need to look at them all. That perfect candidate could be buried in the third stack on your left.

There's help.

Software uses Optical Character Recognition (OCR) to search for key words in résumés and can be programmed to pinpoint specific job skills and experience. This paperless technique can help your business cull through the countless flow of résumés you receive, and accumulate a database of candidates qualified for various positions.

> ## PITFALLS TO AVOID WHEN ADVERTISING FOR A POSITION
> ●●●●●●●●●●●●●●●●●●●●●●●●●●●●●●●
> *Avoid legal pitfalls in job advertisements. Use "salesperson," not "salesman"; use "energetic," not "young"; use "part-time work," not "college student…"*
>
> *Requiring a high school or college degree may be discriminatory. Better to say an applicant must have a "degree or equivalent experience."*
>
> *Government positions require that all qualified applicants will receive consideration regardless of race, color, religion, sex, or national origin. The qualifier "Equal Opportunity Employer" usually covers it. You may want to include this phrase in your ads as well.*
>
> *For more information, see the Department of Labor website on legal hiring practices at www.dol.gov/odep/business/recruiti.htm.*

Automated résumé screening has its share of snags as well. To suit your requirements, about 75 percent of résumés will be rejected as unfit for a particular position. Some could be gems poorly written or misread by the OCR.

## BAD COVER LETTERS
....................

- *"My résumé has been updated so it is more appalling to employers."*

- *"My career have made me adept at communicating skills."*

- *"I am sure you have lots of résumés and cover letters with information about work experience, education, and things . . . I am not going to bore you with any of that stuff."*

- *Experience: "Computer games tester (still reigning Frogger champion)."*

- *"If you don't hire me, I'll eat a bug."*

Others represent candidates whose skills may not fit the position, but could be a good fit in another department.

Work experience can be a problem, too. The time a candidate spent in a position fluctuates in different economic climates, and résumé-screening software can't look beyond the sheer numbers and weigh in factors to make value judgments. That takes a human touch.

What to look for? Résumés fall into two categories: chronological and functional. The **chronological résumé** is easier to follow, with most recent work experience listed first. The **functional résumé** first lists skills and experience most relevant to the position.

In the chronological résumé, look for gaps in work history. A job held from 1998 to 1999 could have lasted two weeks or two years.

For the functional résumé, look for vague job descriptions or a complete lack of job title. An applicant may not actually have acquired the work experience.

Next, scan for related work experience and any educational requirements. Peruse more carefully those most compulsory. Watch for errors. No typos. No misspellings. No grammar problems. Mistakes demonstrate a lack of desire and attention to detail. Be wary of phrases like "exposure to" or "familiar with" and other qualifiers. They could mean a lack of hands-on experience.

### Interview

Before inviting candidates for an interview, you might contact job seekers by telephone to narrow the field. It's a time-saver and can eliminate still more candidates from that stack of résumés.

In the interview, begin with the résumé. A question about "other interests" or "hobbies" is a good way to break the ice. Look for outside interests related to job skills. A musician might be creative, or excel at working in teams. Success in competitive sports might indicate a hard-charging, type A personality.

Tell the applicant about the job—responsibilities, hours, pay range (be careful here), benefits, and career opportunities. Ask the applicant to compare the résumé—work experience, education, responsibilities—with the job you just described.

When talking pay, ask the applicant what is expected. The response can be low (good), realistic (good), or absurd (bad listening skills; you already mentioned the pay range).

You can reduce the risk of later being accused of preferential treatment by preparing a list of questions to ask each candidate. Then summarize the answers (jot a few notes on the résumé itself) for your files. Follow up on answers the applicant gives that seem ambiguous or evasive.

> ## INTERVIEW QUESTIONS
> ......................................
> *Prepare a series of question before interviewing a job applicant*
>
> - *"Tell me about your experience running a _____."*
>
> - *"How well did you do making cold calls on your last job?"*
>
> - *"Tell me how you go about prioritizing your workday."*
>
> - *"Have any of your previous positions required strong leadership skills?"*

After the interview, **investigate**. Check references. Jude M. Werra and Associates, an executive search firm in Brookfield, Wisconsin, publishes a semiannual *Liars Index* to track the number of misrepresentations of education on résumés. The percentage with gaps, exaggerations, and outright fabrications is staggering. Or at the very least, disheartening.

References seldom say anything negative (otherwise they wouldn't have been asked to serve as references). Ask anyway. "If you could think of one negative thing about Pat, what would it be?" You can learn some interesting quirks that could prove useful in evaluating the applicant.

Dependent upon the level of responsibility, you may need to dig deeper. But be sure any information you seek is actually useful. Transcripts and credit reports are a waste of time unless the candidate is fresh out of school or a bookkeeper, respectively.

Personality tests and drug tests can be useful, too. But they can also be trouble. Some jurisdictions restrict your right to use them. Talk to your attorney before requiring.

## THE UNUSUAL CANDIDATE

*Sometimes, unusual circumstances can lead to a personnel gem.*

- *The immigrant willing to accept a position for which he may be overqualified until he has an opportunity to learn the language*

*Oleg spent twenty years as a mechanic on Russian submarines before immigrating to the U.S. After serving an apprenticeship, he quickly learned the language and is now an expert mechanic at JONCO Industries, responsible for all equipment maintenance.*

- *The convicted felon who is grateful for the job*

*At Hausmann McNally, partner Chuck Hausmann claims that one of their top investigators had once been convicted of embezzlement. She doesn't work with company funds, but her intelligence, and perseverance are second to none.*

- *The disabled candidate*

*The blind serve as receptionists. The deaf proofread text. The wheelchair-bound do almost anything in an office you or I can do. Don't discriminate. You might miss a gem. (Besides, it's illegal).*

# TERMINATION

Just as hiring can be tricky, termination is fraught with legal complications and psychological implications.

Telling someone he's fired is not easy. Yet a majority of managers agree that, once a termination is complete, they wish they had done it sooner.

Once you have made the decision to let an employee go, recognize the likely emotional impact you will cause. It's OK to be firm, but prepare for the emotional outburst, the tantrum, or the recrimination. Be patient with the emotional outburst. Seek help for the tantrum. Prepare in advance for any future recriminations with the **exit interview**.

In the exit interview, give a reason for the termination (poor performance, tardiness, failure to meet goals, downsizing, etc.). Remind him of past conversations or formal reviews in which his poor performance or tardiness had been addressed. While termination may be effective immediately, offer him severance (a few weeks' pay, health benefits, etc.) if appropriate.

Then, sit back and listen. Let him rant. Do not argue with him. But don't agree with him either. Simply say that you are sorry it had to come to this.

Get any company documents and records (especially client lists) or keys from him immediately and remind him that company business should remain confidential after his departure. Make arrangements for him to retrieve his personal belongings at a mutually convenient time. It's best to give him a check right then for all accrued compensation, including any accrued vacation time, sick time, or commissions due. One option offered increasingly is early retirement. Comparing the cost of dismissing a loyal long-time employee, allowing him to do make-work jobs at full salary until retirement, or offering early retirement with attractive benefits, many older employees opt for early retirement.

# LEADERSHIP

You need managers who can lead your growing company. Some say leaders are born that way. Don't believe it. Most scholars agree, leadership can be acquired through training and hard work.

Do a Web search on "leadership." There are over 170,000,000 results. Everyone's got something to say about it—how to emulate the good ones, how to avoid the bad ones, or how to be one yourself.

What makes a good leader? Psychologists have pondered the question for decades. Researchers study traits of effective leaders. Much of their study proves disappointing. Traits related to leadership in one situation are not related in others. Characteristics that make for a good symphony orchestra conductor might be missing from those of a football coach, factory foreman, or country club manager.

Most contend that leaders are made, not born. Leadership can be developed through a never-ending process of education, training, and support.

Leadership is a process by which a person influences others to accomplish an objective. Leaders accomplish goals through:

- **Authority**
- **Knowledge**
- **Ethics**
- **Skill**s

## Authority

Best when it is granted by the followers. Your position as manager or supervisor may grant you the authority to give orders to

---

## DRUG TESTING
........................................

*Blood tests can weed out problems before they're hired. But they can also create problems.*

*The American Disabilities Act (ADA) prohibits you from discriminating against people who had drug problems in their past, including those currently in treatment.*

*Random testing of current employees can pose similar problems. You must prove that there is a high probability of danger to others should a candidate use drugs or alcohol (flight attendants, heavy machinery operators, etc.).*

---

## ON LEADERSHIP
........................................

*"Leadership and learning are indispensable to each other."*

—John F. Kennedy

## ON LEADERSHIP

· · · · · · · · · · · · · · · · · · · · · · · · · · · ·

*"A sense of humor is part of the art of leadership, of getting along with people, of getting things done."*

—Dwight D. Eisenhower

subordinates, but that doesn't make you a leader. It simply makes you the boss. During the American Civil War, leaders were elected by the men. Few soldiers had any military experience, and training was on the field of battle. Those with the most knowledge and skill were chosen by the men to lead.

## Knowledge

Information is power. Your education and wisdom set you apart from your colleagues. It immediately grants you a special place in their minds. Just as knowledge is power, it endows the keeper with an aura of leadership. "She knows more than we do. Let's do what she says."

## Ethics

Critical to leadership. Few will follow willingly down a primrose path of unscrupulous behavior, Nazi Germany notwithstanding. People want to be guided by those they respect. A good value system, one endorsed by those you lead, will garner the most respect.

## Skills

Your unique skills can earn the respect of your subordinates. As a leader, you must know your job and have a solid familiarity with your employees' tasks. The best conductors can play any instrument in an orchestra with proficiency.

Leadership behavior typically follows one of three types:

1. Autocratic
2. Democratic
3. Laissez-Faire

### Autocratic

In a situation where there is high concern for the task and similarly skilled labor, an authority figure may work best. The autocratic shop floor supervisor works well in the apparel industry, where sewers perform similar tasks. Especially in complex, highly charged situations, a single "boss" can increase efficiency. The military is an example.

### Democratic

This style is used in team situations. A task force will reach a consensus. A board of directors will take a vote on company policy. At Leo Burnett, despite disparate titles, each member of the Creative Review Committee has equal say in the quality of the creative product.

### Laissez-Faire

Allow your people to do as they choose. This works best when leading creative people—research and development, advertising copywriters, software designers, and architects—who would rather seek their own path at their own pace.

## MOTIVATION

A good leader knows how to inspire, get the best from employees, and marshal their skills and experience for a common goal.

But how do you create an organization that simultaneously allows your employees to satisfy their individual needs while they work toward the organizational goals you have set?

Face it. Some workers have boring jobs. Most have little or no freedom to make decisions on their own. A few are just lazy. They can all be stubborn from time to time.

There are four alternative methods for motivating your people:

**1. Traditional (Theory X)**
**2. Team (Theory Y)**
**3. Cooperation (Theory Z)**
**4. Competition**

---

## THE ROAD TO LEADERSHIP

### 1. Challenge a Process

*Find a process that you believe needs to be improved, and offer a solution.*

### 2. Inspire Change

*Communicate your vision in words that can be understood by others.*

### 3. Enable Others to Act

*Give them the tools and methods to solve the problem.*

### 4. Model the Way

*Get your hands dirty. A boss tells others what to do, but a leader shows that it can be done.*

### 5. Share the Glory

*Accolades belong to the team, while the pain and disappointment fall to the leader alone.*

Source: Kouzes and Posner (*The Leadership Challenge*)

### Traditional

This long-established method (sometimes called **Theory X**) is one part authority and one part money.

How well workers perform determines their pay. It assumes that workers are inherently lazy and will do as little as possible. They are hired to work, not think. Managers recite the rules, spell out every task, and give the worker no room for discretion. In addition, there is always the underlying threat of termination.

Most large organizations still use this approach in one form or another. Add comprehensive health benefits, onsite daycare, a company cafeteria, and discounts on company products to make the environment mare genial. But it's still, "The more work you do, the more we pay you," and "Do it this way or you're fired!"

The **Traditional** management approach assumes that workers are robots who need to be programmed in order to operate efficiently.

### Team

The Japanese introduced this management method **(Theory Y)** in which groups of line workers assume responsibility for production. The team simply informs management of its intentions. Management may recommend minor changes, or approve. Job satisfaction stems from the work itself, rather than financial rewards.

### Cooperation

**(Theory Z)** combines the best of both the traditional and team approaches. Management establishes goals and specifies budget constraints. The workers determine the manner in which the work is to be performed. Team awards are attached to achievement of specific goals. Meeting those goals becomes the reward. The awards can be monetary, vacation days, or simply prestige among peers.

### Competition

In an organization, rivalry is often more effective among groups than individuals. It can inspire teamwork and support a variety of organizational goals—e.g.,

## Case Study — WILSON PRINTING

### THE PROBLEM

Dale Wilson, president of Wilson Printing, wanted to motivate his staff to achieve minimum profitability goals. He declared that all future bonuses would be paid based upon overall company profitability.

After a year of creating milestones that conserved supplies, limited materials waste, and controlled myriad other costs, he found profits no greater than when he first implemented the plan.

Investigating, he discovered his employees found the system confusing. They could not equate cost control with the monthly bonus.

the department with the best safety rating, the lowest machined-parts rejection rate, or the lowest absenteeism or turnover rate.

Individual departments may use the competition approach, but it may not be practical throughout your entire organization. Aggressive (sometimes called type A) personalities who hunger for challenge often respond well to the prospect of a promotion or pay increase. Management sets a goal ("First one to sell one hundred widgets gets a new color TV") and the employees compete to achieve the goal.

> ### ON LEADERSHIP
> *"What luck for rulers that men do not think."*
>
> —Adolph Hitler

## INTERNAL MARKETING

A good leader will inspire his employees. You can start by promoting the benefits of working for you. Sell your company to your employees. Make them proud to work for a superior organization with superior products and services.

Often, the people in your company who have the greatest impact on your customers' service perceptions are among the lowest ranking. If your employees don't believe in their jobs or your company, their attitude will quickly become apparent to your customers.

Start by selling your products' benefits. Tell your employees what great products or services your company provides so they feel a part of that tradition. They become proud of their company, and glad to work there. They serve as positive spokespersons for the firm, both to customers, and to the community (your labor pool).

**Case Study** ) **WILSON PRINTING**

**THE SOLUTION**

Wilson initiated a simple bonus program based strictly upon sales.

The value of every job was clearly labeled on each job jacket. So the production department knew how much they were producing, the binding department knew how much they were binding, and the shipping department knew exactly how much was shipped out each month.

Productivity increased dramatically, as did profits. The simplest plans often work best.

www.wilprint.com

Sell workplace benefits, too. Explain the advantages of working for your company—the good health benefits, safe work environment, paid sick days, longer vacations, on-site daycare, etc. Your employees will brag to their friends (future employees?), and your reputation as a benevolent boss will spread.

Internal marketing is particularly important when companies are competing for a limited labor pool, such as software engineers or advertising creative people. A little pride in your workplace can have a large impact. When Leo Burnett was first chosen as one of the 100 best companies to work for in America, it purchased copies of the book for every employee in the company (I still have mine). It was management's way of reminding employees that we worked for a good company.

# PASS THE REINS

Part of what makes your company a good place to work is the opportunity for advancement. Most good leaders want their subordinates to succeed. "Hire good people and let them do what they do best," is an oft-quoted axiom. By allowing them to perform more and progressively more important duties, you free up time for yourself to do other things. It's a terrific way to save you time for important strategic planning and administrative duties.

Invariably, the customer always asks for you. Yours is the name on the door. Or yours is the only name she knows, the one she has read about or heard about.

Get outside folks to call your underlings rather than you. When they need a problem solved, put your best people front and center. Let your subordinates handle problems you might have handled in the past.

How?

Simple. Publicity. Make them famous in the marketplace.

## PRODUCT = YOU
·············································

*Ask each of your key subordinates:*

- *Imagine yourself as a product.*

- *What are your attributes, those things of benefit to our constituents—our customers and vendors, our banker, our shareholders?*

- *What do you do that's special?*

- *What do you know that's special?*

- *What is it that distinguishes you from all the other smart, creative, industrious people walking around our company?*

- *What are those attributes?*

*Emphasize their attributes when promoting your key players to your industry.*

Here are four good ways to build your key subordinates' visibility, to make them stand out within your company and in your industry:

## 1. Take on an Extra Project

Assign them tasks outside your organization that will expand their sphere of influence, help them meet new people, showcase their skills to a new set of colleagues, and assume a position of responsibility with a community organization (e.g., YMCA, United Fund, or chamber of commerce). Or allow them one day a month to volunteer for a charitable organization, one where they can make a difference. They expand their network and have a whole new circle of folks singing their (and your company's) praises.

## 2. Give a Speech

Some of your key people are natural presenters. Give them a forum. Suggest they speak to your local Kiwanis or Rotary Club. Sign them up for a panel discussion at a conference, or offer to run a workshop or seminar. From there, it's just a short hop to a major address at your next industry trade convention, and substantial visibility (and credibility) for your company.

## 3. Write a Column or Opinion Piece

Some may be better writers than talkers. Have them pen a piece for publication. They don't have to start with the *Wall Street Journal.* Your industry trade publication, local community weekly, or even the company newsletter all have white space to fill. Use clippings to build your key players' credibility, and your company's visibility. Once published, send a clipping along to a colleague with a note, "Thought you might find this of interest." Guess who she'll call next time she needs some expert advice?

## 4. Teach a Class

Put key executives in charge of teaching others in your company. Encourage them to offer their expertise to your local community college, adult education program, or chamber of commerce. They boost your company's visibility, brand themselves as experts, and increase the probability that people will come to them for advice rather then you. Best of all, your company's reputation for hiring knowledgeable people grows.

These projects are all designed to earn respect and admiration from your industry. Along the way, your managers acquire new skills, gain expertise, develop their capabilities, and grow your company's network of friends and admirers. What more could you want?

You want to be sure there's someone waiting in the wings to take over your job, that's what. If succession is not a planned process, it will be an unplanned crisis.

# SUCCESSION PLANNING

Imagine if you were hit by a car tomorrow. Would your business survive your loss? Or would it be liquidated for whatever it might bring in a fire sale? Do you have a plan for succession?

Your successor might come from any number of sources:
• Your employees (Employee Stock Ownership Program, or ESOP)
• A partner (buy/sell agreement)
• The public (through sale of stock)
• A third party (a competitor, supplier, or customer)
• A family member

By far, the most frequent choice is the family member. You've worked hard to build a successful business, a key component of your family wealth, and you have a strong desire to perpetuate that wealth through succeeding generations.

> ## MAXWELL & DAUGHTER, INC. ..........
> *Only about 27 percent of family businesses are passed to a female heir.*
>
> Source: P. M. Cole, PhD paper, Nova Southeastern University

The odds are against you. Statistically, only about 30 percent of family businesses survive into the second generation, and fewer than 15 percent make it into the third generation. This sad fact reflects poorly on a nation where a majority of the economy is made up of family-owned businesses.

Still, most owners envision a day when they can hand the keys to sonny-boy, throw the clubs in the trunk, and drive on out to the tee box. But succession is a process, not an event. There is no single day when the baton is passed. You must plan for a succession transition over some period of time: typically a year or more.

There are two components to succession planning:
1. **Management Succession** (Transfer of Power)
2. **Ownership Succession** (Transfer of Assets)

## Management Succession

The transfer of power requires both a willing leader and a prepared successor. The leader (you) must allow the successor to make the same mistakes you made as you grew the organization. If the successor has been well prepared, he (or she) will seek counsel—beginning with yours—before making any serious blunders. But the decision must belong to the successor, or the baton has not truly passed.

It's a juggling act, balancing the needs of customers, suppliers, and employees while you pass along the decision process. You've had years of practice, years in which you have nurtured relationships, years of headaches you hope your successor

## TRANSITION TIMING

*Make the transfer of power seamless through good communication and careful planning*

• *Rough out a transition plan or timetable to ensure continuity of management.*

• *Reevaluate periodically to see if goals are being achieved.*

• *Transition over a period of months or even a year, depending upon needs of the business.*

• *The founder should assume an advisory role, allowing more decisions to be made by the successor.*

• *The successor must be prepared to assume responsibility for decisions.*

can avoid. How can you share this experience with your successor?

Teach him. Transfer of power begins with successor training.

Get your progeny involved. Introduce him to key customers and suppliers. Ask new customers and suppliers to work with him rather than you. Pass the reins (see previous).

Training smooths the transfer process. Encourage formal education, not just in the technical skills required of the business, but in accounting, marketing, and management. Some experience at a job outside the family business can be immensely valuable. It brings a fresh perspective, new techniques, and outside networks to the family business.

Grooming your successor is a group effort. Instilling confidence in your successor starts with the confidence of your employees. Exposure to all aspects of the family firm, from sweeping floors to counting inventory, gives the successor credibility, and the respect of coworkers. He started at the bottom; he's earned it.

Key employee involvement is also critical to the transition of power. If they participate in the successor's grooming, a sense of "team" evolves. It's an effective way to retain them through the transition, and retaining them is essential for continuity with customers, vendors, and bankers.

## Ownership Succession

The transfer of assets is like your will. Legal and tax implications are unique to your situation.

It's true; you can't take it with you. But when "it" is your business, the techniques for passing it along should be discussed at length with your accountant or attorney.

One word of caution: don't let tax considerations dictate your decision. Your accountant may make compelling arguments for dodging the IRS. But don't be swayed from the issues most important to you and your family just to keep a few bucks from the tax collector. Determine the result you want. Then let the professionals figure out how best to structure it.

# SHOULD YOU OUTSOURCE HR?

One last work on human resource management. There is a growing trend among small- and medium-size businesses to outsource HR. There are compelling reasons for doing so.

The rules for hiring and managing a varied workforce are complex and exhaustive. Many companies simply avoid dealing with the problems through noncompliance.

If you do not follow the rules, your company could be facing serious problems. Failure to comply with Immigration, IRS, or Department of Labor (DOL) regulations could jeopardize both the company and its employees. Penalties are severe. The IRS, for example, can impose a penalty of $1,000 per day for every day a plan is in noncompliance.

> ## MAKE OR BUY?
> ·····································
> *In rapid-growth mode, your company may experience unusual personnel problems.*
>
> *If you can hire and build a personnel department internally for less than you could outsource it, do so.*
>
> *Otherwise, consider the benefits of outsourcing the HR function.*

Outsourcing your personnel management could be a temporary solution for your firm. In addition to compliance with government regulations, an outside HR specialist can:

- Provide résumé screening
- Present wage opinions
- Bring knowledge of industry benefit and compensation programs
- Remove hiring and promotion bias
- Provide employee assessment and testing
- Manage employment changes

Here are three instances when you might want to outsource your human resources department:

### 1. You Need to Hire a Lot of People Fast

You've just landed that big account. You need to ramp up quickly. Outsourcing provides a fully trained HR team to navigate through the bottleneck. They can help recruit qualified people, screen them quickly, and provide orientation training to new hires.

### 2. Seasonal Fluctuations of 10 Percent or More

Every busy season, bring in the outside firm to help recruit, screen, and orient applicants.

External experts have an eye in the marketplace and can better steer you through radical workforce changes.

### 3. Transition in Your Personnel Department

If you have no one presently capable of assuming the responsibilities of personnel director, you may want to use an outside service until you can bring in a full-time person. The outsource service can bring discipline to the chaos. They can even recruit a full-time personnel director to replace their services.

Long term, no service is as effective as your own personnel department. No one can know your company as well as you do. And no one can explain it to potential employees as well as your own people can. But outsourcing may be a solution when you're faced with an unusual personnel problem.

# CHAPTER 13

## Social Profit

*Purpose: The purpose of this last chapter is to recap the 5 Kick-Ass Strategies required to grow exponentially, review the infrastructure necessary to support your expansion, and provide guidelines for making ethical decisions as your company grows.*

———◆———

**R**eaching the next level of sales and profits demands a commensurate increase in social responsibility. Social profit is the creation of wealth beyond money, beyond any accounting ledger. It is wealth of the soul. The sense that you have done what's right and good. To leave this planet a better place than when you arrived. **Social profit** is the net benefit both your firm and society receive from your firm's ethical practices and social responsibility.

Your company's culture is a reflection of your norms, values, and beliefs. Your behavior can dictate and influence your employees' behavior. Your rules become the rules of conduct for your company and the basic values that guide your firm along its path.

> ## CODE OF ETHICS
> ••••••••••••••••••••••••••••••••
> *An organization's written standard of behavior to which everyone must subscribe.*
>
> *Use a code of ethics to communicate acceptable standards of behavior regarding health, safety, environmental, political, and equal employment opportunity issues.*

Those values become the guideposts your managers use to decide what goes into your company's products; how they are advertised, sold, and delivered; and how they are disposed of.

Employees become socially responsible based upon the policies formally accepted by company management. Service to the community supports your customers and potential employees.

If you insist upon running a quality company with quality employees who make quality products, why not insist upon quality business behavior?

## CREATING SOCIAL PROFIT

There are several ways organizations gain social profit:
- **Cultural Diversity**
- **Cause Marketing**
- **Green Marketing**
- **Community Activism**

But good business ethics is the first step in creating social profit.

Simply stated, good ethics is good business. Stress ethics and social responsibility in your organization. It's the right thing to do, and it makes good financial sense.

If you do not, in the short run, you may get away with it. But you will foster a culture of deceit and deception among your employees.

In the long run, you'll get caught. Either by your customers, your suppliers, or the law. You can suffer financially, or your reputation can suffer, or both. Either way is not worth the loss of your company, or the loss of your personal reputation.

The FTC fined Gateway when it failed to honor a "money-back guarantee" with full refund, as advertised. The computer manufacturer had deducted the cost of shipping from its refund, about $62. The fine cost Gateway $290,000. The loss of reputation cost far more than the fine.

In addition to federal watchdogs, consumers are fighting back, too. The Consumer Products Safety Commission and *Consumer Reports* magazine regularly announce products they find to be unsafe or ineffective.

For example, from 1991 to 2000, there were 130 infant deaths caused by window blinds. Since that time, the Consumer Products Safety Commission worked with manufacturers to eliminate loops on window blind pull cords, the leading cause. Also, owners of existing blinds were given a free repair kit to eliminate the hazard (but not before the product manufacturers had paid off a slew of lawsuits).

In 1993, two groups of U.S. Secret Service agents walked into a Denny's restaurant. One group, the all-white group, was seated and served right away. The African American group waited and waited . . . and waited. One lawsuit later, Denny's coffers were significantly lighter, their business had dropped off dramatically, and their reputation was in tatters.

## Cultural Diversity

As Denny's discovered, cultural diversity is not just the law, it is important to the long-term financial health of your company. It's also the right thing to do.

Adoption of cultural diversity programs assures that everyone has an equal right to hiring and promotion. It rewards people on the basis of merit. Not race, color, or religious belief.

The same holds true for the disabled, a consumer market with over $180 million in discretionary income. Smart marketers recognize the disabled as a valuable prospective target market, and potential labor pool.

Good companies actively recruit diverse customer groups, supplier groups, and employees. Since 1993, Denny's has introduced a number of diversity programs. The result: Today, 28 percent of Denny's managers are minorities; 162 Denny's restaurants are minority owned; and Denny's spends over $100 million annually with minority vendors.

## Cause Marketing

Historically, cause marketing meant running a short-term promotion and donating a portion of the profits to some charity. But long-term gains are hard to generate with short-term promotions. Cause marketing works best when there is a long-term commitment to social change.

Research shows the public takes notice. According to *Sales & Marketing Management* (January 1994) 84 percent of Americans polled said that cause marketing creates a positive image of a company, and 78 percent said they would

## THE CONSUMERISM MOVEMENT
...........................

*Two best-selling books, Rachel Carlson's Silent Spring, attacking the use of pesticides, and Ralph Nader's Unsafe at Any Speed, exposing safety defects in automobiles, launched the modern consumerism movement in the 1960s.*

*President Kennedy's 1961 inaugural speech outlined the Consumer Bill of Rights:*

- *The right to be safe from defective products.*

- *The right to be informed, including warning labels and lists of ingredients.*

- *The right to be heard and to receive redress for defective products.*

- *The right to choose freely.*

be more likely to buy from a company associated with an important cause.

Avon's Breast Cancer Awareness Crusade (through the sale of pink ribbon pins), McDonald's Children's Charities, and other cause marketing efforts have resulted in both benefits for the charities and goodwill for the companies—a win-win situation.

## Green Marketing

This is a strategy that supports environmental stewardship by creating products from recycled old products, or that use significantly less energy.

More and more consumers favor environmentally friendly products, whether or not the price is higher. Electrolux, the appliance maker, found that, despite higher prices, their profits from solar-powered lawn mowers and water-conserving washing machines actually were 4 percent higher than their other product lines.

Toyota's Prius and Honda's Insight, hybrid gas-electric automobiles, have both proven winners with consumers, especially as gasoline prices continue to escalate.

Is environmental friendliness self-serving? That is, do companies practice environmental stewardship out of a sense of righteousness or because it's good business? The answer is: Yes.

Many business leaders simply believe in doing right by the environment, whatever the excess cost. There are customers who are concerned about the environment who will pay the premium to preserve our planet. Many pay the premium regardless of the environmental benefits. Unilever subsidiary Ben & Jerry's makes a premium-priced ice cream. Ben & Jerry's has long been noted for its commitment to the environment. Most consumers don't care. They simply like their "Cherry Garcia" or "Chunky Monkey" flavors.

## Community Activism

Get active in your community. The benefits are many:

- Achieve greater visibility for yourself and your company.
- Have a significant impact on your company's sales.
- Enlarge your network of business contacts.
- Enhance your image in the community.

There are many ways to get involved in the community. There is a whole gaggle of charitable and nonprofit organizations, and all have a crying need for volunteers.

You may have a pet charity, one that has a personal appeal to you. Or you may choose a charitable organization whose constituents fit your target market profile (as Avon did with its Breast Cancer Awareness Crusade and McDonald's with its Children's Charities).

Once you have chosen the organization, work with them and make them work for you, too. If the charity has access to any celebrities, ask if they can arrange an appearance at your next function as a part of the fundraising program. You might want to set up an autograph table or have a photographer take instant pictures in exchange for a donation.

Just as giant corporations donate huge resources (think: naming rights, charitable foundations, endowment of university chairs), your smaller company can gain from active support of select community organizations. Community activism enhances your image, creates name recognition, and enlarges your network of contacts. Besides, it's a great way to meet some nice people.

### GREEN MARKETING

*Dixon Ticonderoga makes crayons from soybeans rather than paraffin, an oil byproduct. They claim the soybean crayons are brighter and richer with a smoother texture.*

*Boeing changed all their light fixtures from incandescent to fluorescent, saving 100,000 tons of carbon dioxide a year, one of the main causes of global warming.*

*Shaklee and Interface, Inc., are making friends by paying to upgrade public school boilers from coal to natural gas, which produces fewer greenhouse gases.*

## TRUTH IN ADVERTISING

••••••••••••••••••••••••••••••

*At Leo Burnett, we filmed a television commercial for Glad Trash Bags in which an elephant stepped on two bags of garbage, a Glad bag and a generic bag. (The generic bag broke; the Glad bag did not.)*

*Before we could air this TV spot, we had to prove to the National Association of Broadcasters that we had used relatively the same garbage in each bag, and that the garbage was representative of garbage found in trash cans on the street.*

*The first part was easy. Use the same trash in each bag. But how could we prove our garbage was just "average" garbage?*

*We hired a West Coast research firm to determine the size, weight, and content of the average bag of trash. Somebody actually looked in several hundred San Francisco trash cans; counted the number of bottles, cans, pizza cartons, and banana peels; and concluded that the "average" bag of garbage consists of:*

- *1.6 percent plastic*

- *8.3 percent metal products (cans and lids)*

(continued next page)

# TRUST ADVERTISING

Wandering through the halls of a local advertising agency one day, I noticed a sign on one of the cubicles: "Without advertising, you wouldn't know."

This struck me as arrogant. Do we, as advertisers, truly believe we are the purveyors of all knowledge and information for this planet? Yet, as I began to think about it, there is more than a kernel of truth here.

Consumers are inundated with advertisements. Much of what we learn about the world comes from ads. For instance, you probably learned that gas was recently selling for an extraordinarily high price because you saw a sign at a local station. Maybe you later read about the reasons why in the newspaper, or heard it mentioned on the TV news. But you first learned of it through advertising.

This puts an enormous burden on advertisers to tell the truth. And the fact is, most do. Many advertisers go to great lengths to assure accuracy in their claims. The media serve as watchdogs, disallowing ads that make false or unprovable claims.

Think about the last time you saw an ad for medicine, and the page of small type following it with all sorts of legal caveats, warnings, and medical mumbo jumbo. Magazines won't print advertisements for medications unless they contain mention of dosages, possible side effects, contraindications, etc.

The National Association of Broadcasters (NAB) has strict guidelines on which ads will be allowed on television and which will not.

For example, you can't claim your product is "best" unless it has been tested against all other leading brands in the category by an independent research group.

Despite these efforts at truthfulness, the public remains skeptical. Research suggests half of all consumers don't trust advertisements.

While only a small percentage believe most ads are out-and-out lies, many simply believe the advertiser isn't telling the whole truth, or is leaving out significant facts in order to show the product in its best light.

(continued from previous)

- *12.5 percent glass*

- *3.8 percent wood*

- *12.5 percent yard waste*

- *25.0 percent food waste*

- *36.3 percent paper products (including at least one pizza box)*

Source: Leo Burnett Company

And for good reason. It only takes one lie to destroy the trust built by hundreds or even thousands of truthful ads.

The Volvo case is a classic example. At a big-wheel truck rally in Pennsylvania, one monster truck roared over a long line of cars, crushing them flat. All except one. An old Volvo station wagon remained intact. Unfortunately, there were no cameras to record this event. To recreate the scene, Volvo and its advertising agency structurally reinforced a Volvo station wagon, while structural supports in other cars were cut. The NAB found out and fined both Volvo and its agency for the rigged demonstration.

The incident garnered substantial press. Consumer skepticism soared.

Another form of deception is one perpetrated by Bristol-Myers Squibb. For years, Bristol-Myers has sold the popular Excedrin Extra Strength tablets for headaches. The active ingredients include:
- acetaminophen (250 mg)
- aspirin (250 mg)
- caffeine (65 mg)

When the company introduced Excedrin Migraine—attractive new package, with a big ad campaign—it specifically targeted sufferers of migraine headaches. It sold for $1.00 more than Excedrin Extra Strength.

For anyone who has ever had a migraine headache, an over-the-counter product that relieves the misery would be a godsend, even if it's $10.00 more. I looked at the active ingredients:

<table>
<tr><td>

**WHO TRUSTS WHAT?**

·····································

*Older Americans don't trust television or radio, but may feel more inclined to trust print.*

*The youth of America seldom read. While they are less skeptical of broadcast news than their parents, they place more credence in online sources.*

</td><td>

- acetaminophen (250 mg)
- aspirin (250 mg)
- caffeine (65 mg)

I called Bristol-Myers to find out if there was anything unique about Excedrin Migraine or were these simply identical products. "Yes, they are," said Jennica who answered my queries. I asked her if she thought such a practice might be deceptive to the public. "Well, the FDA [Federal Drug Administration] says we can do it," was her reply. "But I'll be glad to send you the dollar."

</td></tr>
</table>

I considered telling Jennica that her company's advertising claim was a sham, that she should be ashamed of herself, and that deceptive advertising hurts the credibility of all advertisers. But I didn't.

Instead, I'm telling you. Please don't judge all advertising by the deceptions of the few. As you plan your promotion strategies, tell the truth. To do otherwise hurts us all.

## EXPONENTIAL GROWTH

You've decided. You're heading for exponential growth. You're going to devote the time to develop a plan that will maximize each of these 5 Kick-Ass Strategies in your business, establish the infrastructure to support the resulting growth, and propel yourself and your company to wealth and happiness.

So you turn to this, the last chapter, expecting to find everything neatly wrapped up, completely summarized, hoping it would be that easy to grow exponentially.

It isn't.

The 5 Kick-Ass Strategies are as much attitude as aspiration. They are a mind-set, focused like a laser on growth—wary of the strain you can expect on your people, your systems, and your checkbook—but clearly focused on growth.

Growth through acquisition, through new product development. Growth from farming your field of customers and hunting new targets. Growth by simply buying customers' patronage.

1. **Buy Market Share**
2. **Hunt**
3. **Farm**
4. **New Products**
5. **Merge or Acquire**

That's it in a nutshell. The 5 Kick-Ass Strategies: buy market share, hunt, farm, new products, and merge or acquire. Without them, your company is a ship without wind in its sails. With them, you can steer your organization to exponential growth.

There is no substitute for being your own boss. Your vision becomes reality. You feel the joy of watching your company grow, watching your people grow with it. It's a natural high, a euphoric sense of pride in growing exponentially.

I'd like to share it with you. Follow the 5 Kick-Ass Strategies. Formulate and implement your marketing plan, manage your infrastructure, and contact me with your results (rg@thegredecompany.com). I'll publish your comments on my website, good or bad.

# GLOSSARY OF TERMS

**Actual Product:** The specific thing you receive in exchange for money (or barter). If you buy shampoo, it's the container and the liquid itself. If you buy a drill bit, it's the twisting piece of hardened steel.

**Affordable:** One method of determining a promotion budget, used by more than half of all companies, and the least effective.

**Attention Deficit Economics:** Customer attention is constantly in demand. Using promotion messages to grab just a limited amount of that attention.

**Attribute Modification:** A method for creating new products that addresses its specific features and benefits, and modifies them (magnify, micro-fy, reverse, combine, etc.).

**Augmented Product:** The unique product difference, the characteristic that makes that product distinctive, better than anyone else's product. If you buy shampoo, it's the shiny hair, the tangle-free hair, or the dandruff control. If you buy a drill bit, it's the hardened carbon steel, or the carbide tip.

**Baby Boomers:** The largest demographic group, born between 1945 and 1965, these people dominate U.S. buying habits.

**Brainstorming:** A small group meeting to share ideas for new products or strategic plans.

**Brand Focus:**  A broader definition of your business than simply product focus. A brand focus imagines the benefits. For example, Standard Oil no longer sells gasoline, but rather supplies energy. Encyclopaedia Britannica went from selling encyclopedias to information distribution.

**Brand Loyalty:**  Purchase of the same brand consistently. Someone who is loyal to a particular brand skips the information search and the evaluation of alternatives.

**Branding:**  Creating an image for your company, product, or service. An image burned (or "branded," if you will) into the minds of customers and prospects.

**Broadcast Media:**  Radio and television.

**Budget:**  The last part of the marketing plan. It is the sum cost of all the Tactics required to achieve an organization's goals.

**Buying Market Share:**  Selling more of the same products or services to your current target market, taking those customers from your competition. Requires an increase in promotion spending or decrease in price.

**Buying Process:**  Five-part process every customer experiences when purchasing a product to satisfy a need or want: problem recognition, information search, evaluation of alternatives, purchase decision, post-purchase evaluation.

**Buzz Marketing:**  Creating a "buzz" among a target segment through word-of-mouth techniques, especially effective using the Internet.

**Buzzwords:**  Catch words or phrases that come to be associated with a product or brand image. Examples include "Fly the Friendly Skies of United," "Melts in Your Mouth, Not in Your Hands," and Homer's "D'oh!"

**Cash Cow:**  One segment of the market share matrix. These strategic business units produce cash for a company. Often used to fund other SBUs in higher-growth markets.

**Chronic Bottleneck:** Recurring bottleneck that requires long-term planning to fix, usually caused by either materials problems or process problems.

**Competitive Analysis:** Your company's strengths and weaknesses compared to key competitors and product substitutes.

**Conversion Rate:** The number of orders received divided by the number of offers mailed, or, in broadcast, the total viewership of the program.

**Core Competencies:** The unique products or characteristics that make your organization a success—those that set it apart from any others.

**Core Product:** The primary product benefit you receive. If you buy shampoo, it's the clean hair. If you buy a drill bit, it's the hole.

**Credit Policy:** A policy, established in advance, that helps protect a company from bad debt.

**Critters:** Animals, cartoon characters, or imaginary beings that represent or embody a brand. Examples include the Pillsbury Doughboy, Tony the Tiger, the Marlboro Man, and Ronald McDonald.

**Customized Market:** A market of one. It is the ultimate level of market segmentation.

**Debt Financing:** Borrowing money in order to finance an organization.

**Demographics:** The statistics that measure a population, including: age, gender, income, education, ethnicity, and location.

**Dogs:** One segment of the market share matrix—these strategic business units have weak market share in slow-growth markets.

**Doodad:** A product. See "Gimcrack."

**Decline Stage:** The last stage of the product life cycle when profits become elusive due to market saturation and increased competition.

**Delegation:** Allowing someone else the authority to act on your behalf.

**Due Diligence:** The process of carefully examining all submissions and financial statements of a company for the purpose of a merger or acquisition.

**Early Adopters:** Those who are among the first to buy a new product, usually about 10 percent of all target customers.

**Environment Analysis:** An analysis of the environment in which your company operates, including technology, government regulations, economic factors, supply chain analysis, and broad industry trends.

**Episodic Bottlenecks:** Shifting bottlenecks that appear to have no cause, usually caused either by labor shortage, material shortage, or machine breakdown.

**Equity Financing:** Granting an ownership position to another party in exchange for money to finance an organization.

**Evaluation of Alternatives:** The second step in the buying process, after problem recognition and information search. Price, features, reputation, and a variety of other criteria influence purchase choice.

**Exit Interview:** Used to help eliminate problems that may arise from the termination of an employee.

**Extraordinary Service:** Beyond good service. The ability to exceed customer expectations.

**Farming:** One of the 5 Strategies. Selling different stuff to the same customers. Examples include: rotation farming, suggestive selling, and trading up.

**Flighting:** Concentrated bursts of advertising with a hiatus (no advertising) in between. For example, run ads for four weeks, then be off the air for four weeks before repeating the ads. In print, skip an issue or two before running the ads again.

**Finance:** One of the four fundamental parts of any business (along with operations, marketing, and human resources) that is responsible for managing the money that flows through the organization.

**Four I's:** The process of creativity: Information, Incubation, Inspiration, and Implementation.

**Four P's:** Product, Place, Promotion, and Price—the fundamental building blocks of a marketing program—that must be balanced wisely for maximum impact.

**Front Loading:** Spending the lion's share of a media budget in the early stages of an advertising campaign.

**Future Value:** The value of a lump sum at a given interest rate at some point in the future.

**Generation X:** One of the names given this demographic group (also called the Lost Generation) born between 1965 and 1985.

**Generation Y:** One of the names given this demographic group (also known as Echo Boomers) born between 1985 and 2000.

**Gewgaw:** A product. See "Doodad."

**Gimcrack:** A product. See "Widget."

**Gizmo:** A product. See "Gewgaw."

**Growth Stage:**  One of the four stages of the product life cycle characterized by positive cash flow and profits, and early product acceptance.

**Horizontal Coordination:**  A method of internal communication. Examples include: meetings, task forces, and networks.

**Horizontal Integration:**  The merger or acquisition of a company at the same level in the supply chain.

**Human Resources:**  One of the four fundamental parts of any business (along with operations, finance, and marketing) that represents all the employees within an organization.

**Hunt:**  One of the 5 Strategies. Selling more of your products or services to different markets. Hunting new customers requires a change in a demographic, e.g., new location, new age group, new income level, etc.

**Information Search:**  The second step in the decision process, after problem recognition, when we begin to gather data on the universe of choices available to meet some perceived need. This process could include our memory of advertisements, a friend's recommendation, an Internet search, or myriad other information sources.

**Introduction Stage:**  One of the four stages of the product life cycle characterized by product testing and little or no profit.

**Late Adopters:**  The last group to purchase a new product. They will do so only when there is little at risk.

**Licensing:**  Allowing another firm to produce and market your goods for a specific purpose for a specific period of time.

**Magazines:**  The most specialized of all media.

**Market Segment:**  A group of customers with a similar set of needs and wants.

**Market Share Matrix:** An analytical tool used to analyze the growth potential of each strategic business unit.

**Marketing:** The satisfaction of needs and wants through the sale of your products or services. Also, one of the four fundamental parts of any business (along with operations, finance, and human resources) responsible for attracting, retaining, and growing profitable customers.

**Mass Customization:** The ability for a company to customize a product to suit individual customers. Examples include: customized computers over the Internet, custom automobile accessories ordered through a dealer, a special mix of coffee beans ground to your specifications.

**Mass Market:** Includes all buyers in a category.

**Mass Marketing:** Targeting all consumers rather than specializing in market segments or specialty niches.

**Maturity Stage:** One of the four stages of the product life cycle characterized by full product acceptance in the market, peak sales, and profits.

**Merge or Acquire:** One of the 5 Strategies. Merger or acquisition of another company may include all the other four strategies.

**Middle Majority:** Not the first to buy the product. They need to be persuaded that a new product isn't simply new, but better than what they are currently using.

**Middlescents:** The smallest demographic group in the U.S. These people were born between 1930 and 1945.

**Mission Statement:** A written document that states the guiding principles by which your organization operates. It defines who you are as a company.

**Morphological Analysis:** A method for developing new products where a product's key attributes are dissected, analyzed, and changed (morphed) individually.

**New Products:** One of the 5 Strategies. It is essential to introduce new products because customers prefer to work with innovative suppliers, and new products replace those that have grown obsolete.

**Newspapers:** One of the most frequently used advertising media.

**Niche Market:** A small market segment, more narrowly defined. Customers have distinctive needs and wants and will pay a premium price to satisfy them.

**Objective-Task (or Zero-Base Budgeting):** The method of determining a promotion budget favored by academicians and major companies by first establishing sales goals, then determining the tasks necessary to achieve those goals.

**Objectives:** The second part of the marketing plan, after the situation analysis. The goals set by your organization. They should be quantifiable, measurable, and attainable.

**Operations:** One of the four fundamental parts of any business (along with finance, marketing, and human resources) that makes the products the company sells. Responsible for all the direct labor and materials that go into production.

**Out-of-Home Media:** Lower cost compared to most traditional media. Examples include transit, billboards, sports stadiums, and outdoor posters.

**Outsourcing:** The process of obtaining outside vendors to provide goods and services that might otherwise be obtained in-house.

**Percent-of-Sales:** One method of determining a promotion budget. A percentage of annual sales.

**Present Value:** The value today of a lump sum at a given interest rate received at some point in the future

**Print Media:**   Newspapers and magazines.

**Psychographics:**   The psychological factors that separate consumers. These include lifestyle, beliefs, habits, hobbies, and personality differences. Terms like yuppie, Christian, numismatist, liberal, jet-setter, gay, and straight are all psychographic descriptions.

**Planning:** The process of anticipating future events and conditions, and then determining the best way to achieve your objectives.

**Post-Purchase Evaluation:** The last part of the buying process. It begins the moment you own it, whatever "it" is. Two factors contribute to our feelings of satisfaction/dissatisfaction: perception—how we "feel" about ourselves as a result of our purchase—and empirical evidence—the product's performance.

**Practice Spectrum:** The process of delineating services based upon their level of complexity, from commodity service (e.g., haircut, auto mechanic) to expertise service (e.g., industry consultant).

**Problem Recognition:** The first part of the buying process. It occurs whenever we feel there is something lacking in our lives. We have a need, a problem we wish to solve.

**Product Life Cycle:** Product categories and specific brands have limited life expectancies. This process of obsolescence has four distinct stages from birth to death: introduction, growth, maturity, and decline.

**Productivity:** The rate at which input is transformed into output. Examples include: parts and materials are transformed into automobiles, patients at a hospital are cured, or browsers at a store become customers.

**Purchase Choice:** The third step in the buying process, after problem recognition, information search, and evaluation of alternatives. The satisfaction of the need or want.

**Q, S, & P:** Quality, service, and price. Successful companies determine which two out of these three they will offer their customers. High quality and exceptional service justifies a higher price. A low price is necessary whenever the quality is inferior or service is substandard. Any company that fails to offer at least two out of the three will soon be out of business. Likewise, any company that tries to offer all three will also soon be out of business.

**Question Marks:** One segment in the market share matrix. These strategic business units operate in high-growth markets but have a small market share.

**Quintile Analysis:** Dividing customers into five distinct groups and analyzing each for profitability.

**Radio:** Targets consumers using primarily psychographic criteria.

**Rotation Farming:** A simple way to instill brand loyalty by providing an incentive to buy products that lend themselves to periodic purchase. Examples include: car wash, oil change, haircut, tanning salon, etc.

**Sales Analysis:** An examination of recent sales and profit results, target market analysis, and sales estimates.

**Sensory Modification:** A method for developing new products that tests a product against the five senses.

**Service Bottleneck:** A bottleneck in a service organization causing long waiting times.

**Share of Voice:** The percentage of media spending in a particular category that comes from one brand. It is the most often used method of gaining market share. The objective is to create a stronger presence in a market than your direct competitor, a greater share of voice in the media.

**Silvers:** Those people in the U.S. born before 1930 (sometimes called the GI Generation), this demographic group suffered through the Great Depression and fought World War II.

**Situation Analysis:** The first part of the strategic marketing plan, it has three parts: sales analysis, competitive analysis, and environment analysis.

**Social Profit:** The net benefit an organization and society receive from the organization's ethical practices and social responsibility.

**Specialty Store:** Retail establishment that specializes in a single product category (sometimes referred to derogatorily by rivals as "category killer"). Examples include the Gap for basic clothes for younger adults, Foot Locker for athletic shoes, Staples for office supplies, and Home Depot for home-repair supplies.

**Stars:** One segment in the market share matrix, these are market leaders in high-growth markets.

**Strategic Business Plan:** A plan for the future of your organization that encompasses all aspects: operations, finance, human resources, and marketing.

**Strategic Business Unit**, or **SBU:** Multiple product lines that satisfy many diverse market segments.

**Strategic Marketing Plan:** A plan that focuses solely on sales and marketing goals, goals you set after a thorough analysis of your customers, your competition, and your industry.

**Strategies:** The third part of the marketing plan, after the situation analysis and objectives. Strategies are the route you need to take to achieve your objectives. There are five strategies, and only five strategies, that can build any business.

**Stress:** A physical or emotional state resulting from an unexpected change; harmful physical and emotional response that occurs when requirements do not match resources.

**Suggestive Selling:** Suggesting additional items to current customers. Offering accessories, warranties, or service contracts when selling your primary product or service.

**Tactics:** The fourth part of a marketing plan, after the situation analysis, objectives, and strategies. These are specific actions. Examples include: TV commercials, publicity, coupons, a brochure, or attendance at a trade show.

**Television:** The most intrusive medium.

**Theory X:** An authoritarian management approach where it is assumed employees dislike work and need firm direction and control.

**Theory Y:** A management approach where it is assumed employees are more committed to the company and its mission if they participate in the decision-making process.

**Theory Z:** A combination of Theories X and Y where employees are given attainable goals and asked to offer plans designed to achieve those goals.

**Three R's of Service:** Recognition, remedy, and reinforcement. The process of creating loyal customers from among those who voice a complaint.

**Top of Mind:** The all-important measurement that assures you customers will remember your name first when it comes time to make a purchase decision.

**Total Cost of Ownership (TCO):** A principle of determining the lowest cost that takes into account all three elements of cost: quality, service, and price (Q, S, & P).

**Vertical Coordination:** A method to control the work of subordinates through authority, rules and policies, and planning and control systems.

**Vertical Integration:** The merger or acquisition of a customer or supplier.

**Widget:** A product. See "Gizmo."

**Yellow Pages:** A directional media not useful for creating awareness or problem recognition. Soon to be replaced by Internet sources.

# INDEX